T0287859

Fractur

'An important and timely analysis rich in historical detail. It challenges crude denunciations of "identity politics" on both right and left, and reiterates that intersectionality is indeed political economy.'
—Alison Phipps, Professor of Sociology at Newcastle University, author of *Me, Not You: The Trouble With Mainstream Feminism*

'In these pages, Michael Richmond and Alex Charnley draw on the living communisms that are Black feminism, decolonial struggle, and trans solidarity to create a new revolutionary synthesis for a working class that, as they remind us, has always been divided. Combining years of experience of left organising with theoretic sophistication, this book demonstrates why, in material terms, capitalism produces constantly shifting relations (between oppressions) that take the appearance of divisions, and also how movements right now are labouring in and against those fractures. As new forms of *soi-disant* "anti-identity politics" rise up in the colonial heartlands (from gender-critical feminism to nativism), *Fractured* issues a powerfully argued appeal to the left to finally understand that "Prioritising solidarity for those most marginalised or under attack is not about guilt or charity or 'virtue-signalling'. It is part of what can get everyone free."'
—Sophie Lewis, author of *Full Surrogacy Now: Feminism Against Family* and *Abolish The Family: A Manifesto For Care and Liberation*. Her essays have appeared in the *New York Times, Harper's, Boston Review, n+1,* the *London Review of Books* and *Salvage*

'Provides us with an astute, readable and utterly compelling history of our present predicament. This sharp, thoughtful, generous little book helps us see the many roads that lead to better worlds, arguing that to get there we need to abandon those noisy, nasty, noxious debates on "identity politics". It clears ground, carefully tracing histories of resistance and reaction, reminding us that the working class is and always has been manifold - and therein lies our strength.'
—Luke de Noronha, academic and writer at the Sarah Parker Remond Centre, University College London and author of *Deporting Black Britons: Portraits of Deportation to Jamaica* and co-author, with Gracie Mae Bradley, of *Against Borders: The Case for Abolition*

'This is a stirring book, full of inspiration, insight, provocation. *Fractured* insists that if we are to grasp the radical possibilities of connection, we must first understand the political legacy of division. Expect to be educated, made to think, or better still, urged to reconsider.'
—Vron Ware, author of *Beyond the Pale: White Women, Racism and History* and *Out of Whiteness: Color, Politics, and Culture*

'A sharp and lucid rejoinder to all the political trends that in recent years have imbued "identity politics" with magically divisive powers. *Fractured* is essential to understanding anti-racist politics today.'
—Arun Kundnani, author of *The Muslims are Coming!: Islamophobia, Extremism, and the Domestic War on Terror* and *The End of Tolerance: Racism in 21st Century Britain*

'A searing materialist critique of the historical origins of attacks on Identity Politics from the right, a clarifying text that analyses the strategic purpose of the imagined "culture war" that continues to engulf mainstream politics. Richmond and Charnley understand, fundamentally, that the purview of the left should be the creation, cultivation, and fierce defence of a liveable life for all. This book is evidence of an unshakeable commitment to those principles.'
—Lola Olufemi, a black feminist writer, researcher and organiser from London and author of *Feminism, Interrupted: Disrupting Power* and *Experiments in Imagining Otherwise*

'Class reductionism sheds little light on our crisis-ridden times. Instead, *Fractured* uncovers both the historical entanglements of class and race and the multitude of solidarities that continually rise to oppose oppression. Richmond and Charnley gift us with the analysis, and hope, we need to fight on.'
—Alana Lentin, a scholar who works on the critical theorisation of race, racism and anti-racism and co-author with Gavan Titley of *The Crises of Multiculturalism: Racism in a Neoliberal Age* and author of *Why Race Still Matters*

Fractured

Race, Class, Gender and
the Hatred of Identity Politics

Michael Richmond and Alex Charnley

PLUTO PRESS

First published 2022 by Pluto Press
New Wing, Somerset House, Strand, London WC2R 1LA

www.plutobooks.com

Copyright © Michael Richmond and Alex Charnley 2022

The right of Michael Richmond and Alex Charnley to be identified as the
authors of this work has been asserted in accordance with the Copyright,
Designs and Patents Act 1988.

British Library Cataloguing in Publication Data
A catalogue record for this book is available from the British Library

ISBN   978 0 7453 4657 1   Hardback
ISBN   978 0 7453 4656 4   Paperback
ISBN   978 0 7453 4660 1   PDF
ISBN   978 0 7453 4658 8   EPUB

This book is printed on paper suitable for recycling and made from fully
managed and sustained forest sources. Logging, pulping and manufacturing processes are expected to conform to the environmental standards of the
country of origin.

Typeset by Stanford DTP Services, Northampton, England

Simultaneously printed in the United Kingdom and United States of America

Contents

Acknowledgements

We would both like to thank our editor, Neda Tehrani, who took on a pair of first-time authors and helped us chop up and reimagine a very unwieldy initial manuscript. You are so good at what you do. And we are grateful to everyone else at Pluto Press and in the extended production process, who have helped to bring this book to publication.

We want to acknowledge our wonderful comrades – Chloë, Jaemie, Mark, Tzortzis, Lazo – with whom we produced *The Occupied Times* and *Base Publication* for many years. The environment of radical pedagogy and communal production we all shared was what allowed the two of us to begin writing together. We would also like to thank early readers and encouragers who convinced us to persist with seeking a publisher: Sami, Harry Stopes, Tamar, Angela Mitropoulos. Particular thanks go to Kerem Nişancıoğlu, Lou Thatcher and Mike from libcom for incisive feedback that helped us transform the project. Much love to Alana Lentin for all her support and teachings. Love and thanks to fellow members of the Left Twitter rabble. We've learned so much from connecting on that hellsite for over a decade. You were told again and again to 'log off' and bravely you resisted. Thank you more generally to online and irl movement archives and resources like libcom.org, 56a Infoshop in Elephant & Castle and the Institute of Race Relations in King's Cross who are dedicated to keeping radical histories alive as well as to struggle in the here and now. Such spaces are only kept going through the hard work, volunteered time and comradeship of their collectives.

Michael would like to give thanks for his grandparents. Arthur Rubenstein, who instilled in me a love of history and a passion for social justice, and Ruth Rubenstein, my hero, who died before seeing this published but who believed that it would, even when I didn't. May both of your memories be a blessing. Thank you to my parents for your unending love and support, and your help in the darkest of times. I owe you everything. And what I don't owe to you, I owe to our dearly missed Milo. Love and congratulations to Matthew and Evelin on your new little comrade. Welcome to the world, Ilana. Get ready for the struggle! And to my number one Alex, who by the time this comes out will be my wife: thank you for being you, my beautiful best friend. Having the calm reassurance of a partner who gets published all the time was invaluable. I couldn't do anything without you; you are my everything.

Alex would like to give thanks to his Mum, for bringing political questions into our lives early. The inspiration we got from watching you hold a room and turn a conversation on its head taught us that there is nothing better than good conversation. To my brothers, for all the times we have laughed together. Dad, for art and the richness of its question. Kev, for telling me about history on long trips and for your wonderful cooking. Moggy, for reminding us 'what a laaarf!!!' life can be. Gabe, thank you for Hathoo. Ness, for a smile as wide as the world. Imo, for all our seaside adventures together. Sophia and Aaron, thank you for the sofa and your generosity for all those years! Thanks to my wider family and friends. To Mike's folks, special thanks for being so warm and accommodating. To David, thank you for your kindness, tenderness and patience. And to my wife Nat, who has been my best mate since we were kids, for loving everyday more because we're together. And finally to Thea and Breya, our little comrades, who we could never imagine life without.

Introduction

In order to build solid political alliances in the future there has to be some awareness of the historical processes that have brought different groups together and kept them apart.[1]

Vron Ware

Solidarity is the best weapon in the struggle of life.[2]

Aaron Lieberman

Throughout this book we examine conservative propagations of 'identity politics' – a political smear that has been monopolised by the right, but also has form on the centre and left. These discourses will often feature other terms: 'culture war', 'political correctness', 'multiculturalism', 'neoliberalism' (mainly on the left), 'cultural Marxism' (mainly on the right), 'free speech', and now 'gender ideology' and 'wokeness'. Each has their own meanings and contexts depending on where the reaction is coming from. 'Identity politics', and these related terms, act as ideological frames for explaining social and political division. We refer to them all at some point and relate them back to histories of class struggle. We call these social divisions 'fractures', which have become antagonised and deepened by a breakdown in the liberal democratic consensus. The following tendencies characterise this escalation:

- More confrontational government frames pitting 'the people' against threats to nation
- A weak or resolutely defeated 'formal' opposition to the right (i.e. social democratic parties and trade unions)
- A discredited model of neoliberal progress or 'centre ground'
- An ethically motivated and environmentalist youth politics
- Black resistance against the police and racism
- Conspiracies about elites

- A convergence of fascist rhetoric and personalities into the mainstream
- Insurrectionary street politics from diverse formations

The ambiguity produced by a breakdown of liberal democratic legitimacy invites ambiguous political framings. Identity politics is a metaphor all political persuasions have been able to rely upon. The term 'identity' allows for multiple meanings in transit. In pejorative discourses of identity politics, one of the main implied meanings is a politics guided by manipulation. This emphasis works through the slipperiness of the word 'identity', especially in an internet age, where persona construction is built into the medium. These terms function as organising points for conspiracies of cultural decline, demographic change and national weakness. Far-right conspiracies of national weakness are then connected to mainstream adjuncts to the far right, such as Jordan Peterson, who claims there has been a 'backlash against masculinity'.[3] 'cultural Marxism', 'Black Lives Matter (BLM)' and 'Anteefa' are wielded by the right as abstractions, mysterious entities, threatening to impose 'woke identity politics' on innocent populations.[*] 'Marxism' hasn't been this talked about in decades, with conservative literature on the subject enjoying bestseller status.[4] Imagery derived from the culture of liberalism – its speeches, corniness, dissimulations, talk shows – fuels a politically fluid hatred of liberals that is nostalgic for a nation governed by pure conservative ideals: strong men, strong state, free speech, nuclear families.

Aspects of this reaction also travel through the political centre. 'Cancel culture' moral panics regularly explode in Britain, one of the main production houses for transphobic conspiracy theory. The proliferation of these conspiracies, as we explore in Chapter 3, has come through liberals, and some on the left. Identity politics

---

[*] 'Antifa', as a set of organising ideas and practices, can trace its lineage back to the anti-fascist movements in interwar Italy and Germany. 'An-TEE-fa', with emphasis on the second syllable, references a tendency today, particularly on the political right, to not only mispronounce the word but also to misrepresent anti-fascist action, particularly in the USA, as more coordinated, hierarchically led and conspiratorial than in it is. 'An-TEE-fa', are regularly blamed for acts of violence or 'false flags', many on the right claimed that they were responsible for the 6 January Capitol Insurrection.

and wokeness are conservative propagations, then, but they are not limited to the right. Conservative discourses can drag others into them, while the discourses themselves are blended with left terminology. Centrist free speech absolutists have travelled deeper into this territory as their opposition to anti-fascist movements became more pronounced. In 2021, journalist Glenn Greenwald, lionised for his defence of WikiLeaks and Edward Snowden, reacted to the use of BLM and Pride imagery in government recruitment videos, tweeting,

> Contempt for it on the merits aside, one has to acknowledge the propagandistic genius of exploiting harmless-to-power identity politics as the feel-good cover for perpetuating and even strengthening the neoliberal order and further entrenching corporate and imperial power.
>
> From GCHQ bathing itself in the rainbow flag to CIA celebrating Women's Day to General Dynamics waving the BLM banner, this tactic is now perfectly honed to make liberals swoon and believe they're supporting revolutionary change as they actually cheer for status quo power.[5]

The anti-capitalism of 'masks' (and the performance of their unveiling) is no longer a minor canon of left theory and culture. These kinds of oppositional discourses are now a widespread part of popular culture and popular conspiracism. This ideological haywire is typical of our times. The spurious ways these discourses shift and re-attach produces its own trivilisation effect. Suffering is trivialised. Where examples of suffering are raised, one can easily ask who benefits and what the agenda is. This cynicism is a problem for left-wing traditions that must make arguments under the most hostile conditions. Left figureheads and media cultures, to make matters worse, have become dependent on these discourses to exert influence and grow media subscriptions (with a view that some presence is better than none). Charges of disunity, even sabotage, are projected onto trans people by some feminists and socialists. Common to all is a bitterness and resentment over the direction of left-wing politics, a dire certainty that 'identity politics' divides or repulses the working class. But the working class has always been divided.

Jacobin, the most successful English-language socialist magazine of the last decade, became a platform for anti-identity politics and anti-woke discourses. This began in reaction to Obama, but was also propelled by an interest in new right populist movements like the Tea Party (and Trump voters in the 'rustbelt'). The factional stresses that accompanied a new socialist accommodation with electoral politics also became a factor. After the Ferguson insurrections of 2014, the liberal appropriation of 'woke' in popular culture constructed a symbolic screen that the right used to prove the left dominated the mainstream.[6] The US political left – keen to maintain ideological distance from their rivals in the Democratic Party – attempted to steer anti-elite momentum towards a critique of neoliberal elites. This strategy was expressed in polemics opposing 'neoliberal identity politics' – a supposed hangover from liberation movements of the 1960s and 1970s – to a longer socialist tradition. Adolph Reed has been a stalwart of this position. His critiques of anti-racism have been persistently used to remind socialists that Black Lives Matter (BLM) was a distraction:

Notwithstanding its performative evocations of the 1960s Black Power populist 'militancy', this antiracist politics is neither leftist in itself nor particularly compatible with a left politics as conventionally understood. At this political juncture, it is, like bourgeois feminism and other groupist tendencies, an oppositional epicycle *within* hegemonic neoliberalism, one might say a component of neoliberalism's critical self-consciousness; it is thus in fact fundamentally *anti*-leftist. Black political elites' attacks on the Bernie Sanders 2016 presidential nomination campaign's call for decommodified public higher education as frivolous, irresponsible, or even un-American underscores how deeply embedded this politics is within neoliberalism.[7]

As the traditional means of organising left programmes became more restrictive (i.e. conservative and corporatised labour unions became more service-oriented), explanations for the weakness of the left have been found in some of the new movements and identities that have emerged: BLM, in particular. Reed has blamed anti-racism for divisions on the left since the late 1970s and he is only one among many. The impression that neoliberalism is somehow 'fundamentally' serviced by a deployment of minority concerns is a more free-floating conspiracy today and one with an undeniable structure familiar to a particular strand of quasi-Marxist thinking. The problem here is not the simple relaying of facts. There *are* Black political elites, there *are* corporate feminists, there *are* reactionaries who are queer/trans. Identities *can* be used to ward off class privileges, especially in a public sphere that selects for diverse representation at the surface level. But this is also the case for ex-socialists like Tony Blair, who used his socialist identity to ward off challenges from the left and scale the heights of Davos. Indeed, socialist parties across Europe have used their historical identifications with progressive movements to cement their place in 'hegemonic neoliberalism'. The same 'fundamentally anti-leftist' features were part of the most militant early socialist and trade union movements of the nineteenth and early twentieth centuries (featured in Chapters 4 and 5).

The easiest thing to communicate is that power corrupts. The problem is that the hypervisibility of a liberal multiracial public sphere is now being used as evidence to propagate a reactionary myth: that *minorities rule, minorities corrupt.* The tendency of the electoral left to look to centrist politicians for signs of 'hegemonic neoliberalism' has meant they have become politically blind to the international spread of neoliberal *anti-identity politics.* The corny proclamations of racial justice that are daily churn in US politics are, if anything, a distraction from forms of anti-cosmopolitanism now being innovated in the USA, Britain and elsewhere (including within left movements themselves). Angela Nagle, formerly within political left circles, was recruited by conservative platforms to perform this exact function. Now appearing on *Fox News*, Nagle has form arguing the 'Left Case Against Open Borders', while pivoting to mock socialist movements.[8] Imagining that every kind of contemporary anti-racist or feminist politics is yet another vital expression of neoliberalism verges on the reactionary and fast-tracks some comrades right over to the other side.

UNQUALIFIED UNIVERSALISM

It would be easier if this was just a problem of social media, but there are structural blindspots on the left that have become more obvious with time. Liberation struggles of the 1960s and 1970s have been a major neurosis of socialist historiography and are part of the reason these conservative currents keep coming back around. The structuring assumption for many is that the post-war compact made workers movements stronger, while liberation movements, by the late 1970s, had become debased and incorporated within a new neoliberal regime. We look at different versions of this claim throughout this book and challenge the assumption. It is understandable why it stuck. If it is assumed that socialist traditions were defeated or corrupted by class enemies (and were not themselves internally contradictory and subject to *challenges*, as we argue), then they may return every decade to re-enact similar lines and programmes. Robin D.G. Kelley picked up on the tendency early. When Todd Gitlin complained: 'much of the left is so preoccupied with debunking generalizations and affirming the differences among groups – real as they often are – that it has ceded the very language of universality that is its birthright',[9] Kelley answered:

> The idea that race, gender, and sexuality are particular whereas class is universal not only presumes that class struggle is some sort of race and gender-neutral terrain but takes for granted that movements focused on race, gender, or sexuality necessarily undermine class unity and, by definition, cannot be emancipatory for the whole ... Thus, when black gays and lesbians take to the streets to protest violence against them, that's 'identity politics'. When angry white males claim that affirmative action is taking jobs from them, that's class politics muffled beneath a racial blanket they themselves don't understand. When white people vote for David Duke and Pat Buchanan, that's class politics, not 'identity politics'. Something's wrong with this picture.[10]

The 1990s were dominated by this sort of schematisation. Identity politics underwent a pejorative turn after the social movements of the 1960s–1980s dispersed and a massive deskilling of industrial labour was facilitated, freeing capital to exploit labour across the world. Rights-based discourses and social justice issues were gradually limited to campaigns within the state or NGOs. There were massive Western restructures of former Soviet economies, new imperialist wars in the Middle East, Northern Ireland peace processes, the Srebrenica massacre and Rwandan genocide. Nancy Fraser argued that a 'post-socialist' split between a politics of 'recognition' (the establishing of minority or cultural rights) and (economic) 'redistribution' had expanded globally with potentially genocidal forms of 'recognition' part of the new terrain: the world had entered an 'age of identity politics'.[11]

What was suggestive about this global theory of identity politics is that it surveyed an increasingly fragmented and violent world that was supposedly united by a new consensus of Western, liberal democratic values. However, such theories of fragmentation could also become introspective and project back a false image of past unities, against a new tide of minority causes. In 1996, Marxist historian Eric Hobsbawm declared: 'The political project of the Left is universalist: it is for *all* human beings.' Adding, 'identity politics is essentially not for everybody but for the members of a specific group only'.[12] Hobsbawm ascribed inordinate power to unspecified identity groups, imputing they had the desire and ability to sideline or steamroller others: 'Identity politics assumes that one among the many identities we all have is the one that determines, or at least dominates our politics ... and of course that you have to get rid of the others.'[13] His point was that socialism is rooted in universal principles and 'identity politics' threatened to fragment it:

Today both the Right and the Left are saddled with identity politics. Unfortunately, the danger of disintegrating into a pure alliance of minorities is unusually great on the Left because the decline of the great universalist slogans of the Enlightenment, which were essentially slogans of the Left, leaves it without any obvious way of formulating a common interest across sectional boundaries.[14]

7

This was the stem of a wider structure of resentment some socialists fell into and failed to properly differentiate. The idea that 'Right and Left are saddled with identity politics' is precisely how the Trump era has been portrayed by liberals. It is an equivalence that explains nothing. Socialist explanations for the 1990s transition identified a fracturing of political traditions but tended to separate 'economic' and 'cultural' lefts, with the latter meaning any politics including a focus on race, gender, sex, disability, ethnicity. This could keep alive a traditional focus on labour movement politics – just as labour parties and institutions further turned against workers. These theories also risked adapting conservative divisions of tradition and cosmopolitan ideologies of race and sexuality into an economic/cultural split. They rested on unqualified forms of universalism that were themselves cut loose from the changing character of working-class conditions during this transition.

PLAIN EXISTING

An interesting exception is a remarkable polemic against identity politics by long-time director of London's Institute of Race Relations (IRR), Ambalavaner Sivanandan.[15] In the late 1980s, the journal *Marxism Today* tried to forge a broad left vision, anticipating that Tory rule had finally run out of steam. They envisioned a more flexible class politics organised around multiple single-issues and 'identities' from within the Labour Party. Many of these figures went on to court New Labour positions. Some, like Stuart Hall, remained critical. Sivanandan argued against this approach and for a return to class, as many socialists sceptical of identity politics do today. But he also argued that relevant class perspectives were 'eviscerated' by a political focus 'thrashing around for a showing at the polls'. Indeed, any electoral, issue-based politics – environment, class, race, gender, anti-imperialism, sexuality – was distorted when not related back to the 'exploitation of workers ... all the bits and pieces of the working class that the new productive forces have dispersed and dissipated of their strength'. The electoral focus narrows in on the national, where an international perspective was needed more than ever, 'the centre of gravity of that exploitation has shifted from the centre to the periphery and, within the centre, to peripheral workers, home workers, ad hoc workers, casual, temporary, part-time workers.[16]

Sivanandan's response is interesting because he was unattached to more sensitive defenses of the workers' movement under strain of new intellectual trends. He was reacting to a specific interpretation of Gramsci, Althusser, Lacan (sometimes veering off into generalisations), alongside his criticism of a 'working class movement' that had 'turned its face against' the 'profoundly socialist' aspirations of new social movements. Sivanandan's arguments weren't nostalgic for traditional socialist movements or determined by US-centric anti-racism discourse. His barbs can sound like those of Reed and Fraser, but as a post-war immigrant to Britain, he had no illusions about the racist character of national politics and trade unions. He suspected, like Fraser, that economic determinism was being substituted for forms of cultural determinism, but unlike Fraser, he did not wish for a return to a traditional politics of redistribution, nor did he think state recognition of identities was a fortuitous thing. He spent his life analysing and fighting the British state, the Labour Party and trade unions, which collaborated to impose racial division on the working class *in the name of redistributionary principles*. He railed against an individualist turn in politics, but whereas Reed envisions working-class universalism in one country and favours immigration controls, Sivandandan studied and fought them throughout his life. Reed dismisses 'anti-racism' as neoliberal ideology *tout court*, while Sivanandan differentiated 'state anti-racism' from the grassroots cultures of anti-racism he experienced and contributed to. Familiar critiques of identity politics turn up alongside a more discrete emphasis on race and class issues, as is evident in this passage:

The 'personal is the political' has also had the effect of shifting the gravitational pull of black struggle from the community to the individual at a time when black was already breaking up into ethnics. It gave the individual an out not to take part in issues that affected the community: immigration raids, deportations, deaths in custody, racial violence, the rise of fascism, as well as everyday things that concerned housing and schooling and plain existing. There was now another venue for politics: oneself, and another politics: of one's sexuality, ethnicity, gender – a politics of identity as opposed to a politics of identification.[17]

It has become conventional today to write off personal or subjective experience as a symptom of neoliberal individualism and consumerism. But Sivanandan's polemic was not limited to pointing at the speech of some Clintonite lackey or a CIA advert to unmask neoliberal ideology. Crucially, he maintained a distinction between grassroots political cultures and the electoral formation of individual and group identities, 'The personal is the political may produce radical individualism, the political is personal produces a radical society.'[18] This gets us to the nub of the identity problem: what working-class vantage points and perspectives were innovated by participants who brought their own personal experiences to them? If they became overshadowed and overpowered by conformist trends and identity-thinking – nationalism, careerism, sectarianism – how did this occur? These same questions should be applied to socialist movements which, Sivanandan acknowledges, repressed the kind of expanded analytical frames that feminist enquiries innovated. This matters not because bad actors need rooting out, but because we can understand more concretely how liberal societies are constituted by fracture: polarisation is nothing new, on the contrary, it is the point.

Despite his polemical and caustic style, Sivanandan left open a fuller idea of working-class problems of 'plain existing' (including deportations, deaths in custody) that are not accommodated in other socialist framings of class. In the Sanders' movement in particular, an orthodox view of class sought to mobilise a colourblind alliance of voters. This identification with the working class was of a centrist technocratic design: made to land well with Democratic voters who moved to Trump, while attacking the 'wokeness' of centrist factions within the party. Defunding or abolishing the police were not issues socialists could 'pitch to voters'. These issues were also doubled down on in Corbyn's manifestos, where increases in police numbers were promised. This is not surprising: social democratic programmes are functionally limited in what they can do. What is more concerning is how 'anti-wokeness' became a popular socialist snide. It has been strange to see left-wing US tropes of 'identity politics' and 'cancel culture' reach into the heart of public discourse in Britain. Contexts for these discourses vary from place to place, as we examine in Chapter 1, with the toppling of the Colston Statue and the reaction that followed. This direct action produced a new enthusiasm for anti-colonial histories of abolition. It also sparked spiraling anti-woke discourses that went right to the summit of politics and entered into policymaking. Centrists and tabloids took hold of the identity politics charge and used it to band together *socialists and anti-racists* as woke extremists who hated Britain. As we argue throughout, the left cannot control how these discourses evolve and they do not universalise well. Conservatives promote a conspiracy of liberal elites and signpost 'progressive' language as the cause. The most witless/reactionary left currents have imitated this reaction and found themselves swallowed whole by it. The most witless/reactionary left currents have imitated this reaction and found themselves swallowed whole by it. Strands of left populism now lie marooned within jaded and pointless oppositions, having achieved nothing but rancour, suspicion, intellectual stagnation, yet growing media platforms for a few.[19] When all is marked by inauthenticity, revealing the inauthenticity of the world is comforting, but class mantras offer no alternative. If these projects were working, they would not need strawmen to qualify them. There must be other ways.

IDENTITY POLITICS REVISITED

In Chapters 2 and 3 we revisit the original identity politics concept. We look at the work of Black feminists in the USA and Britain and compare how identity politics was conceived and related to very different Black experiences and histories. The Combahee River Collective – who coined the term – published a statement in 1977 outlining a sophisticated appreciation of the interrelationship between exploitation under capitalism and racial/gendered/sexual oppressions:

The most general statement of our politics at the present time would be that we are actively committed to struggling against racial, sexual, heterosexual, and class oppression, and see as our particular task the development of integrated analysis and practice based upon the fact that the major systems of oppression are interlocking. The synthesis of these oppressions creates the conditions of our lives.[20]

We explore the context of these debates to underline their enduring relevance, because the problem of identity is essential to what 'class struggle' means today. This writing is also far more interesting and thoughtful about class relations than most 'socialist class analysis'. The Black feminists we highlight kept relationships between 'the left', the 'working class' and 'liberation' subject to critique. Their writings troubled identity in order to think about different forms of exploitation and oppression through *concrete examinations* of everyday life. The best observations were grounded in historical critiques of colonial relations.

US hegemony over 'culture war' insignia has enabled British commentators and politicians to complain that 'identity politics' or 'intersectionality' are merely US exports. Yet Black and Asian women in Britain responded to their conditions by starting their own groups and developing their own theory, similar to Black feminists in America. By providing accounts of Black women's struggles for their basic needs and those of their children, Beverley Bryan, Stella Dadzie and Suzanne Scafe, in *The Heart of the Race*, exposed contradictions internal to the identities 'women' *and* 'working class'.[21] In *Dreams, Questions, Struggles*, Amrit Wilson described, in similar terms, the conditions that motivated South Asian women to organise autonomously:

Many of us had earlier belonged to the predominantly male black movement or the predominantly white women's movement. By forming Awaz, in 1977, we had taken a stand against the sexism of the former and the racism of the latter. But these were not the reasons why we, a handful of mainly young Asian women, had set up the group. It was rather that we desperately needed a way of addressing our needs and those of other Asian women ... It was a time when Asians in Britain, with few exceptions, were working class, doing some of the hardest and lowest-paid jobs.[22]

These struggles informed a critique of universal identity-thinking around 'womanhood' taking hold in a white, middle-class-led Women's Liberation Movement. Black feminist critiques of 'white feminism' then, continue to offer crucial insight into the imperialist thinking organising white feminisms today. Contrary to contemporary reactions to identity as a homing device for the self or dogmatic groupthink, a major contribution of Black feminism was how it *problematised* identity, its affirmations and unlockings but also its confines. Black feminists in both societies could find no 'home' in the given frameworks of liberation, facing exclusion or subordination in Women's Liberation, and Black Power movements often unwilling to actively address patriarchy.

BORDERING THE MASSES

In every scene this book visits, the nation-state appears as a strangulation on revolutionary solidarity. Chapters 4 and 5 present the border as a state jurisdiction to exploit labour. We think of these jurisdictions as 'regimes of identification' and relate questions of identity back to the border – a major technology of modern state-building. The historical scenes we select show the birth of modern border controls in Britain and America. First we detail the struggles of the Jewish working class in Edwardian Britain, then Chinese immigrants in nineteenth-century California. These histories and their echoes force us to question the tenability of a 'class-based universalism' within the nation. What compromises helped secure welfare provision and collective bargaining? How far did the universalism of socialist movements stretch? Has a class-based universalism ever actually existed? Nostalgia for a more coherent national politics is partly a desire for the world to return to an idea of something, at least, more coherent. This stimulates nationalist feeling in socialist currents (via imagery of post-war class compromise) and centrists (mourning their pre-Trump/Brexit Shangri-La). But the insecurity carries through to most, if not all, political traditions. Marxist, liberal, feminist, environmentalist and anarchist traditions all have tendencies that stress an unqualified universality under threat from divisive neoliberal identity politics.[23] Thinking through our divisions historically allows some distance from periodisations of neoliberalism that overstate a novel break from the past.

In Chapters 6 and 7, we follow historicisations of the border with an analysis of racist violence. How does racism become structural? Chapter 6 looks at forms of racial violence that have been a regular feature in the last century in Britain, where riots are routinely met with racist legislation and the increasing of state powers. Chapter 7 follows up an analysis of Britain's racist riots of 1919 with those that took place in the USA. What we are interested in here are fascist modalities particular to each country and its colonial setting. We refer to them as 'whiteness riots' to determine more accurately what they set out to defend. These riots provoked international responses from Black and anti-colonial resistance movements and intersected with highpoints of worker struggle, showing how moments of revolutionary upsurge are unpredictable.

In each chapter, we try and circle some of the ambiguities produced by what we refer to as 'Revolutionary Time'. No analogies with the past can be made, but these histories are not so far gone either. We live in a period of class antagonism and fascist reaction that borrows from the historical insignia of the past and is stuck in a spiral of escalating crises. There have been millions strong strikes globally, but in Britain and America, a more mixed picture. There are intriguing upswells in workplace organising that do not conform to traditional paradigms. Strikes are often spontaneous and fragmented – sometimes simply responding to new capitalist offensives.[24] The most radical unions in both countries are marginalised by mainstream ones, even when (perhaps *because*) they have been the best at getting wins.[25] The future of all political movements will be just as unpredictable. The last decade has been characterised by global struggles from below against the police and widespread demands for climate justice. Rebellion has broadened horizons, illuminating the possibility of a different kind of society. One that capitalism cannot accommodate. But many of our current socialist projects cannot either. The framing of identity politics and wokeness has succeeded in trivialising some of the most vital social struggles of our time and drawn us into petty attachments. Every upswell in political intrigue returns to 'identity' as a mark of decadence – with 'culture war' division marking a decline from better days. But how much better were these 'better days'? It is seductive to look on past eras as periods of strength, especially when living through periods of desolation. It is understandable to call for unity in troubled times. But this has often led to blaming new social movements for the defeats of the left. Such projection is now common. This book argues that artefacts of colonialism are continuous and developing through an era of capitalist barbarity. The barbarism associated with the 'early stages' of capitalism changed in character. It was developed through new technologies and supply lines, formalised within new legal powers of the liberal state, but we cannot say with any confidence that capitalism has qualitively progressed. That is why barbaric formations keep bouncing back, seemingly rejuvenated, but also looking to the past, howling for the heroes of past slaughters. We should be ready for them.

1

Whiteness as Historiography

The center of activity of abolitionism lay in the movement of the slaves for their own liberation.[1]

C.L.R. James

Not even the dead will be safe from the enemy if he wins.[2]

Walter Benjamin

One of the signal moments of backlash against the first Black Lives Matter (BLM) wave of uprisings was the June 2015 massacre at the Emanuel African Methodist Episcopal Church. That day in Charleston, South Carolina, nine Black people were murdered during their bible study. Their killer, Dylan Roof, joined the study session before pulling out a handgun and opening fire. He reportedly told his victims: 'I have to do it. You rape our women and you're taking over our country. And you have to go.'[3] Roof targeted 'Mother Emanuel', as the church is known, specifically for its historic significance.[4] Established in 1816, it is one of America's oldest Black churches, co-founded by former slave and abolitionist, Denmark Vesey. Accused of plotting an insurrection, Vesey was executed in 1822 after a secret trial. Thirty-five suspected conspirators were also executed, several more were deported. The church was burned to the ground. Black churches were outlawed, their congregations had to meet in secret. 'Mother Emanuel' would not be rebuilt until after the Civil War. After the 2015 massacre, writings by Roof were found online. One picture saw him posing with a Confederate flag, among other white supremacist insignia, leading to renewed demands that the flag be removed from all government buildings.*

Two years later, with Confederate flags and monuments being removed across the country, local officials in Charlottesville, Virginia, agreed to take down a statue of Confederate general Robert E. Lee. Some locals protested. President Trump tweeted it was 'sad to see the history and culture of our great country being ripped apart, with the removal of our beautiful statues and monuments.'[5] The proposed removal of the Lee statue led white supremacists to organise the 'Unite the Right' rally in August 2017, bringing thousands of fascists, and anti-fascists, to Charlottesville. White supremacists holding torches encircled and attacked a group of mostly Black counterprotesters, chanting 'White Lives Matter', 'Blood and Soil' and 'Jews will not replace us'. One white supremacist drove into a crowd of counterprotesters, killing one, Heather Heyer, and injuring many more. Afterwards, Trump notoriously condemned 'both sides'. 'Not all of those people were white supremacists by any stretch,' he told a press conference:

> Those people were also there because they wanted to protest the taking down of a statue of Robert E. Lee ... So this week, it's Robert E. Lee ... I wonder, is it George Washington next week? And is it Thomas Jefferson the week after. You know, you really do have to ask yourself, where does it stop?

Despite Heather Heyer's murder and the brazen gatherings of neo-Nazis, Trump's 'both sides' intervention was barely challenged. The moral equivalence he made between Founding Fathers and Confederate generals was more offensive to the assembled journalists. 'George Washington and Robert E. Lee are not the same,' commented one. Trump replied:

> Oh no? George Washington was a slave owner. Was George Washington a slave owner? So will George Washington now lose

---

* This received predictable pushback. Ten days after the shootings, Bree Newsome took matters into her own hands, scaling a flagpole at South Carolina's State House and tearing down the Confederate flag. Upon descending, she was arrested.

his status? Are we going to take down ... statues to George Washington? How about Thomas Jefferson? What do you think of Thomas Jefferson? You like him? Okay, good. Are we going to take down his statue? He was a major slave owner. Are we going to take down his statue? You know what? It's fine, you're changing history, you're changing culture ...[6]

By 2020, an anti-racist uprising spread across the country and the world, sparked by police murders: Breonna Taylor in Louisville in March and George Floyd in Minneapolis in May. Floyd's murder was caught on film. The video showed policeman Derek Chauvin kneeling on George Floyd's neck while he cried for his mother, uttering the same words as another Black victim of police murder, Eric Garner: 'I can't breathe.' Chauvin knelt on Floyd's neck for nearly ten minutes until he died. The video spread across the globe in hours. Millions hit the streets in the USA, and elsewhere – all in the midst of a global pandemic.[7] Police stations were set on fire, with surprising levels of support.[8] Protesters were killed and journalists were arrested amidst a furious backlash.[9] White vigilantes and militias drove vehicles into and fired shots at BLM crowds. Residents came out visibly armed to 'protect their property', while attacks on Black people soared.[10]

While nearly 40 statues across the USA were being torn down, in Bristol, in the UK, on 8 June, a statue of the slave trader Edward Colston was dragged to the ground, rolled down to the harbour and dumped into the water. The images and sounds of this exhilarating act rebounded around the world via social media. Tory Home Secretary, Priti Patel, called the actions 'utterly disgraceful'.[11] Leader of the opposition Labour Party, Keir Starmer, agreed it was 'completely wrong'; the statue 'should have been brought down properly, with consent'.[12] Every toppled statue was a livewire of political euphoria. The domino effect Trump had predicted was happening and dominos fell beyond America.[13] For a tantalising, intoxicating moment, a palpable fear was spreading that the toppling might never let up; that there was hardly a monument that did not commemorate some racist or atrocity. This moment re-emphasised what was already known to many locals: that Bristol was a city built upon its position as a nerve centre of the Atlantic

Slave Trade. This did not come out of nowhere, local anti-racists had been petitioning to remove the statue for years. Before this, public debates over statues had been isolated to university campuses, occasions for media caricatures of students and academics as 'snowflakes', too fragile to engage with the past. Tearing down statues supposedly alienated ordinary people and yet ordinary people had just dumped Colston in the harbour. What was powerful about the action was not only the ethical intervention against the racism of British life, but the ease and comedy with which the thing fell apart. Bristol poet Vanessa Kisuule wrote:

Countless times I passed that plinth,
Its heavy threat of metal and marble.
But as you landed, a piece of you fell off, broke away,
And inside, nothing but air.[14]

The hollowness of the claim that 'history was under attack' was captured in the brittleness of the Victorian casting. As to Colston's empty plinth, few suggested re-erecting him. While many thought the statue belonged in a museum, discussion locally turned to the countless streets and schools still bearing his name. Marginalised histories of migration and resistance started being retold. Bristol's 1963 bus boycott, led by Black workers, was revealed to new generations. Atlantic histories of migration, abolition and slave revolt, had a revived political nucleus. Across Britain, however, many worried, like Trump, that Colston was the tip of the iceberg. Vox pops circulated about how Britain 'freed the slaves' and 'defeated the Nazis'. Stirrings of an 'All Lives Matter' reaction followed. This reaction from below was accompanied by conspiratorial attacks from the government, echoing the New Right of the 1980s. We want to look at the quality of the backlash against 'anti-racism', 'wokeness' and 'identity politics' following this upsurge. What histories of slavery and abolition were unsettled by protest and what myths were disturbed?

HATRED OF BRITAIN

A week after Colston fell, *Bristol Cable* journalist, Priyanka Raval, approached a 'Protect the Cenotaph' demonstration in Bristol city centre. National demonstrations were called to defend statues and cenotaphs – one of the largest far-right mobilisations in a generation. Islamophobes, fascist networks and football firms piled into London. They were present in Bristol too, but Raval's interviews captured a more politically diverse crowd. The consistent reason respondents gave for attending was 'heritage'. Veterans gathered, claiming they had also been at the recent BLM protest, but wanted to stand guard to make sure the cenotaph wasn't damaged. Some felt BLM protests had overstepped their bounds:

it's great we can protest, another thing we can do in this country … [but] we are being force-fed the Black Lives Matter thing too much … rather than focus on one group, we should be looking at … all sorts.[15]

Others referred to the BLM protesters as 'fascists' wanting to incite an uprising:

I so respect this country … I will defend this culture to the death … we got normal people out here … protecting British culture, and heritage, and history, stopping, the next thing it's Isis in this country tearing down more statues … it's like a Communist uprising … if you look at General Mao … all these kinds of people they destroy history. We're gonna end up with Gulags in this country if someone doesn't stand up so that's what's happening … we're trying to stop a Communist uprising.[16]

Media attacks on Jeremy Corbyn in recent years, as well as initial reaction to BLM, had textured racist conspiracism. In a bid to marshall the discourse of Brexit and destroy a left-wing Labour leader, the press targeted Corbyn as a man who 'hates Britain' and sympathised with the IRA.[17] White supremacist Darren Osborne, who in 2017 killed Makram Ali and injured nine others by driving his van through a crowd outside Finsbury Park mosque, claimed his original plan was to kill Corbyn. 'One less terrorist off our streets,' he said.[18] In 2019, John Woodcock, who left Labour in opposition to Corbyn, told *The Mail*: 'Putin's malignant Russian regime and the Islamists who hate our way of life would be elated knowing we had just elected a man who has sided with Britain's enemies his whole life.'[19] Decades of liberal and fascist ideological crosshatching had allowed these fantasies to enmesh. Centrist politicians and New Labour-supporting columnists, as Arun Kundnani has laid out with clarity, were instrumental in driving anti-Muslim paranoia through policy, metaphor and action.[20] Tabloid talkshow cultures have mobilised this racist inventory around 'cancel culture' conspiracies that feel trivial and innocuous but keep the core victimisation narrative watered. One cenotaph-defender in Bristol complained:

I mean Little Britain, Inbetweeners, taken off TV, what the fuck?*
... All Lives Matter! ... racism is a problem everywhere, you're gonna pick on Britain? ... George Floyd was a criminal, a mugger ... is this the person that should be a martyr ... I don't think so.[21]

Conspiracies of hard left entryism, Islamophobia and anti-Blackness operated as an ideological trequartista. Another interrupted, targeting Raval personally for not being grateful: 'We're here, right, to protect the people who fought for you to be here today ... so you could have a voice.' Raval responded: 'what about the other things ... this country has done, like slavery and empire?' Another man flaps his hand behind her, 'that's in the past'. The moment the progressive foundation for Britain was questioned, Raval was told to 'fuck off! Fuck off then!' and had the camera knocked out of her hand. Raval noted a brooding paranoia organising the atmosphere, an insecurity that words would be taken out of context, that protesters would be presented as racist.[22] One sarcastically yells: 'Got what you want did you? ... snowflake cunt.'[23]

Brashly misogynist and aggressively confident Islamophobes shared political space with those who felt BLM protesters had breached core democratic values of tolerance, inclusivity and equality for all. The shared feeling of victimisation and censorship came from ideas of a mythical purdah over speaking openly about

---

* Media companies began removing content from streaming sites that featured blackface or racist jokes. These strategic, reactive measures by corporations and states were conflated with BLM demands as liberals/white people in power approximated what they thought they should be doing.

national pride, for fear of being seen as racist. Alana Lentin argues that the common claim that something is 'not racist' invariably acts as an opening for the debatability of racism's existence, and counter-accusations of 'reverse racism' or 'anti-white racism'.[24] The 'not racism' of cenotaph guardians was organised through a broad defence of national heritage. Historiographies of whiteness in Britain bond the formation of a 'British people' to a more ancestral root, indeed, they are meant to evoke this bond. Conservative MP Simon Clarke reached back to humbler origins, before colonialism, before the Norman Conquest, to relativise the question of modern foundations that the Colston direct action established: 'Our history is complex, as is inevitably the case for any nation state of at least 1,200 years.'[25] The irony was that Colston's slave-trading began in England, before 'Britain' even existed. 'Britain' was supposed to be self-evident but became a question that nationalists struggled to answer. Some fumbled, others saw an opportunity to be more direct. Douglas Murray rose to the occasion: 'I wouldn't say just statues … our holy places as a nation were being assailed.' Murray lambasted the government for not opposing BLM protesters more forcefully: 'they are our holy places and we provide no apology for it'.[26]

'Whiteness,' Sara Ahmed writes, 'gets reproduced by being seen as a form of positive residence: as if it were a property of persons, cultures and places.'[27] Eternalising 'the nation' with ancestral beginnings is the basis for modern 'white genocide' conspiracies. But such conspiracies are modelled on rudimentary liberal arguments that secularise colonialism through progressive narratives. The assumption that colonial 'periods' were transitional moments in a longer arc of pan-European Enlightenment is an uncontroversial one. What these historiographies occlude are the formal continuities and adaptations of hereditary-thinking to modern relations of property and race. Holly Brewer has shown that colonial laws 'enshrining hereditary slavery' followed the restoration of hereditary monarchy in England in 1660, as slave traders and plantation owners struggled to legitimise the legal exchange of people as commodities in the seventeenth century.[28] Before these colonial laws, white and Black labourers were formally ascribed the identity of 'servants', even if most Africans were treated and sold as slaves. Formalising a market for African slaves, which would be common to buyers, sellers, and legal enforcers and insurers of commodity exchange, required new policy and innovations in property law. Restoration monarchs strived to develop generalisable forms of hereditary ownership in English law that no longer tied people to feudal bonds, but to mobile forms of private property. This created multiple problems of identity for a legal system reacting opportunistically to commercial interests and labour problems, while experimenting with racial classification as a necessary part of the process. Differences between indentured servitude, slavery and free men, including class antagonisms posed by universalising Christian hereditary privileges over the enslaved, were in dispute amid English revolution and restoration. A need for a legal form of generalisable 'slave' property was distinguished, but was not easily implemented. Theories of economic development that see feudalism and capitalism as opposites, Brewer argues, 'are misleading; in the case of American slavery, they developed together, with terrible consequences: Stuart kings manipulated feudal laws and principles to promote not only hereditary property in people but also trade in them.'[29]

Histories of abolition that draw a progressive line from feudalism to the modern era of rights are just as easily used to defend colonialism. William Wilberforce was the leading parliamentary abolitionist of his age, but he and others like him, were actually at great pains to put forward a limited, moral case for abolition of the slave trade – though, for decades, not of slavery itself. Revolutionary currents among enslaved populations and wage-workers had generated significant labour unrest that parliamentary abolitionists had to finely balance. Wilberforce was the archetypal bourgeois evangelist, the most conservative of reformers imaginable, and so of course has come to personify the self-congratulation of nineteenth-century British state abolition. Eric Williams wrote:

> Wilberforce was familiar with all that went on in the hold of a slave ship but ignored what went on in a mineshaft. He supported the Corn Laws, was a member of the secret committee which investigated and repressed working class discontent in

FRACTURED

1817, opposed feminine anti-slavery associations, and thought the First Reform Bill too radical.[30]

Williams' incisive examination of capitalist slavery in the Caribbean captures critical throughlines for this development. Caribbean plantations became capitalist enterprises dedicated to exploiting the racialised labour of enslaved people only after combinations of enslaved Africans, as well as indentured servants, convicts and deportees, from England and Ireland, had arrived: 'In 1606 Bacon emphasised that by emigration England would gain "a double commodity, in the avoidance of people here, and in making use of them there".'[31] From the 1640s, there was an onward supply of religious Nonconformists and Irish prisoners of Cromwell. Williams writes that Bristol, specifically, saw 'a regular traffic in indentured servants ... [from] 1654–1685 10,000 sailed from Bristol alone for West Indies and Virginia.'[32] The routes for indentured servitude between Bristol and the Caribbean were adapted to a more concentrated trade in captured, enslaved Africans through the same ports by the 1680s. Plantation capital in the Caribbean modernised and expanded through a concentrated supply of enslaved people. Atlantic trade and agricultural technologies were reformed by capital to exact a finer, more instrumental calculus over the absolute exploitation of labour-power through slavery. 'Britain' was established as a key commercial identity and administrative centre of capital and racialised labour-power in the Atlantic, while US chattel slavery later developed its hereditary argument and legal precedent as the basis for a slavers' police state.[*]

The moral convictions of abolitionism in Britain remained commercially focused and flexible to economic shifts. Moderate abolitionists persistently distanced themselves from elements of

---

[*] English involvement in the slave trade began in 1563. The trade was formalised under state auspices with the advent of royal chartered companies. The Royal Adventurers in 1663, and its successor, the Royal African Company, saw profits flow to 'the king and queen, queen mother, a prince, 3 dukes, 7 earls, a countess, 6 lords, and 25 knights'. A lucrative investment for many MPs, the father of British liberalism himself, John Locke, had £600 invested in the Royal African Company. Peter Fryer, *Staying Power: The History of Black People in Britain* (London: Pluto Press, 1984), 21.

popular abolitionism and other reform causes. Wilberforce was a leading architect of early anti-trade union legislation, outlawing 'combinations' and strikes. He was close friends with Prime Minister William Pitt the Younger and a pious scourge against the 'immorality' of the lower orders.[33] Large sections of capital, the landed gentry and the Crown never supported abolition, fighting it tooth and nail right up until it happened. And as Williams notes: 'One year after the emancipation of the Negro slaves, transportation was the penalty for trade union activity.'[34] The myth of a centuries old 'British people' is recast through Williams' tracing of a global proletariat trafficked from shoreline to shoreline by the English Crown. There has never been any nationally bounded British identity of people, workers or industries that has not been actively differentiated through racism. Just as panics today around 'free speech' never seem to focus on wage suppression by employers or the rightlessness of immigration detainees, what is worth remembering about abolition are the hymns Wilberforce sang at Mass, not the workers he suppressed.[35] The lives of enslaved people have been conscripted under the same progressive birdsong. Did they do anything to abolish their own social relations? As C.L.R. James wrote, 'these whites despised the slaves too much to believe them capable of organising a mass movement on a grand scale'.[36] Legislation halted the slave trade in British-controlled territories in 1807, after parliamentary debates and votes had failed in preceding decades. The abolition of slavery itself was not legislated until 1834, or actuated until 1838. It was pushed into existence by a flurry of slave revolts – Barbados' 'Bussa Rebellion' (1816), Demerara (1823) and Jamaica's 'Christmas Rebellion' or 'Baptist War' (1831). All were partly motivated by the spread of rumour among enslaved people that they had been freed by royal decree in London but this was being hidden from them by colonial and plantation authorities. Rebellions were put down with ruthless violence. Hundreds of slaves were murdered, their bodies displayed as warnings to others.[37] History, it seems, is always in the process of being 'cancelled'. The downing of Colston, far from presenting a rupture with the past, marked a welcome return to historicisation.

WHO FREED THE SLAVES?

US histories of slavery and racism play a key role in the story Britain tells itself. Slavery happened over there, as does violent policing. If racism does exist in Britain, it is far worse over there, so why are people chanting 'Black Lives Matter' over here? Some on the left jumped on BLM as a new permutation of the 'identity politics' delusion, a cultural Americanism exported to the world. Keir Starmer rowed back on an initial gesture of support, keen to stress he knelt in respect for George Floyd, but only for this particular incident, that took place over there.

One of the most pernicious aspects of white supremacy is its power to erase histories of Black agency and self-emancipation. What BLM electrified in its insurrectionary phase (here was the heresy commentators desperately wanted ridiculed or suppressed) is the desire to abolish a world, a whole world: its social mores, its media; its police lines, colour lines, property lines. The USA had police stations burning, cops fleeing. Racist police are no less hated here.*

The intensity of this revolutionary temporality and the spreading enthusiasm for insurrectionist acts was dangerous for all governments. BLM 2020 was an expression of cross-border struggle, able to connect contemporary abolitionism – of police, prisons, race, class, gender – with the colonial sediments of slavery. Liberation struggles have always crossed borders and cast doubt over the settled status of imperialist nations. The grassroots of abolition had its own cultural flows before a British polity even existed. Indeed, the compulsion to bring public debate back to questions of 'Britain' or 'America', even where the debate was sympathetic, threatened to tidy up the messier details of abolition and liberation

---

* There is a history of British police being besieged too. In Manchester's Moss Side, amid the nationwide uprisings of 1981, a police station was bombarded by Black and white youth, led by a nine-year-old boy. Britain's first regular police force was founded in 1798 to police London's docks, that is, dockers' commoning and pilfering. Established by West India and Virginia slavers, with help from Jeremy Bentham, the Thames River Police show modern policing growing from a double concern: exploiting wage-labour and protecting private property but also providing security for slave-trading. The early river police were beset by dockworkers who rejected their authority and tried to burn down their stations.

as struggles that were outraged by these national jurisdictions and fought across them.

The extra-legal force of Black self-emancipation – that is, enslaved people continually escaping their masters and refusing to be recaptured – made slavery untenable on English soil, and later in the colonies. It happened in rebellions in West Africa against capture and transportation, and aboard ships crossing the ocean.[38] There was constant slave rebellion on the territory now known as the 'United States' before and after independence. From the very beginnings of European settlement of the Americas, there was resistance from slaves and Indigenous people. Syncretic cultures of struggle and survival developed among enslaved people. Combined elements from memories, knowledges and practices were pre-served from before enslavement and mixed with the different cultures of other slaves and of European colonisers. As Cedric Robinson wrote: 'African labor brought the past with it.'[39] Reli-gious practices from Obeah, Islam, Voodoo and reinterpretations of Christianity provided ideological structures to live by, and resist through. Black Christianity partly revolved around messianic visions of emancipation and 'Jubilee' for the enslaved, cast as mod-ern-day Israelites. Maroon societies were communities of resistance and refuge established by escaped slaves, often with Indigenous people and sometimes joined by fugitive European labourers. Organised as egalitarian subsistence cultures, marronage seeded everywhere from present-day Florida, across the Caribbean, Central and South America. The practice became less viable with capitalist settler expansion squeezing out any spaces for escape but it survived right up to legal emancipation.

Herbert Aptheker catalogued approximately 250 rebellions by slaves/indentured servants in the present-day USA between 1619–1865.[40] Aside from full-blown insurrection were more everyday forms of resistance – the 'broken and misplaced tools, the burning of crops, the work slowdowns, the assistance and protection afforded to "runaways", stealing, flight … even self-mutilation and suicide'.[41] Slave resistance was sensitive to rumours that came to take on a 'material force'.[42] Whispers allowed enslaved people to make sense of their wider political landscape, to gauge the mistrust of masters and build alliances with common enemies of their captors. The Haitian Revolution (1791–1804) was a source of inspiration for slaves everywhere. Planned revolts by Gabriel Prosser in Virginia in 1800 and the aforementioned Denmark Vesey in Charleston were directly inspired by events in Saint Domingue. Both conspiracies were discovered beforehand, their accused leaders hanged. Southern states further restricted education and church for slaves, and made life harder for free Black people as 'legally any black was to be assumed a slave unless he or she could prove otherwise'.[43] Slaves and free Black people were the central historical actors in the abolition of slavery but also in the improved conditions of all people oppressed and exploited under racial capitalism.

Abolitionism initially got some formal legal grounding through cases in English and Scottish courts taken up in the eighteenth century by slaves who had escaped their legal owners on British soil. They challenged the legality of their enslavement under metropole jurisdiction, and with some success. There had been a growing Black community in Britain since the seventeenth century. Most Black people early on had arrived as enslaved people. Having a Black slave had become a popular mark of status for the wealthy and slaves brought from West Africa or the Americas were usually children, ripped from their families at an early age. Slavery existed openly in English society in the 1600s and 1700s. Public sales of slaves were regular occurrences in port cities. Even more common were instances of slaves escaping. 'Hue and Cry' announcements dotted English newspapers – young slaves had run away, forced to eke out an existence in the cracks of urban poverty. Their prospects were made harder by racist exclusion. The year 1731 saw Britain's first official colour bar, introduced by London's Lord Mayor: 'It is Ordered by this Court, That for the future no Negroes or other Blacks be suffered to be bound Apprentices at any of the Companies of this City to any Freeman thereof.'[44] An unofficial colour bar had tended to prevail regardless. Most Black men, women and children were restricted to employment in service, 'entertainment' or sex work.

Black abolitionists in Britain, like Ottobah Cugoano and Olaudah Equiano, were at the heart of the movement. Both men had intimate connections to radical and working-class anti-slavery forces as well as elite abolitionists. Equiano's 1789 autobiography tells the extraordinary story of his life as a slave.[45] It was a huge publishing success, becoming an invaluable resource for the abolitionist cause and earning him fame in his own lifetime. Married to a white Englishwoman with whom he had two daughters, Equiano publicly defended the legitimacy of interracial marriage at a time when he was much attacked for it. Equiano was a tireless speaker and activist, and assumed a leadership role in Britain's Black community. As did Cugoano, who also wrote powerfully for abolition and more radically than most white abolitionists. He demanded, in 1787, the immediate abolition of slavery and strongly refuted pervasive claims of Black inferiority. 'The enslaver is a robber,' Cugoano stated simply.[46] More importantly, he argued, the slave had a moral duty to resist:

> it is as much the duty of a man who is robbed in that manner to get out of the hands of his enslaver, as it is for an honest community of men to get out of the hands of rogues and villains.[47]

He urged every man in Britain to take responsibility for the horrors of slavery and to rise up against it.[48] He foresaw a great rising up of the enslaved to win their own freedom.[49] Such strands of a more radical early abolitionism were those prepared to confront property rights and state power. Influential agrarian proto-communist Thomas Spence and his followers, including Black men such as William Davidson and Robert Wedderburn, linked abolitionism to a more generalised fight for social justice. So did other strains of radicalism and early socialism at the time which also called for immediate abolition. There is evidence of racially mixed crowds preventing the recapture of escaped slaves in Britain, as there was in the US North.

Such histories are largely suppressed in the British mainstream, where ink and tears are reserved for agonising over the hollow bronze carcasses of slave merchants and white abolitionists. Indeed, celebrations of Colstons and Wilberforces continue to exist side-by-side. When Black people in Britain bring up slavery or reparations today they are often met with responses like 'actually we abolished slavery first!' Before being told they should 'move on'.

Clear links can be made between the coterminous rise of European abolitionism, capitalist industrial development and class struggle in the highpoints of the movement in both the USA and Britain. Sections of the ascendant bourgeoisie had begun to challenge slavery.[50] But it was also true that global capitalism overall, from its earliest development, 'needed regimes of unfree labour' while also 'unleash[ing] forces' that aided slavery's overthrow.[51] Abolitionism was not a class struggle, apart from when carried out by enslaved people themselves. At times, it was emphasised as an emollient during periods of metropolitan strife. But different sections of these divided societies found various ways to relate to the anti-slavery cause. Bursts of popular pressure for abolition in the metropolis tended to coincide with crises of state and democracy, when common cause was easier to build.[52] Such crises were openings often brought on by slave revolts.

REVOLUTIONARY TIME

There was no legal switch that turned the lights out on American slavery. Abolition was inconceivable to most people, right up until it happened.* While slaves had struggled against slavery from the start, immediate and uncompensated abolition was an extremely fringe position among US whites. Even within the abolitionist movement, a key divide centred on the strategic and moral question of gradual or immediate emancipation. When the radical white abolitionist John Brown and his comrades, some of them former slaves, raided the armoury at Harpers Ferry, Virginia in 1859, they hoped to instigate slave rebellion across the South. Those who were not killed in the failed attempt either escaped or were detained and executed. Within six years, 4 million enslaved people – nine

---

* Frederick Douglass described the lay of the land as he fled to Britain in November 1859, fearing capture for his (non)involvement in John Brown's plot:

> Slavery seemed to be at the very top of its power; the national government with all its powers and appliances, was in its hands, and it bade fair to wield them for many years to come. Nobody could then see that in the short space of four years this power would be broken and the slave system destroyed.

Frederick Douglass, *Life and Times of Frederick Douglass: The Complete Autobiography* (New York: Crowell-Collier, 1968), 321.

out of every ten of whom were illiterate – were free from bondage. This is what W.E.B. Du Bois called 'the General Strike of the Slaves'.[53] The strike entailed mass refusal of work and escape from plantations, first at a trickle then by an almighty flood. In some cases slaves sacked the plantations that had held them.[54] Others could not or chose not to, particularly those in the Deep South, furthest away from the Union Army's advance. Unable to leave, many nevertheless acted to force a shift in the power dynamics of the plantation system. As more and more Southern white men directly involved in owning and managing plantations had to join the Confederate army, enslaved people were able to assert more rights for themselves, refuse tasks and defend themselves from the extreme violence that had always been required to maintain slave society.[55] Diaries of the time show a slaveholding class horrified and flabbergasted that their slaves would rebel or escape.[56] The micro-level social control powers of the planter were fatally undermined. An expanded interventionist federal state would eventually seek to superintend a new regime of labour discipline, but in the meantime Black freedom-seeking spread out into all areas of American life. Some Black men in the South voted and were elected to local, state and national office, even becoming part of the state's policing function. But autodidactism also flourished in local and mutual aid organising. Black churches built on their autonomy, while Black labour resisted and went on strike and the tiny Black minority in the North secured new democratic rights.

This revolutionary break for an expansive freedom, a massive slave rebellion, was appropriated and rearticulated through other movements of the day. It blew wind into struggles everywhere. David Roediger refers to this as 'Revolutionary Time', a period 'in which the pace of change and the possibility of freedom accelerated the very experience of time'.[57] Roediger's work on this period provides an alternative to reductive left critiques of contemporary 'identity politics' or 'wokeness', which are treated as a fashion, a moralising internet trend distracting from the universality of class. The problem with this argument is there has never been a self-conscious universal class of workers in the history of capitalism. In the nineteenth century, nascent US and UK workers movements were, in fact, profoundly impacted by slave rebellions and the moral arguments they posed. The watchword of the slaves' fight for emancipation was the cyclical Biblical tradition of 'Jubilee' which signalled the freeing of slaves and cancelling of debts. Roediger notes how worker strikes were inspired by the rolling bid for freedom that the slave strike initiated: 'Those making the demand [for an eight-hour day] had seen with the slave's unfolding emancipation that the impossible could be made real.'[58] Some workers involved in the eight-hour-day movement had been active, if often equivocal, abolitionists, including labour leaders like Ira Steward and Joseph Weydemeyer. Radical Republicans like Wendell Phillips and Thaddeus Stevens even came to support the eight-hour-day demand. Workers borrowed the language and songs of slave self-emancipation. Steward spoke of the need for slaves' and women's emancipation as a prerequisite for the struggle of the workers movement, echoing Marx's sentiments that 'labour in a white skin cannot emancipate itself where it is branded in a black skin'.[59] Black labour leader Isaac Myers addressed the National Labor Union in 1869, connecting the enslaved labour of the Black person to the waged labour of the white, and underlining the role of enslaved people in their own emancipation.[*]

Slavery, or slave labor, the main cause of the degradation of white labor, is no more. And it is the proud boast of my life that the slave himself had a large share in the work of striking off the fetters that bound him by the ankle, while the other end bound you by the neck.[60]

In the aftermath of war, there was a growing movement of Black workers forming organisations, resisting and struggling over the length of the working day.[61] There was widespread agitation among the freedpeople of the South for contemporary reparations in the form of land.[62] The Republican bourgeoisie, however, shied away from the seizure of further land and capital from former slaveholders which would have been required for the millions of

---

[*] The National Labor Union (NLU), founded in 1866, viewed 'free' Black workers as ill-disciplined, ignorant and liable to be manipulated by capital. Union rhetoric was at times more calculated than white workers' actions but the solidifying postbellum racial division of labour was characterised by twin disciplining forces: the 'colour bar' and the 'hate strike'.

free Black people to gain a foothold in postbellum society. There would be no significant land redistribution, no '40 acres and a mule' to every freedman, as promised during the war. This passing of 'Revolutionary Time' marks a catastrophic fork in the road, a counter-revolution against the General Strike of the Slaves. What was achieved during the brief window of what Du Bois called 'Black Reconstruction' was extraordinary. Comprehensive education and Black male enfranchisement and representation within existing political structures improved Black quality of life. Radical Republicans in Congress, the military and state governments seized control of the process of Reconstruction from President Andrew Johnson after he showed his determination to re-empower defeated Confederates in the former slave states, waving through new 'Black Codes' to all but reinstitute slavery. Johnson tried to shut down the Freedmen's Bureau, responsible for the life-saving healthcare and education infrastructure for freedpeople (and poor whites). He also vetoed much of the legislation proposed by Radical Republicans in Congress. Popular support for Radical Reconstruction grew in the North, with many horrified by Johnson's indulgence of Southern rebels. This battle played out over several years between warring factions of the Republican bourgeoisie who held differing visions for the future roles of both Black labour and disgraced Confederates. Disagreement also centred on the necessity or length of the military occupation in a postbellum South still plagued by violence.

The promise of a Radical Reconstruction, however, was defeated by a bourgeoisie allergic to land redistribution and by white terror – vigilante massacres, assassinations and intimidations perpetrated by the newly formed Ku Klux Klan among others.[63] White supremacy finds its 'Redemption' – the word used by those forces who secured white domination and instituted racial apartheid – following this period of contestation, uneven democratisation, Black self-education and self-organisation. This temporary, partial Black liberation amid ever-present white revanchism and ressentiment, nevertheless marks an extraordinary window of history, one forced open by slave struggles from below. Slave self-activity and the prowess of Black soldiers and spies in the Union war effort, crucial in defeating the Confederates, terrified the authorities who quickly demobilised and disarmed Black militias. Slavery did not return – a testament to the collective struggle of African Americans for every inch of autonomy they could grasp hold of, but also to capital developing new regimes of accumulation and social control. Federal withdrawal from the South marked a new settlement – one characterised by continued, if modified, white supremacy, leaving the vast majority of Black people without land, freedom or the most basic of civil rights, remaining exposed to constant state and popular violence. Saidiya Hartman describes the coming of emancipation as 'less the grand event of liberation than a point of transition between modes of servitude and racial subjection'.[64] Hartman treads delicately in helping us make sense of the 'tragic continuities in antebellum and postbellum constitutions of blackness'.[65] She is careful to make clear that what follows is not identical to antebellum slavery but that the postbellum regime of debt peonage, sharecropping, convict-leasing and other forms of coerced labour kept nearly all Black people in the South rooted to the plantation as a subjugated 'race' controlled by threat, violence and contract.[66] The maintenance of a near monoculture in the cotton cash crop helped to hold many of the prevailing power relations in place. Gradually, Black male suffrage, where it had ever fully existed, was extinguished from statute books and political practice, and 'Black Reconstruction' was extinguished from memory. Northern capitalists decided they could happily work with Jim Crow and the Supreme Court helped along the way. Convergence and consensus formed between ruling classes over a shared interest in labour discipline and ideological agreement about Black inferiority. Popular pressure was also applied as the vast majority of whites, across the land, opposed Black equality.[*]

This reaction greatly impacted the US workers movement. In the quarter century following emancipation, white workers were the more likely to scab on Black workers. The general rule with

---

[*] Northern bourgeois radicalism shrivelled and disappeared, replaced by a conservative lionising of free markets, part of a wider capitalist class offensive against a growing and varied labour militancy. Many reformers grew tired of the 'Negro Question', blaming Black Americans for failing to grasp the opportunities they had been 'given'. Reconstruction was increasingly seen as a cautionary tale of 'too much democracy' for those incapable/undeserving of it.

white unions – North and South – was to prefer segregation to joint organisation, biracial workplaces and common struggles. US labour history after slave self-emancipation saw biracial alliances become the exception as 'Revolutionary Time' faded into distant memory. Cooperation never reached the extent of the multiracial rebellions of 'motley crews' of sailors, slaves, servants and Indigenous people during the colonial period, when racial categories, national ideologies and class positions were more in flux. Linebaugh and Rediker write:

> The emphasis in modern labor history on the white, male, skilled, waged, nationalist, propertied artisan/citizen or industrial worker has hidden the history of the Atlantic proletariat of seventeenth, eighteenth and early nineteenth centuries. That proletariat was not a monster, it was not a unified cultural class, and it was not a race. This class was anonymous, nameless.[67]

Racism was a key basis of working-class disunity in the nineteenth century and beyond. Representatives of Black labour were hardly demanding much. The original demands of the Colored National Labor Union (CNLU) – formed in 1869 following the exclusion of Black workers from the NLU – were incredibly moderate. They included land reform and the protection of Black people's basic rights like freedom from violence. Isaac Myers, the CNLU's first president, spoke at the NLU's Philadelphia congress, trying to persuade white workers not to racially segregate the postbellum labour movement. His plea was illustrative of the moderate platform of class compromise and basic rights sought by the CNLU and other Black leaders affiliated to the Republican Party:

> white laboring men of the country have nothing to fear from the colored laboring men. We desire to see labor elevated and made respectable; we desire to have the hours of labor regulated as well to the interest of the laborer as to the capitalist. Mr. President, American citizenship for the black man is a complete failure if he is proscribed from the workshops of the country.[68]

Racial segmentation of the labour movement might have been to white workers' own detriment overall but this is part of the ambiguity of race–class composition in US history. The combination of material, status and imaginary advantages accrued to the white worker in comparison to the enslaved or oppressed Black worker, was all bundled into what Du Bois called the 'public and psychological wage'.[69] White supremacy did not just trickle down onto the white American worker. It had to be participated in and actively reproduced. This history is relevant to the contemporary scene. Black self-activity, not only in the 1860s, but in the 1960s and now, has been a consistent catalyst and inspiration for both overlapping and entirely distinct movements for liberation within a wider politics of class struggle. If in the US Civil War period autonomous Black freedom-seeking movements helped to foster other movements of women/workers, the same was true for Civil Rights and Black Power in the 1950s–1970s, in both the USA and Britain. These movements inspired other anti-racist struggles, women's and gay liberation movements, just as Black music, even when played by whites, helped to soundtrack generational rebellion. BLM mobilised multiracial crowds capable of potent insurrectionary upheaval and generative of a powerful global pedagogy. This is how revolutionary histories are kept alive.

STATE ANTI-RACISM

Some time after the 2020 protests, during Black History Month, Black British Tory Minister for Equalities, Kemi Badenoch, presented recommendations for a ban on 'critical race theory' in British schools. The 'over there' framing – that BLM in Britain was a dangerous, fabricated imitation of US politics – was now being used for a state attack on anti-racist education. By using 'critical race theory' as a placeholder for 'anti-racism', Badenoch could target anti-racists, and potentially teachers, for any flare-ups in Britain. At the same time, she claimed anti-racism was effectively racist. It had no relevance for Black people in Britain, other than as a method for indoctrinating innocent minds, or worse, promoting victimhood and 'segregation'.[70] Colston's toppling kicked off this reaction, but it took some months before the government could regain some ground and start caricaturing UK anti-racists as US doppelgängers. None of it made any sense, of course. If BLM really was just a US import, why were calls to remove the statue ignored for decades? The kind of euphoria experienced by multiracial crowds, live and digital, all over Britain, could hardly be understood as a merely libidinal, internet-driven copycat of US protests. Colston was one of the first to fall in the 2020 wave worldwide and certainly one of the more spectacular. A few days after, protesters pulled down a Christopher Columbus statue that had stood in Richmond, Virginia, since 1927. They placed a burning American flag on top of it before rolling it to a nearby lake and dumping it in, in homage to Bristol.

The way British anti-racist legacies were managed by the state was under very different conditions than in the USA. Under New Labour, issues of race and gender were baked into a whitewashed iconography of 'diversity' and 'equal opportunities'. This was not incorporation, but erasure. Sanitised, sanctified paeans to Gandhi and Martin Luther King Jr. could be taught in schools, but not a peep about the anti-racist militancy of Black and Asian movements in Britain and its colonies. 'Diversity and inclusion' benchmarks provided the assimilation rhetoric that 'non-white' people might find recognition within the neutral legal dominion of the state, but any 'integration' paths have always been twinned with aggressive immigration controls and racist policing. Racism was made into an individualised sickness, unrelated to colonial histories and white nationalist bordering. Diversity training dovetailed with a supercharged cultural declinism, mournful of a divided Britain under siege. Broadsheets and tabloids demonised asylum seekers and spoke openly of the problems of assimilating 'Islam' into Britain's 'tolerant' culture.

'Debating' multiculturalism, from the 1980s to the Credit Crunch, was a central means of defining 'race' as a relational issue of 'the races' that make up the national population, not the colonial relation of a nation to the people of a world it subjugated.[71] The problem was 'hate speech', 'hate crime' and prejudiced individuals. But when thousands took to the streets to confront racist police, they were hated for it. The deliberate denial of racism in Britain, and the bracketing of real racism to America, is part of what makes 'anti-racism' so incendiary for the liberal press and conservative Right in a period of rampant nationalism. For Blairism, 'racism' was all but extracted from mainstream discourse, except to signify isolated and aberrant examples of 'extremism'. While race in America is something much harder to ignore, it has rarely been a central part of how the past or present of Britain is understood or discussed – central though it is. A 'colourblind' emphasis on 'multiculturalism' would be the mechanism to exorcise race and racism from the British mainstream after the murder of Stephen Lawrence, even as it laundered the racism of Thatcherism through a language of culture and assimilation.

Therefore, many Brits ask: where has this focus on racism come from? Who is doing this? Who is polarising us? The feigned ignorance and jealous maintenance of British 'tolerance' is a major discursive structure of self-imposed historical amnesia. The conspiracy of anti-identity politics discourse relies on a public sphere already primed to aggressively resist any assertion that sexism/homophobia/racism are systemic. When racism is made systematic to a critique of a nation, it conflicts with the idea that a nation is just a collection of individuals who may or may not commit a 'hate crime'. This definition of racism provides ideological grounds to deny it exists at all, excepting the 'ignorance' of 'a few idiots'.

The banishment of British colonialism and race-making to the past is also not new. In the 1980s, the same arguments against anti-racism Tory ministers like Badenoch and others now mobilise were used to attack Black and Asian scholars and activists in Britain. Back then, Thatcher's henchman, Norman Tebbit, claimed 'most people in Britain did not want to live in a multicultural, multiracial society, but it has been foisted on them'.[72] Britain's 'New Right' saw themselves as bravely taking on hegemonic shibboleths, including 'the ideology of anti-racism', as well as other such enemies of free expression. Jenny Bourne of the Institute of Race Relations takes up the story:

> From 1982–1986, when the Institute of Race Relations produced three booklets for young people filling the lacuna about the derivation of racism (and immigration to the UK) in slavery, colonialism and imperial endeavours, attempts were made not

just to ban those books from schools and shops but to close down the IRR run by the 'racially mischievous Sri Lankan Marxist' A. Sivanandan (who had coined the phrase 'we are here because you were there').

This was not a culture war, it felt, to those of us who lived through the vilification in the press, parliament, on our doorstep, and then by funders who took fright, like a real war for our very existence ...

... Where, for example, was William Wilberforce in the IRR's account? Where were the massive infrastructural developments Britain had brought to her colonies? That was the rumble that was begun by a teacher in an association for the teaching of history and was summed up in a leader in the Spectator in July 1985 which asserted that Roots presented 'a particularly chilling example of a "history" textbook for schools' which revealed a 'hatred of "capitalist" civilisation'. 'Europeans generally, and the British particularly are presented ... as plundering barbarians ... The British ... never do anything but from the vilest of commercial motives – even the slave trade was abolished only because wage labour was more profitable.' ...

... Antiracism was a particular bugbear for all factions of the New Right – encompassing as it did issues relating to national culture, cultural relativism, and so-called values as well as their hatred of social engineering and state intervention. For the New Right, as for Thatcher, there was no such thing as society, only the individual, and this belief seeped into its understanding of racism.[73]

The New Right saw anti-racism, as many on the right (and beyond) see identity politics today, as a politics of asking for special treatment, of asking to be a special case, outside of the majority. This is simultaneously a denial of racism and a claim of unfair advantages for 'minorities' that has persisted. John Casey, a leading New Right commentator, celebrated a favoured theme, and a favoured form through which to launder New Right racism, that is, the naturalness of patriotism and 'a feeling for persons of one's own kind'.[74] This claim to 'natural' affinity sits well with the academic racism peddled today by figures like Eric Kaufmann, Matthew Goodwin and David Goodhart. Kaufmann staked a claim of wanting to differentiate between, on the one hand, 'racial self-interest',[75] something understandable among all races, and, on the other hand, racism, something he and many others locate in the individual psyche or moral compass of ignorant or extreme people. Goodhart, Kaufmann and Goodwin assume that racism is progressively disappearing, while anti-racism – always a conflation of liberal and more radical impulses – has been institutionally hegemonic for years and is now engaged in a domineering, woke overreach that alienates white majorities for their reasonable concerns about immigration and purported demographic overturnings. These men are just some of many who position themselves as tribunes and racism-whisperers for a silenced white working class, defending them from the depredations of globalism and multiculturalism. Far from identity politics and anti-racism being artificially exported from the USA to Britain, there is a need in Britain for America to be its eternally worse poor relation. BLM's global spread is reduced to an Americanism foisted upon British children, whereas UK shockjocks of anti-wokeness are only too happy to use parallel US moral panics to attack any sniff of liberation movements. Are we supposed to believe anti-racism in Britain never existed until #BLM went viral? Even as similar moral panics gained structure in 1980s newspapers? Attacks on the symbolic architecture of racism and nationalism, on the living history it is designed to erase, should be celebrated, precisely for this estrangement of nationalism. Drowning Colston provided a public history lesson, an articulation of a global historical struggle against white supremacy. In our own era of 'Revolutionary Time', where capitalist norms come under constant stress, the gathering of crowds to raze police stations to the ground and topple statues, to loot back the colonial loot, and much else besides, retains a utopian kernel of abolition, an incendiary promise of more to come. The current wave of reckoning with the origins of racial capitalism and its ongoing mutations makes multiple demands – for abolition, redirection of resources, decolonisation, reparations. It is not just that a celebratory architecture remains standing, taunting the descendants of enslaved and colonised people today, nor even that our rulers are necessarily descended from those who ruled before – it is that the USA and modern Britain have a commercial identity built upon these accumulations. And the emasculation of national symbolism reveals nationalism as symbolism pure and simple, intensely and emotionally dependent on organising racist policies around a 'history of the victors'. We are in a new phase of explosive global politics and resurgent imperialist competition across the world. BLM 2020 was one crucial moment of rearticulation in this dangerous period. The moral intensity of this movement provides inspiration and clarity for others; tactics of organising and direct action posed by one struggle, find another. There are also failures of solidarity and limitations. There is no authentic passage for class struggles; there will always be fallouts and shortcomings. We will see it again and again in the coming chapters. Nineteenth-century struggles composed around gender, race and class continually overlapped. Movement actors repel, betray, inspire and intersect with each other in histories that might be new to readers but may also feel eerily familiar. We will see how periods of war, revolution, political instability and social strife opened up new possibilities for differently oppressed and exploited people to seek paradigm shifts in social relations, in contradiction with the state, but also under the stress of collaboration with it. This is not to say that the nineteenth- and early twentieth-century timeline is analogous to our own. It simply gives us some humble bearings. The supposed problem of identity politics is not a rupture with the past. As long as there has been resistance and social movements against capitalism, there have been political collectivities struggling to compose themselves as an identity of common interests. As long as there has been racism and imperialism, there have been forms of white identity politics. Organising our thinking around concrete situations of class struggle in history reveals plenty of continuities, both in the way uprisings play out, and how they are put out.

2

Qualities of Testimony

The triply-oppressed status of Negro women is a barometer of the status of all women, and that the fight for the full, economic, political and social equality of the Negro woman is in the vital self-interest of white workers, in the vital interest of the fight to realize equality for all women.[1]

Claudia Jones, 1949

One way identity politics is discussed today is to lament how personal frames are used by individuals to control the language or actions of others. Accusations that activists manipulate words or control speech help kindle the fires for moral panics around 'trans ideology', 'anti-racism', free speech and 'cancel culture', stoked by liberal, conservative and far-right media. In Chapter 1, we saw mixed crowds who felt their 'heritage' was under attack from politically correct language and protest. Manipulation of language is also one of the more contentious meanings of identity politics on the left. One effect of overbearing conservative conspiracies of left culture as politically correct (including from left conservatives) is that it is more difficult to thoughtfully reflect on how militant political traditions are subject to 'political correction' in a very specific sense. The liberal state seeks to neutralise militancy and upsurge by rehabilitating some of its radical emphases. These are filtered through more conformist wings and integrated back into the society they set out to oppose. The language and concepts of historical movements can be turned and distorted through this process. Jackie Wang, in her essay 'Against Innocence', engages with this problem using an organising experience, where a feminist language of personal safety was used:

The phrase 'I don't feel safe' is easy to manipulate because it frames the situation in terms of the speaker's personal feelings, making it difficult to respond critically (even when the person is, say, being racist) because it will injure their personal sense of security. Conversation often ends when people politicize their feelings of discomfort by using safe space language. The most ludicrous example of this that comes to mind was when a woman from Occupy Baltimore manipulated feminist language to defend the police after an 'occupier' called the cops on a homeless man. When the police arrived ... they were verbally confronted by a group of protesters. During the confrontation the woman made an effort to protect the police by inserting herself between the police and the protesters, telling those who were angry about the cops that it was unjustified to exclude the police. In the Baltimore City Paper she was quoted saying, 'they were violating, I thought, the cops' space'.[2]

The feminist creation of safe spaces has been part of a long struggle to recognise victims of domestic abuse, rape and misogyny. There were also conformist defences of personal safety in women's movements that were overwhelmingly white, lacking race literacy about how rape threats and crime were and are racialised. Some were more openly hostile to Black women and communities. The coding of whiteness as 'innocent' was a feature of white women's movements, which, in the 1970s, developed personal safety campaigns at the same time as Black men began being incarcerated at unprecedented rates. 'Carceral feminism' is a concept used to describe the historical entanglement of feminism and the state: between claims to secure the safety of women and girls, on the one hand, as the justification for enhancing state powers of violence, on the other.

Terms like 'safe spaces' now float more freely in a liberal public sphere that selects for discourses that pit victims and universalise harms. When the language of safety and violation transcends concrete situations, where power relations are observed, cops can be reconstructed as victims of harassment. Expanding legal protections for police in hate crime statutes has been a significant strategy of 'blue reformers' to undermine grassroots challenges to police killings after the insurrections of 2020.[3] At this level of abstraction, the language of social justice can be used to justify anything, including the thing being opposed. This was palpable in Nancy Pelosi's speech, following Derek Chauvin's conviction for murder: 'Thank you, George Floyd, for sacrificing your life for justice.'[4] That George Floyd could be reconstructed as a martyr of the system that murdered him speaks to the unwavering carceral logic of liberal assimilationist framings of social justice. There seems to be no situation where 'state justice' cannot be advanced as the solution to state organised violence.

Democratic Party elites have such form for manipulating social justice language that identity politics has become a watchword for exactly this kind of manipulation. But the assumption that universalist messaging can escape liberal assimilationist social justice frames and the homogenous interest groups reproduced by elites also does not track.[5] Problems of identity are not resolved by disavowing personal experience and projecting universal fronts. This is just a form of universal identity-thinking, riveted to the same gaming of electoral compositions and groups. It is impossible to think of a revolutionary politics somehow liberated from personal experience – as if people are not already galvanised by the complex reasoning that our experiences can offer. We arrived at a reading of identity politics, and of racial capitalism, partly because of our experiences of family incarceration and psychiatric institutions. These experiences were isolated fragments of our experience until we found that by questioning the legitimacy of incarceration, and the state, both together and with others, our questions could be reposed as abolition questions.[*] It is through a kind of stitching together of fragments, as Ruth Wilson Gilmore argues, that we work through our fragmentation.[6] We have only this world, a wrong world, with which to work. Bad conditions for living and organising can be excuses to close ranks, or hold up a bigger banner, but they should prompt us to keep our mind open to the fact that solidarity does not mean bringing the same old glass to every spring. The broadness of a class struggle will depend, ulti-

---

[*] Wang has a brother incarcerated, making her attuned to the way identification with personal safety can be used to advance forms of carceral justice.

mately, on forms of solidarity that are mindful of the quality of different struggles.

Identity Politics, originally named by the Combahee River Collective (CRC), recognised the identity problem and made it a solidarity problem. It was not about 'identifying with a racial community' or 'exploring identity' through assimilationist frames, as is often perceived. It called for concrete reasoning about why movements and people were divided. The qualitative analytical value of testimony was key. Manipulations of identity instrumentalise the personal, whereas instructive testimony differentiates the universal. Identity politics was a concept that allowed for an exploration of multiple historical realities through group reporting and testimony, which was required to *elucidate complexity*. The next two chapters explore the Black feminist origins of identity politics with this in mind. There is no denying elite manipulations of identity today, but there are also dangers posed by conflating our own identities, our fundamental characteristics and qualities, with social forms of identity-thinking, which are not inevitable or natural, but are historically constituted and irreducible to a much richer plane of lived experience. Careful appreciation of its initial framing at the very least provides some distance from bitter and overheated resentments, if not hatred, many feel towards identity politics. Is it possible to rethink identity as a more complex problem today – one that gets into the grain of the problem of division? Can respect for the divisions that exist generate a more resilient 'identity of purpose' that resists identity-thinking?[*]

INTERGENERATIONAL BLACK FEMINISM

The Black Women's Alliance, later the Third World Women's Alliance (broadening to a 'women of colour' framework), became independent from New York's Student Nonviolent Coordinating Committee (SNCC) in 1969. The more mainstream National Black

---

[*] Ruth Wilson Gilmore uses the phrase, 'the developing identity of purpose', in her review of Mothers Reclaiming Our Children (Mothers ROC), a 1990s abolitionist group in LA involved in gang reconciliation and directing community resistance towards the police. Ruth Wilson Gilmore, *Golden Gulag: Prisons, Surplus, Crisis, and Opposition in Globalizing California* (Berkeley, CA: University of California Press, 2007), 202.

Feminist Organization (NBFO) was founded in 1973. The CRC began life in 1974 as the Boston chapter of the NBFO but soon broke away, finding themselves more revolutionary on questions of political economy and sexuality. These groups and others were involved in community organising or political lobbying, around reproductive rights, sexual violence, welfare, etc. Some organised consciousness-raising and reading groups.

> This focusing upon our own oppression is embodied in the concept of identity politics. We believe that the most profound and potentially the most radical politics come directly out of our identity, as opposed to working to end somebody else's oppression.[7]

This quote helps us get into some of the contention around identity politics. The claim that the most 'radical politics' comes 'out of our identity' suggests it comes out of the identity of each writer personally, but this is only because the collective were dialoguing with a militant intellectual tradition. This intervention was the product of a historical context. From the late 1960s, the iconic power of Angela Davis and the solidarity movements organised around her incarceration, as well as the writings of Frances Beal, Toni Cade and others helped kick-start a new Black feminist movement. Historian Kimberly Springer is clear on the movement's innovation: 'black feminists are, historically, the first activists in the United States to theorize and act upon the intersections of race, gender, and class'.[8] Black feminism develops in reaction to the racism of Women's Liberation[9] and to 'limits on black women's roles in the civil rights movement and to the rise of black masculinist rhetoric'.[10] Black feminism and the Women's Liberation Movement (WLM) develop concurrently[11] and interrelatedly.[12] But Black women almost entirely rejected joining WLM organisations.[13] Though most supported the basic cause, they saw the WLM as not for them. Sometimes critiques were to the point. Assata Shakur:

> Most of us rejected the white women's movement. Miss ann was still Miss ann to us whether she burned her bras or not. We could not muster sympathy for the fact that she was trapped in her

mansion and oppressed by her husband ... we had no desire to sit in some consciousness raising group with white women and bare our souls.[14]

Many saw Women's Liberation as separating gender, race and class, when Black women could not separate *themselves* from that oppressive triad. Black women's liberation was entangled with the segregated geographies of America, so that was where they organised. They played leading roles in Civil Rights and Black Power movements, and forced improvements in the gender politics of organisations, which differed from group to group, branch to branch.[15] The Black Panther Party brought people in from everywhere. Teachers joined workers, the unemployed and students. Many Black women were attracted by the militancy and confidence with which members armed themselves and confronted police, with several women in leading roles. Robyn C. Spencer, historian of the Oakland Panthers, interviewed Elendar Barnes, who joined in her teens:

I became very involved ... because it was an extension of what I knew, an extension of what they called the Deacons [for Defense] down South. And my grandfather wasn't necessarily a member of the Deacons, but our family's stance was, you know, you protect your family by any means necessary and, you know, you use guns. So my involvement in the party came from me seeing things that occurred in terms of my family organizing down South and that stuff being carried. I remember asking, 'Papa, why you always got a gun?' He'd reply, 'It's for the white folks, baby.' That is from very young. That's why I joined the Panthers. I came from that idea of standing up. And I think a lot of people in Oakland have these southern roots.[16]

Barnes' testimony connects Black Power to earlier struggles against white supremacy. Through migration, memories of the South arrived in Oakland. Black Power militancy is given different traces here. It was a *revival* of something Barnes remembered 'from very young'. This testimony carries through into how Black women related to men in the movement. Assata Shakur reportedly said in

1970: 'the absence of feminist ideology ... did not translate into an acceptance of inequality'. Divisions existed among Black women about their role in the struggle – over how much to emphasise gender within groups primarily focused on fighting racism. Angela Davis did not see feminism as a 'popular subject' among most Black women in revolutionary organisations. Authoritarian forms of misogyny persisted. Davis was attacked as 'domineering' by some Black men who 'feared she was out to "rob them of their manhood"'.[17] Black women revolutionaries were sensitive to charges that they were 'betraying' the community, knowing that providing testimony of misogyny in Black movements could be used by the white public sphere to further target and vilify Black men.[18] The feeling of being made to 'choose' is part of what leads to the development of Black feminist organisations, even if many still felt feminism was for white women and worried it would divide and co-opt Black struggle. Nevertheless, some Black and 'Third World' women, especially younger women, began peeling off from existing groups – SNCC, the Panthers and others – into early Black feminist groupings by the turn of the decade.[19]

In this sense, Black feminism represented a preservation of late 1960s/early 1970s 'Revolutionary Time'. More theory and organising began to develop along Black feminist lines, with new problems raised. The lesbian 'question' divided the movement – so did issues of class, and strategic questions of reform versus revolution.[20] This included, implicitly, and sometimes explicitly, a revision of the labour question. The CRC wrote:

> we are in essential agreement with Marx's theory as it applied to the very specific economic relationships he analyzed, we know that his analysis must be extended further in order for us to understand our specific economic situation as Black women.[21]

The struggle of various social movements to compose themselves within a class formation is simultaneously held in tension by their non-identity, or historical separation, as a result of colonial and capitalist development. This contribution opened out the Marxist problem of class formation more thoroughly than homogenising notions of 'class consciousness' were doing in the American

Marxism of the period. The original aim of the CRC's identity politics was to engage a more concrete focus on differentiated working-class conditions. Crucial to this was testimony, the banding of experiences, from which concrete analysis of historical conditions could be made.

CONSTITUTIONS OF WHITE FEMINISM

The CRC named themselves after the 1863 Civil War raid led by Harriet Tubman, freeing 750 slaves near the Combahee River in South Carolina. This historical link was itself a testament to the agency of Black women in their own emancipation.[*] The CRC identified a continuum between the service roles Black women were so long confined to and their historical separation from both the white industrial working-class and white women's suffragism. The 'extending' the CRC highlighted in their reference to Marx, related to an underdeveloped class analysis of Black women. The majority of enslaved people, especially in the Deep South, worked in the fields, where a less gendered division of labour prevailed. There was also a less strictly gendered division of reproductive labour in slave quarters. A division of public and private spheres characterised the bourgeois focus of white women's suffragism, which 'all but ignored the predicament of white working class women, as it ignored the condition of Black women in the South and North alike'.[22]

The construction of womanhood, and of feminism, was and is a contested and differently lived modality. The notion of 'public and private spheres', men and women's work and roles, was largely irrelevant to the lived experience of most Black women for much of US history. Today's conspiracies around 'Gender Ideology' seek to preserve a nineteenth-century gender ideology built on this patriarchal nuclear family – a mode of existence forcibly and legally denied to most Black people for centuries.[23] Millions of women in America (and before under British rule) were held and sold as chattel, with no bodily autonomy, no freedom, no escape from

---

[*] It also showed Black women activists constantly making connections to longer-term continuities and organising traditions.

violence. Millions of women had to suffer having their children, and other loved ones, being sold off to far away places, at any time, knowing in all likelihood they would never see them again. The political goal for white middle-class women, by contrast, was to get the vote and more agency in the liberal public sphere. This quality of freedom was alien to the experience of enslaved women, or 'free' Black women in the North, coerced into some form of wage system.

Most histories of the US women's movement tend to begin at Seneca Falls where, in 1848, the first convention explicitly to discuss women's rights was held. It was hosted by Elizabeth Cady Stanton who, like most of the movement's leading lights, came to women's rights through an involvement in abolitionism. Lucretia Mott and Susan B. Anthony were influenced by backgrounds in Nonconformist Christianity and the spiritualist revivalism of the 1830s and 1840s. However, as abolitionism and the women's movement got closer to the state, leading figures, unwilling to address composite framings of womanhood, became ever more abstracted from the concrete experience of enslaved, racialised women, as well as domestic and factory workers, Black, immigrant and white.* At Seneca Falls, Frederick Douglass was initially the only attendee to support Stanton's call for the convention to demand *women's right to vote*. There were no Black or Indigenous women in attendance, nor any mention of them.

The movement-building of women's suffrage and the 'General Strike of the Slaves' in the crisis of Civil War meant 'Revolutionary Time' was tangible. Attempts were made to work through the compositional divisions of American society. There was an openness to the emancipatory idea of equality; as the possibilities for freedom expanded, alliances between social movements were attempted. Stanton and Anthony supported the entry of Black men into the

---

* The earliest US industrial workers were women and girls in New England. Their first known strike was in Pawtucket, Rhode Island in 1824, years before Seneca Falls. An 1828 New Hampshire strike was led by women who 'shot off gunpowder, in protest against new factory rules, which charged fines for coming late, forbade talking on the job, and required church attendance'. Howard Zinn, *A People's History of the United States: 1492–Present* (New York: Perennial Classics, 2001), 228. Women in Lowell, Massachusetts 'turned out' in 1836, fighting a rent-hike in company boardinghouses. Struggles to shorten the working day near Pittsburgh saw women 'armed with sticks and stones [break] through the wooden gates of a textile mill and [stop] the looms'. Zinn, *A People's History of the United States*, 116.

Union Army and 'attempted to rally masses of women to their position by issuing a call to organize a Women's Loyal League'.[24] Stanton, Anthony and Mott travelled around Northern states rallying support for the Union cause, facing intense hostility from pro-slavery whites. The League collected nearly 400,000 signatures petitioning Congress for immediate abolition which 'represented the largest number of signatures ever introduced on a congressional petition up to that time'.[25] Angelina Grimké proclaimed at an 1863 rally: 'I want to be identified with the Negro ... Until he gets his rights, we shall never have ours.' At the League's founding convention, Grimké, by then a veteran women's rights and anti-slavery campaigner, diagnosed the conflict as 'a war upon the working classes, whether white or black ... the nation is in a death-struggle. It must either become one vast slaveocracy of petty tyrants, or wholly the land of the free'.[26] These upheavals produced a radical equality that premised a concrete universality of particulars.

This changed as these particulars struggled to compose a broad front against a reorganising and empowered central state. The American Equal Rights Association (AERA) was founded in May 1866, again by Stanton and Anthony, as an attempt to combine the struggles of women's rights and Black freedom movements. Politicians pushed back. Republican leaders helped split this fragile alliance, claiming to favour Black male suffrage in what was presented as a zero-sum game. AERA meetings came to be dominated by rancour. Many white delegates emphasised that white women were *more deserving* of suffrage than African Americans, male or female. By 1866, the wheels were already in motion to enfranchise Black men only. The repeated phrase was that it was 'The Negro's Hour', often justified on the basis of Black men's military service. Stanton and other white campaigners, though certainly not all, came to oppose Black male suffrage in reaction. Feelings of bitterness and accusations of betrayal dominated subsequent conventions as many white women had come to see the purveyance of suffrage rights as a moral mark of just deserts. What began as a contingent alliance of political equals – Black men and middle-class white women – who together envisaged something approaching universal emancipation as near and possible, became the rhetorical basis for division. Once the utopian, projective, radical equality between women and men, workers and slaves, was relinquished, an inverse, divisive equality took root, opening up a reactionary drive to reassert racial and sexual difference. How could it be that white women of high standing were now to be subservient not only to men, but to *Black* men, most of whom only months ago had been slaves? 'Equal rights' was reframed by women's movement leaders as a backwards step for women, who were destined to slip down the rungs into a position 'below' the 'Negro'. Indeed, many white women held to the legalistic belief that Emancipation immediately put freed slaves on an equal footing with middle-class white women.

PREHISTORIES OF IDENTITY POLITICS

The CRC pinpointed the identity of 'Black Women' as a central fracture emerging from the historical constitution of male suffrage and the reaction of white women. The construction of gender for Black women under slavery was distinct from that of white women slave-owners *and* white women reformers. As to the role of Black women in resisting slavery, Stephanie McCurry writes,

> [they] were at the very center of slaves' political networks and strategies of resistance, as much a part of the destruction of slavery as men were. That was as true of the Civil War South as it was of every other slave rebellion or liberation struggle in the slave zone ... In Saint-Domingue, Guadeloupe, Jamaica, Cuba, and elsewhere, women were 'equal and active participants in ... insurrectionary conspiracies', party to all of the tactics used by slaves, not excluding membership in armed maroon bands. Nor were women spared the violence that everywhere attended resistance.[27]

When the CRC wrote their statement in 1977, they were tracing a line back to the differentiated experiences of nineteenth-century Black women under slavery, and among the Northern working class. The identity of Black women was an artefact of a representative split that estranged Black women from womanhood and agency. This contradiction was given to how Black women had always framed emancipation through their own experiences. Maria W. Stewart was an early and rare example of an African-American woman who spoke publicly in front of mixed crowds. She was also published in William Lloyd Garrison's *Liberator* in the 1830s. Stewart was keen to point to the racist servitude Black people faced in the 'free' North:

> Few white persons of either sex, who are calculated for anything else, are willing to spend their lives and bury their talents in performing mean, servile labor. And such is the horrible idea that I entertain respecting a life of servitude, that if I conceived of there being no possibility of my rising above the condition of a servant, I would gladly hail death as a welcome messenger.[28]

Stewart spoke of Northern Black women being 'confined by the chains of ignorance and poverty to lives of continual drudgery and toil'.[29] She wrote: 'we feel a common desire to rise above the condition of servants and drudges. I have learnt, by bitter experience, that continual hard labor deadens the energies of the soul, and benumbs the faculties of the mind.'[30] As well as erasing Black women from womanhood, white women's critique of patriarchy particularly concentrated on the threat of racialised male labour, rather than that of bourgeois men. This not only helped to ratify the authority of patriarchal union representatives over labour, but also obscured the agency of women workers, whom they represented negatively as women needing moral rehabilitation. Black women did not register for white middle-class women, Rosalyn Terborg-Penn explains:

> Elite and middle-class white women did not normally work outside of the home. They did not have to contend with the realities of poverty, illiteracy, or menial employment, as did most Black women. Even the more fortunate Black women who were living in a quasi-free status outside of slavery, often had to work for wages or services.[31]

Sharon Harley expands the point, arguing a racial division of labour *among women of the working class* also prevailed. While all proletarian women were marginalised by nineteenth-century suffragism, there was also hierarchical ordering within the class. Black women had to do the hardest wage-labour, for the worst pay.

Since household or domestic work was considered degrading by white women, these jobs were reserved for black females ... Shut off from the factories, unskilled black females, especially in urban areas, were forced to work in domestic service at jobs which were more demanding than those most white female wage earners could imagine.[32]

The CRC were drafting historical ties and the development of Black women as a differentiated subject of the working class to try to explain what was missing in liberation and socialist movements. Long before the CRC, Claudia Jones, a Black communist, was analysing the same historical complexity of identity and how identification regimes of race and gender had sedimented class divisions. Jones had an under-appreciated impact on Black feminist intellectual and activist traditions of following generations.[33] Often written out of US and UK left histories, Jones was born in Trinidad but lived most of her life in Harlem, before spending her final years in London.* With intellect and charisma, she forced Black perspectives and women's rights perspectives into the Party. The Black feminist tradition, or identity politics, is not ideologically opposed to Marxism as some socialists think, nor is it ideologically married to Marxism, as conservatives and fascists like to claim. Jones was part of an interwar generation of Black communists who connected Marx's critique of political economy to America's racial conjuncture of labour. A central question for her was the role of women in revolution, which encouraged her revision of American women's suffrage, writing in 1949:

It was the historic shortcoming of the women's suffrage leaders, predominantly drawn ... from the bourgeoisie and the pet-

---

* Intellectual, journalist and CPUSA member since the 1930s, Claudia Jones joined as a young woman to campaign for the Scottsboro Boys. She was constantly targeted by the state, incarcerated several times before being deported to Britain. There she founded the *West Indian Gazette* and the Notting Hill Carnival, before dying aged just 49.

ty-bourgeoisie, that they failed to link their own struggles to the struggles for the full democratic rights of the Negro people following emancipation.[34]

This 'shortcoming' ran through the generations and was extended by 1960s/1970s Black feminists into critiques of Women's Liberation. Jones was in the Black women's group 'Sojourners for Truth and Justice' in the 1950s that was active in the early Civil Rights Movement. They combined proto-Black feminist perspectives with communist politics.[35] Jones' intellectual work, in advance of the 'interlocking' lens of Black feminism, produced similar theses from the late 1940s onwards.[36] It was never just about 'inclusion'. Jones saw Black women, in the USA and elsewhere, as a 'neglected' revolutionary subject, key to unlocking the global class struggle:

> We can accelerate the militancy of Negro women to the degree with which we demonstrate that the economic, political and social demands of Negro women are not just ordinary demands, but special demands flowing from special discrimination facing Negro women as women, as workers, and as Negroes.[37]

Jones outlined her position on 'super-exploitation', which as Carol Boyce Davies explains, 'refers to the way black women's labor is assumed; the way they are relegated to service work by all sectors of society, with the complicity of progressives and white women's and labor interests (including those on the Left)'.[38] In a 1951 *Daily Worker* piece, Jones and the Sojourners for Truth and Justice wrote:

> There is no state ... in which we can eat, live, work, play, rest, or breathe free of segregation and discrimination, and when the greatest voice we have produced [Du Bois] dares sing out against these indignities, his passport is recalled and he is denied the right to earn a living.[39]

The organisation was named after Sojourner Truth, who was born into slavery and was a regular attendee at abolitionist and women's rights conventions from the 1840s on. Truth consistently argued that *all* women should have the right to vote and equal pay to men.

She said of 'colored women': 'they go out washing, which is about as high as a colored woman gets.'* Bringing up the racial and gendered division of labour, Truth hits upon this seam of Black feminism that extended through generations. If the testimonies of Truth, Maria W. Stewart, Harriet Tubman and others, offer a *prehistory of identity politics*, Jones offered a mid-twentieth-century critique of the same problem. The CRC then gave it a conceptual frame. As we will continue to argue: because the identity problem was *immediate* to the experience of racialised people, particularly Black women, what emerges through these experiences is a textured, historical account of the problem of class composition and formation as such. The identity problem is nothing less than one of fracture, but the concept of fracture offered by Black feminist thinkers is not burdened by socialist anthropomorphisations of 'splitters' or 'betrayers', continually resurrected to explain failure and defeat. Black feminists have shown how lines of fracture open up ways of seeing across separations, but only if the separations are also kept close and alive to the movements that struggle against them. The concept of identity politics helped to do this, where more assimilationist frames sought smoother returns from a cohering national imaginary. This is the root of the contradiction around division and unity. It is to assume division as deceit, that 'the personal' gets in the way of unity. It is nice to imagine some future moment where divisions between people will spontaneously dissolve. But the fractures that divide have to become the canals in which struggles flow. The consequences of overshooting the real and imagining another way of overcoming this shattered palette of human experience is the death of social movements, expressed as a kind of festering disavowal and, eventually, resentment.

LINES OF FRACTURE

Women's Liberation in America exploded out of the forment of multiple, intersecting social uprisings – the 'Revolutionary Time'

---

* Truth spoke, preached and sang at conventions, becoming something of a celebrity in her lifetime. She was known for her sarcastic wit and for the publishing success of her popular narrative of her life, which she dictated to an amanuensis as she could neither read nor write. Nell Irvin Painter's excellent biography exposes the difficulty of grasping Truth the human being versus the symbol she became; *Sojourner Truth: A Life, A Symbol* (New York: W.W. Norton, 1997).

of the 1960s, exactly a century on from the AERA conferences where the alliance between white women's suffrage and the Black freedom struggle collapsed. Historian Alice Echols writes,

> to understand the '60s, one must recognize that at that point in time it really did seem that economic and social justice could be achieved, the family reorganized, and all hierarchies based on gender, race or class erased. The inability of the most technologically advanced country to defeat an army of poorly equipped Vietnamese peasants or to contain dissent at home seemed proof to radicals and conservatives alike of the system's fragility and vulnerability ... at the time it did not seem unreasonable to think that America was on the threshold of revolutionary change.[40]

The WLM's impact was vast, forcing changes in law and in culture. The movement marked a rejection of respectability and an embrace of rage, plotting the course for a confrontation with everyday patriarchy and misogyny. It marched, raised consciousness, sat-in, occupied, interrupted legislative debates, provided illegal abortions and spawned a dynamic print culture. Like nineteenth-century white feminism, the WLM emerged through an interaction with Black freedom politics. Civil Rights organising in the early 1960s was racially integrated. Not without problems and tensions, young Black and white activists worked together in the South, particularly in SNCC.* Women in general encountered misogyny in the Civil Rights Movement,[41] but some white women activists grew more vocal about this. Issues raised by white women in SNCC were taken into the wider student movement, eliciting aggressive and defensive reactions from New Left men who accused them of splitting the movement. At a Washington DC demonstration in 1968, feminist speaker Marilyn Webb was abused by movement men in the crowd, shouting 'Take it off!' 'Take her off the stage and

---

* SNCC was partly led and inspired by Ella Baker who took young organisers under her wing, teaching them 'participatory democracy, an organizing philosophy that emphasized group decision-making over leader-centered organizing' as she had become 'disillusioned with the male and hierarchy-centered leadership' of Civil Rights organisations. Kimberly Springer, *Living for the Revolution: Black Feminist Organizations, 1968–1980* (Durham, NC: Duke University Press, 2005), 23.

fuck her!'[42] Women's Liberation partly grew out of these encounters, the convergences and splits between different people, different movements.[43]

Civil Rights integrationism gave way to Black Power autonomy and, in some cases, separatism. Black Power's inspirational example was consciously followed by white feminists.[44] Young white feminists compared themselves to Black movements as they applied principles of self-activity and autonomy to their own liberation. Echols writes of an early women's liberation group:

> the radical women who began meeting in Chicago that fall took their inspiration from black power ... [it] enabled them to argue that it was valid for women to organize around their own oppression and to define the terms of their struggle.[45]

The word 'liberation' was borrowed from anti-colonial struggles, while consciousness-raising was influenced by Civil Rights Movement practices.[46] With borrowing and appropriation, again came erasive discourses, in near-identical formulations to nineteenth-century movements. The representative split continued. Black or 'Negro' meant male, 'women' meant white, and WLM rhetoric remained reliant on the 'slave analogy' that had organised the 'First Wave'. Roxanne Dunbar (now Dunbar-Ortiz) of Cell 16, now an eminent scholar of settler colonialism whose work we admire, wrote repeatedly at the time of the undifferentiated 'slavery' of 'women': 'Women have just been slaves, chattels for all of History, and have the characteristics of any Slave.'[47] Shulamith Firestone explicitly identified with Stanton and Anthony as forebears to the new feminism.* She set about recovering their

---

* Identification spread beyond Firestone's writings. The radical feminists calling themselves 'Redstockings' were a nod to first wave feminists, 'bluestockings'. The lead affinity group in the New York Radical Feminists were the 'Stanton Anthony Brigade'. Attendees at 1968's Sandy Springs conference 'decided to plan a national conference to commemorate the 120th anniversary of the first women's rights convention at Seneca Falls'. Alice Echols, *Daring to be Bad: Radical Feminism in America 1967–1975* (Minneapolis, MN: University of Minnesota Press, 2019), 107. In *Notes From The Second Year*, editors Firestone and Anne Koedt wrote:

> We needed a movement periodical which would expand with the movement, reflect its growth accurately, and in time become a historical record, function politically much as

reputations as 'radicals'.[48] This was partly a reaction against many on the left who cited the deficiencies of the 'first wave', arguing that autonomous women's movements would inevitably become counter-revolutionary. Historical fault-lines weighed heavily on radical feminist intellectuals. In *Notes From The First Year*, Firestone approvingly cited the self-discovery of 'women' through Black freedom movements: 'it was due to their work in the Abolitionist Movement that many women first became aware of their own slavery', failing to account for those slaves who were Black women, or the part Black women played in ending the capitalist system of slavery. The slave analogy was taken to the point of erasing the conditions of Black women as both slaves and women through a flattening of the 'other half' of the sex: 'today, we hardly remember that less than a century ago, even after the Civil War, more than half of this country's population were still slaves under the law'.

Stanton and Anthony, like 1960s radical feminists, felt sexism was far more oppressive than racism or class exploitation. They saw the power wielded by men over women as *the* key oppression.[49] This is made clear in the very first sentence of their *History of Woman Suffrage*, deploying the slave analogy to state: 'The prolonged slavery of woman is the darkest page in human history.'[50] This framing groups together the oppression of *all* women under a unified 'slavery' during a period in which millions of women actually experienced enslavement, while others, including Stanton, grew up in families that *owned slaves*. From the outset, it was in the interests of wealthy white women to use such sweeping, erasive definitions of 'womanhood'. From the outset – for Black women, immigrant women, working women, Native American women, queer women, or combinations of these – the picture was and is a lot messier. Stanton and Anthony did try to build alliances with workers but their insistence on foregrounding gendered oppression would land them in trouble. Angela Davis writes:

Stanton and Anthony's Revolution exactly a century ago. Notes From the Second Year attempts to fill these needs.

See *Notes from the Second Year*, June 1968, Duke University Libraries, https://tinyurl. com/2rrwfnxz.

Although Susan B. Anthony, Elizabeth Cady Stanton and their colleagues on the paper made important contributions to the cause of working women, they never really accepted the principle of trade unionism ... In the eyes of the suffragists, 'woman' was the ultimate test – if the cause of woman could be furthered, it was no wrong for women to function as scabs when male workers in their trade were on strike. Susan B. Anthony was excluded from the 1869 convention of the Nation Labor Union because she had urged women printers to go to work as scabs.[51]

Stanton said this proved 'what the *Revolution* has said again and again, that the worst enemies of Woman Suffrage will ever be the laboring classes of men'. The history of male-dominated labour movements, and their often enthusiastic reproduction of patriarchal order, is anything but proud. But Stanton's classed and racialised denigration of *certain* men always seemed to flow much easier than the few times she directed her criticisms at the rich white men holding so much more power.[*] For Stanton and Anthony, the betrayal of womanhood by Black male suffrage could only be reduced to a conspiracy of male supremacy between Black and white men. The lesson Stanton took? Woman 'must not put her trust in man'.[52] After the 13th Amendment abolished slavery, the 14th, ratified in 1868, introduced federal protection for some civil and voting rights to emancipated slaves. It also introduced the word 'male' into the Constitution for the first time. Stanton wrote in an 1866 letter, 'if that word "male" be inserted, it will take us a century at least to get it out'.[**][53] While shared patriarchy was likely an element, Black male enfranchisement came about in larger part because the Republicans and the Northern bourgeoisie needed to secure Reconstruction. That is, a calculation was made that Black

---

[*] As Terese Jonsson says of contemporary white feminist 'innocence': 'By investing in discourses of white innocence, white women align themselves with a white supremacist patriarchy in ways which not only enforce the oppression of people of colour, but also their own patriarchal subjugation.' Terese Jonsson, *Innocent Subjects: Feminism and Whiteness* (London: Pluto Press, 2019),166.

[**] It was, in fact, a century before Black Americans of any gender had some of their civil rights enforced by the federal government.

men would vote Republican, while white women could help return the Democrats to power.

The AERA falls apart upon passage of the 14th and 15th Amendments as a result of this *representative split.* The opposing of 'woman' to 'Negro' not only marked a 'splitting' of the idea of universal suffrage down the colour line, and the end of the abolitionist gesture within this part of the women's movement, it erased Black women from the struggle entirely. This 'white blindspot' (or intentional erasure) has been a persistent feature of every feminist 'wave' since, haunting the encounter between white and Black women's movements in America for two centuries. Debates around the rights and wrongs of the 'Reconstruction Amendments' and their exclusion of woman suffrage are complex and wrought. The role of state power and legislation in causing representative splits to antagonise movement alliances was clear to Firestone by the 1960s, but her framing of womanhood reengaged the whiteness of the 'first wave'. As Ellen Carol Dubois intimates, this is hard to disconnect from the social backgrounds of the campaigners themselves: 'Woman suffrage leaders were rarely from the ranks of wage-earners. Some, like [Lucy] Stone and Anthony, were the daughters of small farmers. Others, most notably Stanton, were the children of considerable wealth.'[54] White feminism broadly showed itself consistently unable, in movements a century apart, to make common cause with racially oppressed women, under the complex matrices of US white supremacy and patriarchy, in ways that didn't fundamentally erase or minimise that oppression, helping reproduce it.

IMPENDING EQUALS

We can see from the earliest expressions of a Black feminist politic in America that the impulse for autonomous organising by Black women came as a result of their exclusion from the white women's

---

* This extended the franchise to all men regardless of 'race, color, or previous condition of servitude'. Stanton and Anthony said the enfranchisement of Black men and of women should happen all at once or not at all. They advocated women's suffragists going it alone, cut ties with the Republicans and aligned with pro-slavery Democrats like George Francis Train, who funded their newspaper. The faction led by Lucy Stone and her husband Henry Blackwell saw Black male suffrage as a next step to surely be followed by women's suffrage.

movement and because of their different priorities and struggles. Far from the accusations levelled later against those said to be engaging in identity politics, this was not about Black women's narrow horizons or in-group mentality but the historical exclusivity of 'universal' categories that suppressed historical complexity. Indeed, proto Black feminists of the nineteenth century had the most capacious visions for emancipating the human community. Anna Julia Cooper, born into slavery, spoke at the World's Congress of Representative Women in 1893, as part of the Chicago World's Fair. At a conference attended almost exclusively by white women she called for nothing less than universal emancipation:

> Let woman's claim be as broad in the concrete as in the abstract. We take our stand on the solidarity of humanity, the oneness of life, and the unnaturalness and injustice of all special favoritism, whether of sex, race, country, or condition. If one link of the chain is broken, the chain is broken. A bridge is no stronger than its weakest part, and a cause is not worthier than its weakest element. Least of all can woman's cause afford to decry the weak. We want, then, as toilers for the universal triumph of justice and human rights, to go to our homes from this Congress demanding an entrance not through a gateway for ourselves, our race, our sex, our sect, but a grand highway for humanity. The colored woman feels that woman's cause is one and universal.[55]

Black women like Sojourner Truth and Frances W. Harper supported the 15th Amendment and tried to persuade white women to support it too.[*] The reaction of some white women campaigners to the opposition of the rights of Black men to 'women' was incendiary, with some embarking on a turbocharged white supremacist politics. Stanton asked:

---

[*] Free-born poet, teacher and social reformer, Harper challenged Stanton and Anthony at a convention in 1866. She countered the constant erasure of Black women, drawing attention to the abuse and discrimination they faced every day. She 'describ[ed] a situation in Boston where sixty white women walked off the job to protest the hiring of one Black woman'. Davis, *Women, Race and Class*, 257, fn. 35.

If Saxon men have legislated thus for their own mothers, wives and daughters, what can we hope for at the hands of Chinese, Indians, and Africans? … I protest against the enfranchisement of another man of any race or clime until the daughters of Jefferson, Hancock, and Adams are crowned with their rights.[56]

Frederick Douglass spoke at an AERA convention in 1869, shortly before the 15th Amendment passed:

When women, because they are women, are dragged from their homes and hung upon lamp-posts; when their children are torn from their arms and their brains dashed upon the pavement; when they are objects of insult and outrage at every turn; when they are in danger of having their homes burnt down over their heads; when their children are not allowed to enter schools; then they will have [the same] urgency to obtain the ballot.[57]

This showed a difference in how Douglass (and others) looked to the vote as a strategic factor in a wider liberation struggle. But comparativism had set in, incensed by the formal distribution of rights. The Stanton/Anthony faction increasingly viewed getting the vote as an end in itself, a single-issue focus. These conventions illustrate the kinds of fraught discussions that came to the fore. In response to Douglass' assertion that pervasive racial violence was an argument for prioritising Black male suffrage, as part of a broader strategy, Susan B. Anthony replied: 'Mr. Douglass talks about the wrongs of the negro; but with all the outrages that he today suffers, he would not exchange his sex and take the place of Elizabeth Cady Stanton.'[58] Stanton's personalised conception of 'womanhood' was personal to her struggle, but couldn't be universalised to others. Despite abolitionism inspiring her own struggle, she eventually concluded it was better for Black women 'to be the slave of an educated white man, than of a degenerated, ignorant black one.'[59] She landscaped an apocalyptic future of 'women' overwhelmed by the primal appetites of slaves and immigrants, 'butchers and barbers',[60] warning that Black male suffrage would 'culminate in fearful outrages on womanhood, especially in the Southern states.'[61] Of course, women like Stanton were under threat of rape, though less likely from proletarian men (whom they'd seldom meet) than within the households of their fathers and husbands. This concrete threat – rape by husband or relative – underwent a transference to a phantasmatic social figuration of Black men.

Freedom from racial slavery was different to freedom from the bourgeois private sphere, but these differences didn't derail the abolitionist alliance so long as the aperture of political possibility was open. How then did possibilities narrow and imaginations recede to the extent that suffragist-abolitionists weren't simply withdrawing support for the 15th Amendment, but citing their vulnerability to Black male aggressors and foreigners of all kinds, as a result of the legislation? How could alliances be torn apart so comprehensively that by century's end, Stanton and others would ally the goals and objectives of American 'womanhood' to explicitly white supremacist ideals of racial purity, with white women's roles as moral guardians and biological childbearers of the white race?

The existence of Black women was erased throughout the development of abolitionist and suffragist representation and political discourse. This is why historical figures like Stewart, Truth, and Harper are so important to the Black feminist tradition. They elucidate the complex history of suffragism and feminism. It is not as if Stanton could be ignorant of the conditions of Black women in the North. Given the structural pervasiveness of the nation's racial and gendered division of labour, it is likely she would have employed several Black women servants. Working class suffragists later brought militancy and energy to a faltering movement, helping it reach its goal of enfranchising women in 1920.[62] But only *some* women.* The point at which working class women, most of them immigrants, joined the fight was also a period of intensifying white supremacy in mainstream women's movements. By 1890, both halves of the split women's suffrage movement had reunified under the leadership of Stanton and Anthony. A united

---

* When the 19th Amendment removed the exclusion of 'women' from the franchise, this great lever of emancipation, central demand of a white middle class women's movement whose 'expediency' knew no limit, made no difference to the lives of millions of women.

white women's suffrage movement aligned itself with US imperialism[63] and helped reinforce Jim Crow,[64] with little pushback from socialist suffragists from the inner cities whose campaigns scarcely mentioned race.

The rise of the WLM was therefore less a progressive extension of the 'first wave', as it is sometimes conceived, than the artefact of a highly contritional and divisive abstract equality. The movement had to begin again, excavating the past, reading across separations, rebuilding a vision to overcome a world made from the sediments of a fractured womanhood. It started from scratch, in urban, coastal and university areas, dominated by college-educated white women in their twenties and thirties, with minimal racial and class variation.[65] This subjectivity, the priorities it informed, combined with claims to universalism, and the ignorance or arrogance with which difference was often handled, separated middle class white women and their movement from Black/working-class women once more.[66] Movement forms, including consciousness-raising, played into these separations, these different lives. With an assumed basis of commonality, difference was ignored or treated with suspicion. The movement's recruitment model necessitated that women with different lives and experiences conform to the WLM way – meaning difference was often incorporated through tokenisation or domination, if at all. Inescapably, as Winifred Breines argues: 'Black women felt betrayed and enraged.'

> The way they saw it, white feminists did not genuinely seek out black women on their own terms. They invited them to be speakers at their meetings, conferences, and demonstrations more as tokens than as integral participants. They often only included black women in their political analyses – or meetings – in order to make themselves feel less guilty for being white. Their understanding of the black woman's situation was superficial, and they did little to remedy it.[67]

Of course, this problem varied across groups and individuals, as some white feminists made great efforts to build knowledge and solidarity. Meredith Tax, leader of Bread and Roses – a socialist-feminist group based in Boston, emphasised:

We cannot talk of sisterhood without realizing that the objective
position in society of most of us is different from that of welfare
mothers, of the black maids of our white mothers, and of women
in 3rd World countries. Sisterhood means not saying their fight
is our fight, but making it our fight.[68]

ARTEFACTS OF EQUALITY

The willingness to see across separations and hold them close as
real and material, but approachable, theorisable and therefore
relatable, suggested ways separations could be bridged. Practical
routes were less clear. By the 1970s and 1980s, radical feminism
morphed into a tendency focused on enclaves and lifestylism.[*]
This included self-help or pseudo-religious subcultures, new age
'mother nature' figurations of womanhood 'where patriarchy was
evaded rather than engaged'.[69] Businesses, festivals and organisations grew out of these enterprises but so did a selective
anti-consumerism, including 1980s anti-porn campaigns. A drift
towards biological essentialism is partly where transphobia begins
to harden. Some feminisms turn to a focus on affirming 'matriar-
chy', 'femaleness', 'maternal instincts', 'nature' whereas early radical
feminists were more wedded to social constructionist explanations.[**] These shifts partly worked as pitches for unity, an answer to
composition problems, after years of factional struggles. Reagan-
ism ensured more people had to look to family for pick-ups and
financial support, families already broken apart by overwork,
incarceration and unemployment. The social conservatism of the
nuclear family was extended within an economic vision of the
self-dependency of work, enterprise and welfare.[70] Black work-

---

[*] A conservative, anti-feminist backlash was part of the crushing of 1960s movements
more generally, with pushback against abortion rights, attacks on welfare and the expansion
of mass incarceration and the 'War on Drugs'. While its achievements were huge, some
WLM gains were incorporated as a new common sense, while feminism, more generally,
was 'rendered an anachronism'. Echols, *Daring to be Bad*, 294.

[**] Firestone was perhaps most revolutionary in this area, writing: 'The end goal of feminist
revolution must be, unlike that of the first feminist movement, not just the elimination of
male privilege but of the sex distinction itself: genital difference between human beings
would no longer matter culturally.' Shulamith Firestone, *The Dialectic of Sex: The Case For
Feminist Revolution* (New York: Bantam Books, 1972), 11.

ing-class women had already experienced double or triple burdens under the post-war compact. Unemployment tendencies theorised by Black communist auto-workers in the 1950s and 1960s became familiar to white male workers in the 1970s and 1980s. There was great discrepancy in differentiated relations of exploitation in British and American neoliberalism. Black feminism sits autonomously within the 'Revolutionary Time' of the period. The CRC were reflecting on the period's obstacles and what was yet to come.

There was substantial ideological division and variation *within* radical feminism.[71] The women's movement in general had grown sensitive to 'accusations' of lesbianism, meant to 'discredit' them.[*] Lesbians had to struggle inside and outside the movement for acceptance, recognition and a change of terms as the 'gay–straight split' and political lesbianism shook things up.[72] Early radical feminism broadly operated from a heterosexual presumption, with some homophobic attitudes. Internal divisions that contributed to the movement's demise, split far more along lines of sexuality,[73] class[74] and organisational hierarchy. But a common legacy of radical feminism was its uneasy whiteness, as Black women were largely absent altogether. There was passionate discussion about this absence, sometimes thoughtful or honest about the fact white women were completely cut off from Black women. Some radical feminists sought to handle this by accepting it would be exclusionary. This was a problem from the beginning, which imparted a determination over how feminist factions tried to distinguish their autonomy. Echols provides transcripts from Sandy Springs Conference in 1968 that exemplify the problem. 'No one wants to exclude blacks,' said one delegate. 'We've had black women in our groups.' Another, 'I think if we are really honest about it we don't want to work with black women because we are not sure what our relationship is.' Another,

The reason she said you're opening a can of worms is that they are going to want to discuss different things, have different

---

[*] Particularly its liberal wing, filled with McCarthyite paranoia about the 'Lavender Menace' fuelled by NOW President, Betty Friedan.

concerns. We're going to get so involved with them that we are not going to talk about female liberation.[75]

These testimonies are less important in underwriting the WLM as racist, than in underlining what Black feminists were arguing: that relations of womanhood are historically diverse. Through this necessarily condensed history of US suffragism and feminism, we find campaigners, and women more generally, spending their lives fighting patriarchy. A patriarchy lodged firmly at both the centre of power and domination in American life as well as in the molecular, everyday social relations of human beings and households. Many women have struggled, not by campaigning for suffrage or reforms but through self-defence in the face of male violence in the street, in the home, on the plantation. Women have organised strikes when faced with sexist bosses, low wages and the double burden of waged and caring labour. The specific historical conditions of racial and gendered oppression and the particular exploitation of slavery or super-exploitation, saw Black women develop, over centuries, a radical Black feminist tradition. Autonomy has constantly been proven necessary by the exclusion, erasure, insensitivity and violence they have faced. Universalising the identity of women is premised on historical exclusions of others. Being white didn't stop women being sexually abused by boyfriends, husbands, or comrades in left movements, or from suffering homophobia or being doubly exploited inside and outside work. The whiteness of Women's Liberation was alarming to its participants because it explicitly registered the movement's universalist claims as an obvious contradiction. Whiteness had anchored the WLM in the longitudinal fractures of American constitutional equality, which continued to bite at the universalising projections of a free and liberated *identity of womanhood* from the very beginning. Divisive equality, in this historical sequence, began with the complaint that middle-class white women, the wives and daughters of property owners, had been abandoned by the nation. They were to take their place behind ex-slaves, before the law. Having taken root, legal equality developed, for some suffragists, into a more fully-fledged authoritarian desire to inscribe hierarchies. White women, 'cast under the heel of the lowest orders of manhood', were set to suffer the 'outrages on womanhood' that would inevitably follow. When the WLM rose up to challenge patriarchy anew, they found a fractured womanhood, which the CRC and others argued had to be historically understood. Histories of separation had forced white women to confront the movement's whiteness. These divisions could be confronted, or bundled away and suppressed, with exclusionary consequences. Black feminists in Britain faced the same problem, in different circumstances.

3

Black Feminism and
Class Composition

Of white feminists we must ask, what exactly do you mean by
'we'?[1]

Hazel Carby

The identity politics named by the Combahee River Collective in
Boston was already being experimented with in the British context
of post-war migration. Hazel Carby's 1982 essay '*White Woman
Listen!*' presents the knotted problem of identity in the Women's
Liberation Movement from the perspective of British racial rule.
Carby also highlighted the risks of 'womanhood' standing in place
of historicisation,

> The black women's critique of history has not only involved us in
> coming to terms with 'absences'; we have also been outraged by
> the ways in which it has made us visible, when it has chosen to
> see us. History has constructed our sexuality and our femininity
> as deviating from those qualities with which white women, as
> the prize objects of the Western world, have been endowed. We
> have also been defined in less than human terms ... Our contin-
> uing struggle with History began with its 'discovery' of us.[2]

Carby's essay sets up a critique of universal identity-thinking in the
WLM that first asks how women's identities were formed and constructed. Historical 'absences' of Black women in theories of
womanhood are less outrageous, Carby suggests, than an estranged
hypervisibility, where categories and typologies of Black women
have taken the place of concrete worlds. Carby, and other British

Black feminists of the period were clear, the point was to *trouble* identity-thinking:

Black women do not want to be grafted onto 'feminism' in a tokenistic manner as colorful diversions to 'real' problems ... Neither do we wish our words to be misused in generalities as if what each one of us utters represents the total experience of all black women.[3]

Some of the same problems of identity in US Women's Liberation were as prevalent in Britain, but racialisation worked differently, so the problems of conceptualising womanhood shifted too. British Black feminists prioritised the concrete testimony of Black and Asian women, many of them migrant workers, who offered vantage points on differentiated forms of exploitation in Britain's racial regime. These testimonies also suggested ways to organise collectively against it. 'White feminism' was taken to task by Black feminists on several counts, with each problem used as a funnel to identify problems that have not gone away. Nim Ralph, writing in *Gal-Dem*, relates contemporary 'sex-based rights' campaigns to a longer history of white imperialist feminism:

For centuries, white women have been actively complicit in the oppression of black women and other women of colour. White feminism finds its lineage in the biological determinism, eugenics and scientific racism of the 19th century, which led to the categorisation of bodies within a racial hierarchy that deemed some women inherently more 'human' than others. Therefore white women's social, civil and political rights were fought for while black women were pushed to the back, and often dehumanised; for example in the US based and UK based suffrage movements ... Throughout history, cis, white, middle-class women have utilised their racial and class privilege to become the self-appointed gatekeepers of the feminist movement. We can see sex-based rights feminists carrying this legacy alongside the rest of the radical feminist ideology into today's exclusion of trans folks from women's and feminist spaces.[4]

Lola Olufemi has echoed this argument, writing of the 'ideological links between biological essentialism and scientific racism: both see the body in absolute terms'.[5] Olufemi's capacious vision for an abolitionist feminism states: 'womanhood, the central pillar under which we gather to make our demands, is not real. It is only a vantage point that we use strategically to lessen the brutality we experience'.[6] Some of the most revolutionary feminist positions historically have arisen in opposition to how sexual reproduction and gendered divisions of labour are mediated by the capitalist class relation. Contemporary exclusionary feminisms, by contrast, demand state intervention to establish and maintain a legal identity of sex against perceived threats to it. Today's conspiracies that posit trans women as violent predators seeking access to 'women's spaces' take a similar form to how white supremacy has long constructed racialised men as threats to white women.[7] The rape threat in both narratives is divorced from the primary agents of sexual violence – men at home, men known to the victim.[*] Instead, patriarchy is projected onto an estranged group awarded exaggerated power and agency.

British Black feminists introduced a critique of biological common sense and sex-based universalism to confront the racism and nationalism of 1970s 'white feminism'. White women's movements in Britain struggled to deal with the implications of this critique, with a mix of genuine, hard fought, constructive reassessments, as well as defensiveness and sect-building. By elevating disputes internal to the WLM, we can help preserve the historical memory of this momentous upsurge in feminist militancy and intense theorising. The WLM became a huge, networked space for mutual support and growth in a deeply sexist society in which feminism has never had powerful allies. It transformed and enveloped thousands of women's lives, galvanising fights on several fronts: for reproductive rights, sexual liberation, equal pay, as well as solidarity with other struggles. It grew out of women's experi-

---

[*] A 2018 study: 'More than 90% of rape and sexual assault victims know their attacker, a new study of almost 1,000 victims says. Researchers from Glasgow University said it was a popular misconception that most attackers were strangers.' Lucy Adams, 'Sex Attack Victims Usually Know Attacker, Says New Study', *BBC News*, 1 March 2018, https://tinyurl.com/yey5mvbp.

ences of patriarchal attitudes, structures and violence, both in wider society and within social movements. One self-evident contradiction for Women's Liberation in Britain was race. From the start, the movement revolved around white middle class women, built largely around local consciousness-raising groups and organised through sedimented university networks.

The exclusionary feminists of Britain's liberal public sphere today ignore the granular dimension of these historical conferences and debates entirely. Sara Ahmed refers to contemporary exclusionary feminism as 'gender conservatism', arguing it is 'part of the not-so-new conservative common sense, which has reweaponised "reality" as a "war against the woke", that is, as an effort to restore racial as well as gendered hierarchies by demonizing those who question them'. Harassment of trans people,[*] Ahmed adds, is 'made invisible by appearing to take the form of a debate'.[8] One effect of the upsurge in gender conservative discourse is that historical 'waves' of feminism are in turn subject to distortion. The quality of subterfuge inherent to the internet medium is manipulated by transphobic groups seeking to enlarge their presence and recruitment. Suffragette colours are appropriated to signify a 'sex-based' feminism, while some radical feminists of the 1980s use their own testimony to promote historical revisions of Women's Liberation in support of a transphobic common sense. Militancy, heresy and political conviction are the master signifiers of 'gender critical' groups today, but as we argue, this movement – if we can call it a movement at all – is more mundanely organised by a reaction against social change and a hatred of gender nonconformity, with declinist theories of neoliberalism often a bridge between respectable and more extreme elements. Sarah Clarke and Mallory Moore argue there are 'practical crossovers' emerging between 'gender critical' feminism and the traditional far right, which '[show] the breadth of trans-atlantic collaboration between religious fundamentalists and feminist activists'.[9]

---

[*] A 2018 report by Stonewall and Yougov in Britain: 'Two in five trans people (41 per cent) and three in ten non-binary people (31 per cent) have experienced a hate crime or incident because of their gender identity in the last 12 months.' Chaka L. Bachmann and Becca Gooch, 'LGBT in Britain: Trans Report' (London: Stonewall, 2018), https://tinyurl.com/43y3ver8.

This leads us to a historical interrogation of 'gender critical' feminism and previous feminist 'waves' – is a connection distinguishable? What is the relationship between the identity conflicts of liberal, radical and socialist feminism and Black feminist critique in the 1970s, and the turbo-charged universalist doctrine against 'gender ideology' today?[10] Are we, as Ahmed suggests, dealing with an opportunistic innovation of conservatism, albeit one, perhaps, all the more dangerous, because of its ability to tie women's experiences of patriarchal violence to carceral solutions? In some ways, the polemical fire of 1970s radical feminism are retained in an emphasis on women's bodies; but where many radical feminists prioritised a critique of the patriarchal state, gender conservatism aligns the state to a group of 'sex-conforming' women, many of whom are comfortable in the white habitus of powerful institutions – journalists, lawyers, MPs, Baronesses. What, then, is the relationship between British whiteness and imperialist forms of feminism? How was 'imperialist feminism' – as a particular function of the state – analysed by anti-imperialist feminists in the 1970s and 1980s? The emphasis on white feminism in this chapter might initially be received as a survey of intra-feminist debates and their connection to past and present political questions of gender identity. Crucial as they are, these debates were never limited to a war of position in feminist movements. We find incisive critiques of Marxist historiography, which turned on questions of periodisation, capitalist development and progress, critical to how we historicise capitalism and class composition. Black feminist writers innovated a 'compositionist' class analysis, we argue, that studied forms of exploitation and state social control functions, neglected elsewhere. These critiques preserve the incendiary quality of feminist conceptuality in our strange and disconnected time, where abolitionist feminists who build on this work are subject to sustained reaction from the British media, from the right, centre, and sometimes the left, while continuing to pursue and road-test more fruitful paths to struggle.

BLACK FEMINISM AND THE POST-WAR WORKING CLASS

The first large WLM conference in Britain, held in 1970 in Oxford, made no mention of race on its agenda. Terese Jonsson contextualises this absence: 'issues of race, whiteness and coloniality ... should be seen as central to the construction of feminist politics and theory ... both when they were made explicit and when they were denied'.[11] Attended by 'over 600 women ... only two were Black'. One of those women, Gerlin Bean, 'couldn't really pick on the relevance as it pertained to Black women'.[12] Bean was an influential figure among Black women activists in the early 1970s, when Black women's autonomous organising in Britain began to blossom. The move towards autonomy was not solely a reaction to white women's racism. The movements developed in parallel.[13] Racialised women's groups, often growing out of women's caucuses formed inside Black Power groupings, were founded through experiences of exclusion and oppression from Black/Asian men as well.[14] Women of colour found themselves accused of 'splitting the movement' on two fronts. Gail Lewis and Pratibha Parmar wrote:

> endemic racism in the women's liberation movement and the sexism of the black movement resulted in the desire on the part of political black women both here and in the US to fashion a movement whose central concern was the transformation of social relations based on class, race and gender.[15]

Black women's activism, taking place almost entirely in urban areas, was rooted in working-class community organising. It was less separate from Black men and Black communities. The fight against racism required shared campaigns against police and state violence, deportations, discrimination in education and housing. Women were as central to these struggles as men, if not more. Black and Asian workers also brought a radical edge to workers' struggle. Black women introduced strike action into the NHS in a way never seen before. Black nurses, midwives and carers had to break through not only the structural racism of institutions but also the gendered assumptions of 'caring' work. In health care, in factories and in Britain's Black Power movement, Black and Asian women were at the forefront of struggles against exploitation, racism and sexism, positioned in a racial and gendered division of labour reproduced directly from British colonial societies. Invariably paid less than men *and* white women, they worked night shifts, juggled wage-labour with childcare responsibilities, and most sent off a chunk of their meagre income to family members in remittances.* As one Black woman worker in Southall told *Race Today* in 1975, moving beyond the limited horizons of the mainstream WLM: 'Equal pay with men? We do twice as much work – we should get double pay.'[16]

The family was a main focus for the WLM but some feminist theorists were critiqued for normative assumptions they made about families formed around nuclear, heterosexual and housewife structures of social reproduction. Feminists of colour also critiqued the equivalency drawn between white and Black patriarchs. Carby summarises:

> How … can we account for situations in which black women may be heads of households, or where, because of an economic system that structures high black male unemployment, they are not financially dependent upon a black man? This condition exists in both colonial and metropolitan situations. Ideologies of black female domesticity and motherhood have been constructed through their employment (or chattel position) as domestics and surrogate mothers to white families rather than in relation to their own families. West Indian women still migrate to the United States and Canada as domestics and in Britain are seen to be suitable as office cleaners, National Health Service domestics, etc. In colonial situations Asian women have frequently been forced into prostitution to sexually service the white male invaders, whether in the form of armies of occupation or employees and guests of multinational corporations. How then, in view of all this, can it be argued that black male dominance exists in the same forms as white male dominance? Systems of slavery, colonialism, and imperialism have systematically denied positions in the white male hierarchy to black men.[17]

Many racialised women in Britain lived in single parent or extended family households, and were more likely to be wage-labourers.

---

* Early on, many were still lumbered with the debt incurred by their passage to Britain too.

76

White feminist theorists provided urgent critiques of the violence of the nuclear family, but many racialised women pointed out that *they* could experience the family home as a safer space compared to a racist state and society. There was little recognition that *some* families, even those conforming to the nuclear ideal, were constantly under attack *at the same time* as women experienced the oppression of gendered traditions and hierarchy. Black women's organising challenged the assumptions of the white women's movement and its claim to universality. This provided the foundation for a more far-reaching analysis of class (or better, varied forms of economic exploitation). There were big debates and divides over whether different women of colour saw themselves as 'feminists' (many more did by the 1980s), or if the term was too bound up with whiteness.

Receiving years of sustained critique, Natalie Thomlinson describes a WLM culture 'ill-equipped to engage in auto-critique', which, she finds, 'had significant repercussions when bitter debates around identity politics occurred in the 1980s'.[18] 'Calls for attention to white feminist complicity in racism,' writes Terese Jonsson, 'are often problematically interpreted as calling for a white feminist sense of guilt ... But a focus on guilt stays unhelpfully within the moral framework of innocence, by implying that one must be either innocent or guilty.'[19] Over the years, white feminists have responded in various ways to internal and external critique,[20] but Ruth Frankenburg once commented that the 'predominant response' to Black feminist critique 'has been one of uncomfortable silence'.[21] Some white feminists saw race as a distraction from the cause. The areas chosen for 'Reclaim The Night' marches amid the late 1970s 'Yorkshire Ripper' killings were symptomatic of this. Thomlinson writes:

[organisers'] decision to march through Chapeltown, a mixed-race area, provoked controversy at the socialist feminist conference in Manchester in January of that year. Whilst the Leeds women who had instigated the march felt that their reasons were understood – Chapeltown had been the scene of many of Sutcliffe's abductions – the prospect of white women marching through Black areas calling for an end to male violence raised the uncomfortable spectre of the myth of the Black rapist whose primary victims were white women. This was not helped by one radical feminist's argument that 'As to racism: any man can be a rapist. The colour of the penis forcing its way into you is irrelevant.'[22]

As with the racialised dynamics of lynching, there are numerous examples of British colonial atrocities that leant heavily on the image of protecting white women from sexually violent men of colour. Uprisings in India in 1857 and Jamaica in 1865 abounded in these discourses and were used to justify violent crackdowns. More explicitly, the 'White Women's Protection Ordinance' of 1926, introduced in Papua New Guinea, empowered a racist judicial system ensconced in moral panic to execute native men convicted of raping, or attempting to rape, white women.[23] Alison Phipps argues in her recent book on contemporary 'white feminism' that white women's 'protection' remains 'at the forefront in a world moving rapidly to the right.'[24] Carceral feminist reactions to the 2021 murder of Sarah Everard included Caitlin Moran mirroring the demands during the 'Yorkshire Ripper' murders for a 'curfew for men' in the *Times*.[25] A call for 'more police on the streets' to protect 'women and girls' raised eyebrows, unimpeded as it was by the fact that Everard was killed by a policeman. That such a 'solution' would heap more violence upon racialised people raised no such surprise.

By differentiating the experiences of women, British Black feminism opened up a troubling of British working-class history and the representation of women within it. While accounts of migrant worker struggles in Britain have been around for decades, with participants themselves historicising their impact, trade union histories have only recently – gradually and selectively – incorporated the factory struggles of migrant workers into the timeline of the workers movement, because they were previously opposed, or erased, from the wider picture.[26] The 1970s saw growing labour militancy, which spoke to the contradictions of the time, but also to the end of formal empire, and therefore a growing redundancy of labour institutions and parties as constabularies of the imperial state. The established labour imperialist doctrine in

Britain, spearheaded by the Labour Party and steered by a progressive idealism of social and economic unity, was unsustainable, and reasons had to be given. Inflation and unemployment generated cross-party discord over how national welfare could be funded. James Callaghan, in his first conference speech as Labour leader, found cause for this crisis in the ingratitude of striking workers and working-class dissenters. 'The ordinary worker,' Callaghan claimed, 'is getting more and more outspoken in his opposition to the small bands of disrupters in industry.'[27]

The emphasis on post-war 'fragmentation' used to explain the ascendancy of new social movements and the decline of workers movements suggests a form of periodisation that *externalises* stresses and challenges to the post-war labour movement identity itself. As Jack Saunders has shown, from the 1950s onwards there was an antagonism between 'respectable' formal trade unionism and informal cultures of working-class dissidence. Respectable trade unionism was tolerated insofar as the economic compromise functioned. By the 1970s, this antagonism had developed as a public discourse that 'now doubted that any normative, "responsible" trade unionism really existed.'[28] Labour doctrine disassembled not because of undisciplined splitters, or the rise of identity politics, but because working-class people lost confidence in labourist institutions, which turned one section of the class against another. Systems of cash limits were introduced by the Labour government to cut public expenditure, ensuring 'expansion in one branch of provision could only be at the expense of another.'[29] This broadened working-class militancy to the public sector, where many immigrant workers were, as well as consumers of public services, who resisted losing provisions that were already underfunded and stretched. Where calls for compromise and below inflation pay deals were imposed from above, the lowest paid workers, pushed under basic sustenance, rejected them. Women began taking on leadership roles in the National Union of Public Employees (NUPE), with many white working-class women inspired by the coterminous rise of Women's Liberation. The combination of rising inflation and wage caps had a particular impact on Black and Asian workers, who often did the lowest paid jobs already.[30] These events changed the shape and composition of working-class radicalism and asked questions of the persisting white male homo-geneity of labour representation.

WOMEN MOVED TO WORK

As Tara Martin López has shown, the lowest paid ancillary workers and auxiliary nurses in the NHS included Europeans, white work-ing-class men who had entered the service sector because of deindustrialisation, many Irish women, single mothers, as well as women from Nigeria, Sierra Leone, British Guiana, Mauritius, Trinidad and Jamaica.[31] Inflation and fragmentation of public services brought multiracial crowds of women on strike. Black Feminist writing, as in *The Heart of the Race*, offered an analysis of this transition that emphasised a colonial form of labour differen-tiation that existed from the moment Black women arrived:

> Service work was little more than institutionalised housework, as night and daytime cleaners, canteen workers, laundry workers and chambermaids – an extension of the work we had done under colonialism in the Caribbean. The alternative to this was factory work in small, ununionised sweatshops, where condi-tions were poor and negotiating conditions non-existent. On the assembly line we worked side by side with other immigrants from Asia, Ireland, southern Europe, producing ... the house-hold goods that were so essential to Britain's post-war economic boom.[32]

The Black feminist critique of 'white feminism' was directed at women who generalised the experience of women in Britain. This carried through into more general expectations of patriarchy and working-class culture. Black feminists brought complexity to labour questions and therefore to the uneven experiences of women. These testimonies helped to refocus and concentrate on *working-class women, on class issues.* The focus on poor conditions, struggles for union recognition, the distance from white feminist theories of womanhood, draws comparisons with the early nine-teenth century where women were more active in the strikes, riots and movements of early industrialisation, under the banners of

Chartism, Owenism, abolitionism and beyond. Just as Black and Asian women workers in 1970s Britain were often considered particular and remote from national trade union strategy, women workers, by the late nineteenth century, were ostracised from labour movements. The white male 'hate strike', deployed to force exclusionary measures by state or employer, worked here as effectively against working-class white women, as it did against racialised workers of any gender in the nineteenth and twentieth centuries.[33] Proletarian women in Victorian London had an unstable affinity with the imperialist development of 'whiteness', especially those from colonised Ireland.

The 1888 strike at the Bryant and May factory[*] is one famous, if often undervalued and misunderstood, example of the conditions working-class women faced.[34] Credit, blame and attention for the strike at the time, and in most histories, has tended to revolve around the figure of Annie Besant.[**] A middle-class activist and member of the Fabian Society, Besant penned an article, 'White Slavery in London', in her halfpenny weekly, The Link, about the plight of the 'Matchgirls'.[35] She uses the 'slave analogy' to emphasise the horrendous conditions and abuses suffered by women and girls in the factory. Besant describes some of them cutting open their arms, allowing their blood to cover the statue of Liberal Prime Minister William Gladstone, whose family grew rich from West Indies slaving. The women resented money being taken out of their wages to build the monument. It became something of a tradition for locals to anonymously throw red paint over the statue ever since, commemorating the matchwomen.

The phrase 'white slavery' has long been in the national lexicon, used by campaigners from different classes, often to describe women and children doing factory labour. Besant compared

---

[*] In July 1888, around 700 women and girls walked out following the sacking of a worker. They faced horrendous conditions: long hours, poverty wages, violent and sexist foremen, and health hazards that made many of them sick. The labour force was split between factory hands and workers who assembled matchboxes in their homes. There was unity between them. Some strike demands were met: punitive fines and the docking of wages ceased. Separate eating quarters were provided for safer food consumption. A pay rise was secured. The Matchmaker's Union was established.
[**] A middle-class reformer and sometime socialist involved in the late nineteenth-century London left. A leading figure in the Malthusian League for population control.

owners Bryant and May to slaveholders, repeating the familiar tale that in fact these 'white wage slaves' suffered a *worse* fate than the 'chattel slaves' of the past. The matchwomen were long thought to have been led by this group of reformers with the press at the time accusing Besant of stirring up trouble. Louise Raw provides evidence that the Fabians were not keen on strike action at all.[36] The matchwomen instigated the strike – a response to their experiences of wage-labour and sexism. The impulse for radical action also came from collective memories of anti-colonial resistance and the discrimination they faced in Britain (most being Irish Catholic by birth or descent). It is useful then to consider the innocent framing of the matchwomen and the relationship to slavery Besant and others insisted on. Besant remarked in her autobiography that her idea for starting *The Link* was inspired by a Victor Hugo quotation:

I will speak for the dumb. I will speak of the small to the great and the feeble to the strong ... I will speak for all the despairing silent ones. I will interpret this stammering; I will interpret the grumblings, the murmurs, the tumults of crowds, the complaints ill-pronounced, and all these cries of beasts that, through ignorance and through suffering, man is forced to utter.[37]

By the late nineteenth century, slavery was increasingly associated with white women trafficked as sex workers. This slave analogy was extended by reformers like Besant, George Bernard Shaw and other Fabians, who framed the 'girls' as helpless victims whose conditions was scandalous *because* they were white. 'Who cares for the fate of these white wage slaves?' Besant pleaded, 'born in slums, driven to work while still children, undersized because underfed, oppressed because helpless, flung aside as soon as worked out, who cares if they die'.[38] Alison Phipps notes the development of this discourse today: 'the term modern slavery has replaced white slavery, but this rhetoric remains suffused with race: many trafficking initiatives have innocence in their titles, coding their victimised subjects as white'.[39] These narratives are used to support representative institutions of reform that take hold of women's issues to regulate the labour of working-class women. We see this most clearly when sex workers are refused legal rights as workers by campaigners who claim they are protecting women from exploitation.[40] The matchwomen example is a case in point. They were part of cultures of resistance nurtured in the radical East End, which included working-class women's networks of informal mutual aid: sharing of food and childcare, prisoner support, self-defence against male violence. The projection of innocence was a way of rehabilitating the identity of the women for a white middle-class audience, which could perceive them as white and therefore deserving of help. By championing the cause, reformers were also better positioned to mediate class antagonisms, in a depression, with tensions at boiling point. When a newspaper proved Bryant and May exposed the matchwomen to white phosphorus poisoning, it was also revealed that leading suffragist, Millicent Fawcett, was herself a shareholder. Fawcett took the factory owners' side, denying any risk to workers' health.

This strike was a key catalyst for New Unionism and was closely followed by more radical suffrage movements. Tom Mann, a leader of the dockers' strike in 1889, recognised its impetus, later writing: 'nothing brought any change for the better until the women and girls went on strike'.* Twenty years later, the East End would be a centre of organisation for splinter groups of working-class suffragettes, which further complicated the women's question. Founders

---

* The matchwomen spurred the upturn of militancy that became known as 'New Unionism' – a flurry of late nineteenth-century struggles led by previously excluded sections of the working class, namely, women, Irish, unskilled workers (or all of the above). Mann confirms the influence of the Matchwomen, citing their self-activity and drawing a distinction between the advocacy of 'kindly-disposed' middle-class reformers and direct action by workers:

> The first considerable movement [of New Unionism] came from the women and girls employed at Bryant and May's match factory at Bow. Kindly-disposed persons had written about the awful conditions under which the girls worked ... Lists of shareholders were published showing that a considerable percentage of those were clergymen; but nothing brought any change for the better until the women and girls went on strike.

Tom Mann, *Tom Mann's Memoirs* (London: Labour Publishing, 1923), 79, https://libcom.org/files/tommannsmemoirsoomannuoft.pdf.
Ben Tillett, a dockers union leader of whom more will be written in this book, also acknowledged the matchwomen marked 'the beginning of the social convulsion which produced New Unionism'. Louise Raw, *Striking a Light: The Bryant and May Matchwomen and Their Place in History* (London: Continuum, 2011), 171.

of the Women's Social and Political Union (WSPU), Emmeline Pankhurst and her eldest daughter Christabel, held a narrow suffrage focus, viewing votes for middle-class white women as an end in itself, a movement for itself. Meanwhile the perspectives of Sylvia Pankhurst, Emmeline's middle daughter, continually expanded. She first saw the vote as a vital class and gender question, a way of opening up other paths to social justice, but divisions emerged within the family and the movement.* Christabel insisted that the quest for woman suffrage depended on their neutrality towards the parties, while Sylvia 'detested' her sister's 'incipient Toryism'. Sylvia was expelled from the WSPU in 1914 as she aligned more and more with socialist causes. She was particularly censured for expressing solidarity with Irish workers fighting for their right to unionise in the famous Dublin Lock-Out dispute. Institutional and family ties cut, Sylvia was ensconced in the East End radical scene, and set up one of the best radical newspapers of the period which she edited for a decade, with a circulation of around 10,000 at its height. The changing name of the paper – from the *Woman's Dreadnought* to the *Workers' Dreadnought* – showed the changing ideological basis and political focus of Sylvia and her comrades, mostly working-class women like Charlotte Drake, Melvina Walker, Nellie Cressall as well as the young Jewish sisters Rose and Nellie Cohen.[41]

The divergent paths of the Pankhurst sisters underline that the demand for suffrage alone was no clear indicator of political content or universal womanhood. Emmeline and Christabel settled on a conservative imperialism.[42] The horizon of their ambitions became the enfranchisement of women *like them*. In the end, they envisioned little change to women's roles in society, not to mention the lives of women colonised and exploited across the Empire. Mary Macarthur, organiser with the Women's Trade Union League, said of the women's suffrage movement:

---

* Exclusion of women from public life, from professions, from working (carried out by convention, family hierarchy or trade unions if not directly by state/private institutions) was pervasive. In some ways, it did encompass women across class and other divides. It also made some rich women angry enough to become interested in contentious politics.

We have ... a tremendous suffrage movement in England, but unfortunately the supporters of that movement are mainly middle-class, leisured women. They are asking for the suffrage on a limited basis, a basis that would not enfranchise the women we represent. If the bill were passed, not 5% of the women we represent – 200,000 women – would get the vote.[43]

The enmity between middle-class suffragists and men of the workers movement would increasingly be challenged by the emerging voices of working-class/socialist women who were also suffragists. Socialist feminist and suffragist, Dora Montefiore, wrote: 'Adult Suffragists are in a curious position, they have one day in the week to fight reactionary women and another day to make a stand against apathetic and hostile Socialist men.' Montefiore rejected a suffragism by and for middle-class women, writing of them: 'if they could get votes for propertied women, [they] would light bonfires from one end of England to the other, and say they had won the enfranchisement of women'.[44] White middle-class women innovated a form of white imperialist feminism through their own partial enfranchisement within the state, while other white women of privilege refused to ignore differences in women's exploitation and oppression. This brought them into working-class movements as instigators of more far-reaching, revolutionary change.

The Black and Asian feminist critiques of 'white feminism' in the 1970s can be understood as a revision of earlier critiques of imperialist suffragism for a new era where poor conditions, precarity of contracts and union representation persisted. A century after the matchwomen, in 1992, industrial workers were exposed to similar conditions. Factory workers took strike action against unsafe conditions at the Burnsall factory in Smethwick. The striking workers were mainly South Asian migrant women who had built power by joining forces with refugee and asylum seeker movements. Amrit Wilson gave a snapshot of their conditions: 'The workers had to process pieces of metal by immersing them in baths of chemicals. There were no health and safety provisions – no gloves, no ventilation fans, no clean area where they could eat their food.'[45] The symptoms of 'Phossy Jaw' that so many matchwomen contracted were similar to those of the Burnsall workers.* As Wilson tells us:

> Work-related illnesses, including miscarriages, were frequent (miscarriages are common among women working with pollutants, a result of chemicals accumulating in the foetus). At Burnsall there was no way of avoiding this. When one young woman had a miscarriage, the employer's attitude did not change. His position was that the workers in his factory were treated well.[46]

The GMB union opposed the strikers' tactics and 'ended the strike by withdrawing support. After nine months of standing on the picket line the strikers were not even allowed to vote on the decision.'[47]

RELATIONS OF PATRIARCHY

Organised labour and women's movements in Britain, from the imperialist heights of the 1890s to the defeats of the 1980s, were formed through informal tiers and segregations in the working class that persisted and demanded new feminist theories. While a Marxist feminist focus on waged work and unwaged housework contributed to a better understanding of the relationship between labour-power in the factory and the reproductive labour capitalists depended on to produce value, the Black feminist viewpoint anticipated a more varied terrain of forms of exploitation and relations of patriarchy.[48] The way forms of oppression and exploitation were 'interlocking' for Black and Asian women in Britain, was Hazel Carby's concern and 'the prime reason for not employing parallels that render their position and experience not only marginal but also invisible'.[49] The polemic stress of a unified 'womanhood' was one way this could happen, but Carby also addressed identi-

---

* White phosphorus poisoning was a horrifying, painful condition which disfigured many of the women's bodies and lives, even killing some. The industry's use of the chemical was only outlawed in 1910.

ty-thinking implicit to Marxist theories of 'stages' and 'modes of production' that carried over into feminist theory:

The metropolitan centers of the West define the questions to be asked of other social systems and, at the same time, provide the measure against which all 'foreign' practices are gauged. In a peculiar combination of Marxism and feminism, capitalism becomes the vehicle for reforms that allow for progress toward the emancipation of women. The 'Third World', on the other hand, is viewed as retaining precapitalist forms expressed at the cultural level by traditions which are more oppressive to women.[50]

Marxist schematisations of modern and premodern patriarchy suffered from a categorical reduction. This assertion dovetailed with a liberal hypostatisation of Black and Asian women as victims of 'undeveloped' cultures.[*] Even a latent suspicion that this was the case could factor into how racialised women were perceived, as workers, and in relation to 'modern' women's movements. The crudest 'tics' of Marxist historiography are not representative of Marxism as a whole, but not a small part of it either. The scandal Marxist historian Ellen Meiksins Wood invoked when after years of studying the origins of capitalism, she wrote, 'capitalism is conceivable without racial divisions, but not, by definition, without class', amplifies the problem Carby addressed regarding patriarchy. Wood added, it is only 'for historical reasons' that race happens to be 'a major "extra-economic" mechanism of class reproduction in US capitalism'.[51] Carby was picking up on a prejudice within Marxist historiography that remains at the core of transition debates today. Jairus Banaji, who has produced some of the best

---

[*] Different gender relations have existed in different societies, at different points in history. Carby notes Igbo and Iroquois as liberatory examples that were colonised and suppressed. Eurocentric perceptions of 'barbarous' modes of patriarchy in the 'Third World' rarely factor colonial impositions of the sex-binary. Oyèrónké Oyewùmí argues: 'prior to the infusion of Western notions into Yoruba culture, the body was not the basis of social roles, inclusions, or exclusions; it was not the foundation of social thought and identity' and that 'in precolonial Yoruba society, body-type was not the basis of social hierarchy'. Oyewùmí, *The Invention of Women: Making An African Sense of Western Gender Discourses* (Minneapolis, MN: Minnesota University Press, 1997), preface, x and xii.

critiques of formalistic trends in Marxist historiography, makes a similar claim: 'A widespread Marxist view that lacks any sophistication works back from the form of exploitation to the mode of production.'[52] Carby argued that an unsophisticated theory of capitalist development informed how patriarchy was being theorised,

> Feminist theory in Britain is almost wholly Eurocentric and, when it is not ignoring the experience of black women 'at home' it is trundling 'Third World women' onto the stage only to perform as victims of 'barbarous', 'primitive' practices in 'barbarous', 'primitive' societies ... It should be noted that much feminist work suffers from the assumption that it is only through the development of a Western-style industrial capitalism and the resultant entry of women into waged labor that the potential for the liberation of women can increase.[53]

Black feminists were registering various relations of patriarchy, given to different relations of production. These relations were not modern or pre-modern but concretely formed – different, but contemporary and studiable. The awkward opposition of 'First World' and 'Third World' patriarchy in feminist theory was turned on its head. Living under fear of state violence and racialised exploitation in a modern imperialist society like Britain begged the question: how are modern societies determined? The generalisation of wage-labour and the growth of a modern labour market has been one answer that Marxist theory took forward. Banaji, however, gives the example of the modern slave plantation to challenge this historiographic assumption. The plantation is seemingly governed by a 'slave mode of production' and therefore a 'form of exploitation' different to that of the factory worker in advanced industrial societies.[54] Yet, the capitalist plantation system was uniquely developed by capital, making it distinct from earlier forms of plantation and slavery. It was regulated by a capitalist 'law of motion' and so assumed the speculative, fully engaged character of a capitalist enterprise, even if the immediate form of exploitation was slavery. 'The slave-plantations,' Banaji summarises, 'were commodity-producing enterprises characterised by speculative investments ("centres of commercial speculation") in the production of *absolute* surplus-value on the *basis* of landed property.'[55] Banaji's critique of Marxist formalism troubles 'before or after' arguments about slavery and capitalism, pointing the way to more concrete analysis of local, national and global relations of production. 'Archaic' relations of production weren't superseded by 'productive forces' in any abstract sense but *modernised* by capital. This explains why slavery, indentured and child labour still exist in different forms today, alongside varied forms of 'free' wage-labour. Not as an unfortunate leftover of a more barbaric world, but the development of 'smarter' and more integrated segmentations of labour, including barbaric forms where necessary/possible. Banaji argues,

> if the capitalist enterprises which dominated most of colonial Africa and large parts of Asia utilised coercive forms of exploitation, we must ask whether the laws of motion of capital are not, within certain limits, compatible with 'barbarous forms of labour.'[56]

Similarly, Eurocentric accounts of patriarchy provided little room to theorise how 'barbarism' was constitutive of advanced capitalist nations. This was clear enough to Black and Asian women subjected to medical experiments by the state.[*] The direct coercion of the state over the bodily autonomy of Black and Asian women was a central plank of Black feminist activity in Britain. The Organisation of Women of African and Asian Descent (OWAAD) struggled against 'virginity tests' at Heathrow Airport introduced to 'verify' that South Asian women *really* were arriving as the fiancées of

---

[*]   Britain and America have long histories of racist medical experimentation dating back to slavery, and continuing into prisons and psychiatric settings. Experiments continued in sub-Saharan Africa until the British Empire fell. While Nazi human experimentation was meant to draw an ethical line in the sand, the USA continued to do similar, including infecting Black Americans and Guatemalans with sexually transmitted diseases and sterilising Puerto Rican women as well as using them as test subjects for the birth control pill. See Helen Tilley, 'Medicine, Empires, and Ethics in Colonial Africa', *AMA Journal of Ethics*, July 2017, https://journalofethics.ama-assn.org/article/medicine-empires-and-ethics-colonial-africa/2016-07; and Denise Oliver Velez, 'Women's History Month: Sterilization and Experimental Testing on Puerto Rican Women', *Daily Kos*, 4 March 2018, www.dailykos.com/stories/2018/3/4/1744140/-Women-s-History-Month-Sterilization-and-experimental-testing-on-Puerto-Rican-women.

British Asian residents. Without these insights, the issue of reproductive rights couldn't be properly differentiated. Their publication
FOWAAD! highlighted the different experiences of reproductive
rights for Black and Asian women:

> the wider issues of abortion as it affects us have been ignored by
> the (mainly white) women's movement. Black women have
> demanded abortion, and been forced to have sterilisations! We
> have demanded the right to choose, and we have been injected
> instead with Depo Provera against our will ... When making a
> demand for abortion rights, the women's movement has a duty
> to point out to all women that racism and imperialist population
> control programmes are also being used against black and Third
> World women.[57]

As Natalie Thomlinson, explains, Depo Provera,

> was widely administered to Black and particularly Asian women
> during this period. This was seen to be the result of racist doctors
> in the NHS who deliberately wished to limit the fertility of Black
> women by not explaining fully the functions of the drug and the
> complications that it could cause.[58]

There was no 'capitalist mode of patriarchy' which could explain
the 'universal' oppression of women under capitalism. In Britain,
the historical contexts of migration were central to the fractures
running through these debates. Exposure to different forms of
exploitation left some women with sickness and trauma others
were not experiencing. Forms of state patriarchal violence could
not be easily addressed by the critique of housework or accounts of
women's common biological interest if 'biology' was separated
from social relations. Do experiences like sterilisation change a
person's biology? If so, biology becomes a question of the qualitative, sensuous encounter between bodies and the social relations
imposed on them. If not, 'biology' becomes a form of ableism, a
standard which disregards the various conditions of the body and
the uneven stresses it is put under, to protect the higher reality of
the concept. Black feminist critique achieved its level of nuance in

large part because theories of bodily oppression were derived from *particular experiences*. It is no coincidence that a 'gender critical' complaint against trans people is that 'feelings' are being imposed onto 'biology' – do we not feel our biology?

FEMINISM AND ABOLITION

The emphasis on qualitative testimony in Black feminist publishing was not unlike the 'workers reports' many Marxists understand as a better way to theorise class composition and formation today.[59] Black feminism included workers' reports, but also perspectives on the relationship of the state to the working class, borders and race. Seen in this light, the tension between the 'objective' projects of Marxism and 'affective' or 'interpersonal' projects of 'identity' or 'intersectionality' obscures heterodox organising traditions outside of sectarian disputes in the press or academia and far more attuned to concrete theorising. Race, class and gender questions are about historical approaches to studying capitalism – what are better or worse ways of describing this complexity and the specificity of organising problems within it? The *subjective* position of Black women was crucial to the formation of alternative knowledge. The struggle to form an identity of purpose in feminism wasn't simply the fault of white feminists either. 'Political Blackness' had lost much of its hold on anti-racist praxis in Britain by the 1990s, impacting the role of Black identification within feminist movements. Division existed within the categories 'Black women' or 'Women of Colour'. Differences also surfaced along lines of class, educational attainment, religion, ethnicity, ideology, sexuality and the willingness to identify as 'feminist'. Common to most movements were questions over the individual prominence of voices and leaders, just as there are today. The class position of some leading lights in relation to the women they wrote/spoke about, and the question of how much to air publicly the dirty laundry of 'the community' for the gaze of white liberal readerships were ongoing and unresolved issues. There were also prevailing understandings about autonomy within movements – a respect for the needs of Black people, and Black women specifically, to organise separately.

By the 1980s, consciousness-raising had melded with self-help anti-racism. White women got together to 'explore' their racism. Racism here was conceived largely as a culturally inherited inevitability that white women must individually 'confess' to, before attempting to purge it from their psyches.[60] The 1980s are seen as a time of decline for Women's Liberation but were also a period of growth and dynamism for Black feminism, and for interracial organising and coalition-building.[61] Some feminists of colour joined existing feminist groups and publications, others trade unions and the Labour Party. Society became more mixed. Structures of segregation began breaking down – partly due to the entrance of more racialised people into reformist structures.* Funding became a heated point of contention inside movements, with worries about how activists' relationships to the state were being transformed. Many radical groups dissolved or became NGOs, doing casework as the social state shrank. Tamer community groups formed around 'ethnic' or 'cultural' divisions, which pulled liberation theory into state discrimination projects and muted militant outlooks.[62]

Revisiting the *quality of these divisions* means resisting the hindsight bias or outright reductionism of people who claim this history as their own because they were there. One of the ways feminist struggles are emptied of significance and used to promote conservative ideologies is by *personalising these histories of division*, while valorising a model of feminism that promised unity, but was wrongly besmirched. Feminists from different traditions explained splits in the movement through the lens of a divisive 'identity politics'. Socialist feminist Lynne Segal looked back, decades on, at the 'corrosive notes' that were struck 'with the rise of identity politics, just as Left and feminist forums unravelled in the 1980s'.[63] For radical feminist Julie Bindel, the emphasis is conspiratorial: 'it is narcissism. I lived through the first tranche of identity politics in the proper women's liberation movement, which I joined in 1979. The 80s were dogged with it, it was terrible.'[64] It has become a

---

* This wouldn't have been possible without the success and militancy of autonomous migrant struggles in the 1950s–1970s. These partly stemmed from carrying forward personal experiences or collective memories of anti-colonial struggles as well as being inspired by US movements for Civil Rights and Black Power.

feature of liberal public discourse that people in power denounce identity politics, while simultaneously invoking it in the limited arena that suits them.[65] Bindel continued:

> this is now complete 2nd Wave identity politics … it is the Men's Right Activists who speak through the prism of transgenderism. Who will say, and will be patted on the back for saying it, 'speaking as a trans woman of colour', when they're just a white man with a beard.[66]

From slavery to the Suffragettes to the WLM, gender conservative historiography looks back on a world where sex was binary and *only now* is this binary violated by neoliberalism or social media. These declinist theories are prevalent on parts of the socialist left as well as on the right and are sometimes hard to distinguish. A letter published in *The Morning Star*, stated:

> We very much appreciate your efforts in giving a platform for a sex-class based analysis of women's position, in the face of the convergence of neoliberal individualism and alienation from class consciousness which we believe is very clearly at the heart of gender identity politics.[67]

Making identity politics responsible for the collapse of the labour movement or Women's Liberation is historically scandalous, but the problems of sectarianism on the orthodox left can be disavowed when a portrayal of identity politics as particular and divisive is given to explain whatever it needs to explain. In many ways, today's state-friendly 'gender critical' feminism, more than willing to work with reactionary interests, has more in common with the moral pragmatism of British suffragism than the WLM. Instead of an untenable 'waves' approach to historicising feminism, can we look at gender critical feminism as a modernisation of imperialist forms of feminism? Conspiracy is the main organising unit of this reaction, but these conspiracies have proven capable of steering courtroom judgments and government policy.[68] They have become part of a liberal state reaction to the last guarantees that human rights offered for working-class people and people subject to the racist gender-conforming reactions of a society formed through colonialism.

Lola Olufemi writes, 'feminism is a political project about what *could* be. It's always looking forward, invested in futures we can't quite grasp yet. It's a way of wishing, hoping, aiming, at everything that has been deemed impossible'.[69] Feminism has raised the most imaginative challenges to categories and assumptions that keep checks on the possible. The principles and foundations of Black feminist writing – testimony, experience, critique, concrete universalism – are features of new communist writing today. Introducing *Transgender Marxism*, Jules Joanne Gleeson and Elle O'Rourke write: 'Our struggle is one that must be understood as intimate, concrete, and particular; just as it restlessly casts shadows over more universal questions, upsets attempted settlements between classes, and erodes otherwise tidy attempts at systemic thought.' A viewpoint on 'varied experiences of sexuation' is commensurable with the categorical critique of Marx, but a particular viewpoint on class struggle is required to elucidate this connection.[70] Molly Smith, co-author of *Revolting Prostitutes*, hails the influence of 'second wave' feminism:

> I was re-reading 'Wages Against Housework' the other day, because I'm constantly re-reading it, and I'm always struck by the line: 'we're seen as nagging bitches, not as workers in the struggle.' I think it encapsulates the way in which not recognising something as work limits people's ability to organise against it and around it, and ultimately to refuse it.[71]

Sophie Lewis revises the red thread in radical feminism, in particular the gender abolitionism of Shulamith Firestone, against its trivialisation and appropriation by gender conservative feminists: 'the persistent revolutionary desire and abolitionist drive that run through Dialectic [of Sex] disrupts the race-blind, queerphobic movements in the text. Firestone against Firestone'.[72] The reaction to these revisions – of Black feminism, sex, work, gender, radical feminism, Marx, utopia, revolution – has been fierce. It is sometimes targeted all the fiercer on the left. Where thinking negates the ruling assumptions of a society, it is received as negative.

Because this negation expands the possibility for solidarity, for humour, love, compassion – it is received as divisive. Not only do these challenges persist, they repeat. Repetition was conceived as tragedy by Marx, but repetition also leaves us with a trace, as Olufemi reminds us, to 'everything that has been deemed impossible'. The next chapters, on modern border controls, are a reminder of this. 'Abolish borders' – it bears repeating, and for as long as it takes.

4

Aliens at the Border

There has never been a moment in modern European history (if before) that migratory and/or immigrant labor was not a significant aspect of European economies. That this is not more widely understood seems to be a consequence of conceptualization and analysis: the mistaken use of the nation as a social, historical, and economic category; a resultant and persistent reference to national labor 'pools' (e.g. 'the English working class'); and a subsequent failure of historical investigation.[1]

Cedric Robinson

In 2011, Walter Benn Michaels was interviewed for a *Jacobin* article titled, 'Let Them Eat Diversity'. He argued,

Neoliberal economists are completely for open borders ... [Milton] Friedman said years ago that, 'You can't have a welfare state and open borders', but of course the point of that was 'open the borders, because that'll kill the welfare state' ... Because who's for illegal immigration? ... the only people who are openly for illegal immigration are neoliberal economists.[2]

Neoliberalism became a leftist epithet used to describe a laissez-faire form of capitalism as new markets opened up and commodity production further globalised. This transition saw social provisions cut in Western societies and increased movement of labour globally. It did not reduce the role of the state, it progressed its policing function. The failure to clearly distinguish between *increased funding* for carceral state functions and the *defunding of welfare* has been the basis for 'oppositions' to capitalism that are realised in defences of the nation. British Fire Brigade Union official, Paul Embery, wrote in 2018, 'There was a time when support for open borders was a fringe position on the Left ... having absolutely no control over the numbers of people entering your country was inimical to socialist planning around employment, housing and welfare.'[3] Embery used US discourses to target radical movements in Britain:

> open borders were a dream for bosses intent on reducing labour costs – a point refreshingly recognised by Bernie Sanders, hero to millions on today's Left, who described a borderless world as a Koch brothers proposal that would make working people poorer.[4]

Many right-wing anti-immigration conspiracies have been de rigueur among socialists for some time. Adolph Reed wrote in 2006: 'open borders is a ruling class policy ... no matter how emotionally appealing the "no borders" slogan is to some progressives'. Reed offers a technical case for borders from the left: 'regulating immigration is no different from regulating workplace conditions, wage and hour rates, building codes, interstate commerce or international trade, prohibiting racial or gender discrimination, levying taxes, or any of the many other areas of life that government regulates'.[5] Reed demonstrates the problem of viewing racism as a breach of individual human rights and nothing more. It is all very well prohibiting racial or gender discrimination for individual workers, but how do we account for borders *discriminating between workers* based on a change of place of labour? Sivanandan put it this way,

> Racism is not its own justification. It is necessary only for the purpose of exploitation: you discriminate in order to exploit or, which is the same thing, you exploit by discriminating. So that any other system of discrimination, say on the basis of nationality, would – if available – do equally well.[6]

Sivanandan's analysis of post-war Britain not only troubles grim social democratic ultimatums ('open borders or welfare state?') but provides a more complex account of race and class antagonisms. He refers to the 1950s as an 'era of laissez-faire immigration', with migrant workers from the colonies forced to search for work where they could get it – including *within the institutions of the new welfare state*. Racism functioned on the same 'free market basis ... not [to] debar black people from work per se ... to deskill them, to keep their wages down and to segregate them in the dirty, ill-paid jobs that white workers did not want.'[7] Sivanandan argues racism became more targeted after the 1962 Commonwealth Immigrants Act: 'Racialism was no longer a matter of free enterprise; it was nationalised.'[8] This shift in policy is still felt today by the Windrush generation, who came without passports in the 'laissez-faire era' and were later deported.[9] This also spurred the kinds of liberation and Black feminist theory featured in our last chapter. Sivanandan lucidly summarises:

> During the laissez-faire period of immigration, racism helped capital to make extra profit off black workers (extra in comparison to indigenous workers) – and the state, in the immediate economic interests of the ruling class, was content to leave well enough alone. But in the 1960s the state, in the long term and overall interests of capital (as against its temporary and/or sectional interests), entered into the task of converting immigrant settler labour to migrant contract labour. One of the benefits of such labour, as has been shown, is that it is automatically subject to discrimination on the basis of nationality laws and inter-state agreements ... Hence it resorted to a system of control which, in being specifically (though not overtly) directed against the 'coloured' Commonwealth, was essentially racist.[10]

The transition to neoliberalism in Britain concentrated state powers in nationalised forms of border control. In the USA, this worked differently, as we see in Chapter 5. The critical approach to borders is not to accept what neoliberal economists say they believe, or to bean count human beings, but to reject the inevitability of these violent institutions. Trite theories of neoliberalism that get sucked into open borders conspiracies, far from enabling a critique of capitalism, more often becomes a nationalist substitute for one. Future movements must address the border as a central organising problem – one that improves our understanding of race, class and gender questions. Sivanandan called immigration controls the 'loom' of British racism. The British styling of 'immigration concerns' has also allowed for subtler racist manoeuvring in the centre and distortions of anti-racist history on the left. British centrist 'anti-racists' today have successfully instrumentalised their 'love of Jews' to attack socialists and anti-racists, while supporting immigration controls at every step. The way antisemitism was instrumentalised for a factional war within the Labour Party (despite the philosemitism and antisemitism of the right and centre) strengthened an absurd counterweight from the left: that the Labour Party is 'proudly anti-racist'. Nothing could be further from the truth.[11]

The Aliens Act, our focus this chapter, forces us to think more concretely about how racism changes and new forms are established on the basis of new relations of production. Britain's first modern immigration controls were passed by Arthur James Balfour's Conservative government in 1905 and implemented by the succeeding Liberals.* They submitted Britain's working-class Jewish population to the threat of deportation. Nadine El-Enany has shown how Britain imitated measures taken by its white settler colonies in Canada, Australia and Southern Africa, where early immigration laws took on the appearance of 'race-neutrality' while producing 'racialised effects'.[12] What Satnam Virdee calls 'socialist nationalism' crystallised during this period.[13] As the labour market nationalised so did the identity of labour. British socialist nationalists were willing to work with, and demand violence from, the bourgeois state to police foreign – and British-born – proletarian Jews. They agitated for 'alien control', in part, to regulate the more radical, internationalist elements of the working class.

AGITATING FOR RESTRICTION

'New Unionism' was catalysed by the economic crises of the 1870s. Britain abandoned the free trade regime its hegemony was built

---

* Balfour was central both to Jewish exclusion through the Aliens Act and gave his name to the 1917 Declaration affirming Britain's notional support for Zionism (the first of any major power to do so).

on, seeking to protect profit margins at the expense of working-class conditions. Unemployment soared in major industries. Precarity became more widespread as automation ate into craft worker privileges. Piecework became the norm. This anticipated a structural sea-change in working-class organisation. Previously excluded workers – women, Irish Catholics, 'unskilled' and casual labourers of the so-called 'residuum' – began forcing their way into the institutions of the working class, developing their own organisations and becoming players in national politics.* The main break was with craft union exclusivity. A 'skilled' labour aristocracy had gradually managed to negotiate wage increases and voting rights (for themselves). These conservative workingmen, unprepared and complacent, saw the unskilled masses lay siege to movement hierarchies. Pushback against the 'deserving' section of the nation's working class ripped up their respectability politics playbook and cosy dealings with the Liberal Party top brass. There were demonstrations and riots against unemployment and for Irish Home Rule in 1886 and 1887. Then came victory for the matchwomen, followed by the gasworkers and dockers in 1889. Within a year, nearly 200,000 unskilled workers had been organised into unions. Working-class socialism had arrived as a force. But the rupture of New Unionism also contained within it an embrace of the nation-state.

In 1892, President of the Trades Union Congress (TUC), John Hodge, announced to members: 'the door must be shut against the enormous immigration of destitute aliens into this country … We must protect our own starving work people by refusing to be the asylum for the paupers of Europe'.[14] This emphasis on state patronage of the national worker, on protecting 'our own', was part of an emerging consensus shared by dominant strands of organised labour and parliamentary liberalism as Britain began to nationalise a polity. By late nineteenth century, advanced industrial economies like Germany and the USA threatened British pre-eminence.[15] Economic downturn was rationalised by blaming foreigners for unemployment, low wages and terrible work-

---

* Victorian ruling-class pejorative for the growing urban underclass produced by industrial capitalism.

ALIENS AT THE BORDER

ing-class living conditions. British workers contributed to national prosperity and deserved reward, but the benefits were being reaped by the 'scum of other nations', as Liberal MP Cathcart Wason put it:

What is the use of spending thousands of pounds on building beautiful workmen's dwellings if the places of our own workpeople, the backbone of the country, are to be taken over by the refuse scum of other nations? In the interests of the health and well-being of the nation at large, the standard of civilisation, prosperity, and comfort should be raised to as high a level as possible. But, as the lower organism would always kill the higher, it was the duty of every section of the community to endeavour to protect and foster the highest civilisation we could possibly have in the country.[16]

Founder and leader of the Social Democratic Federation (SDF), Henry Hyndman, was a successful businessman, a former Tory with family wealth partly accrued from the slave trade.[17] He founded the SDF in the early 1880s based on his own peculiar interpretation of Marx's theories.[18] Hyndman's conceptions of capitalism and imperialism were steeped in antisemitism from the start, sometimes couched in Christian morality and traditional Judeophobia, but also conspiratorial explanations for modern economics and world affairs. The SDF's journal, *Justice*, edited for decades by Hyndman's great ally Harry Quelch, consistently trafficked in nativism and antisemitism.[19] 'Jew moneylenders now control every Foreign Office in Europe', *Justice* published in 1884. In 1890, it said Jewish 'control' of Britain's press was 'in accord with their fellow capitalist Jews all over the world'.[20] Many of the era's significant Left figures passed through the SDF on their way to forming breakaway parties, or joining the non-Marxian Christian socialists of the Independent Labour Party (ILP), or later the Labour Party itself.

The ILP exemplified the gains of New Unionism. It integrated Irish-descended workers, but was no better than the SDF when it came to Jews. The party tended to frame questions of class exploitation as national questions. Leonard Hall wrote in *Clarion*, in 1895: 'There is scarcely a town of any dimensions in the country in which the foreign element has not menaced and injured the position of the local workman.' Hall, President of the ILP's Manchester and Salford branch, described immigration control as 'legitimate self-preservation.'[21] Bruce Glasier was one of the ILP's founders, along with Keir Hardie and future Labour Prime Minister Ramsey MacDonald. He later took over from Hardie as editor of ILP journal, *Labour Leader*, writing of Jewish immigration:

> neither the principle of the brotherhood of man nor the principle of social equality implies that brother nations or brother men may crowd upon us in such numbers as to abuse our hospitality, overturn our institutions or violate our customs.[22]

Harry Snell's* 1904 pamphlet, 'The Foreigner in England: An Examination of the Problem of Alien Immigration', outlined the ILP position on the mooted introduction of controls. The author eventually errs against the legislation, but not out of solidarity with Jews: '[The] rich jew ... has done his best to besmirch the fair name of England, and to corrupt the sweetness of our national life and character,' Snell wrote, 'the alien problem in Whitechapel and Stepney is in the main a Jewish problem ... let him go where he will the Jew is always an alien.' Snell added: 'As a Labour Party we are not called upon to contend that all anti-alien feeling is necessarily immoral.'[23] An early airing for the argument: 'it's not racist to have concerns about immigration'.

From 60,000 in 1880, Britain's Jewish population 'approximately quintupled'[24] in 40 years as a result of persecuted Ashkenazi Jews escaping famine and pogroms in the 'Pale of Settlement'.[25] But Jews never constituted more than 1 per cent of Britain's total population. Carrying little more than the clothes on their backs, Yiddish-speaking Jews largely settled in three concentrated areas: Manchester, Leeds and, overwhelmingly, London's East End. A space of profound poverty, with chronic housing shortages and unemployment, East London was also a ferment of working-class

---

* From poor rural beginnings in the East Midlands, Snell moved to London, spending time in the SDF, ILP and the Fabians. He served as Labour MP and in government under both Ramsey Macdonald and Churchill. He was later ennobled, becoming Baron Snell.

militancy. These new arrivals, though, found themselves excluded by employers *and* unions. As the great historian of the radical Jewish East End, William Fishman, put it: ' "Britons first" was the normal response of masters and trade unionists.'[26] And antisemitism extended to the most militant. In 1891, two leaders of the Great Dock Strike, Ben Tillett and Tom Mann, sent letters to the *London Evening News* calling for controls against Jews.[27] Another hero of that strike, John Burns, demanded: 'England was for the English!'[28] A decade later, at a 'Stop the War' rally in Battersea Park, Burns (by then an MP) blamed the Boer War on the 'financial Jew'.[29] Despite widespread railing by trade unionists about Jewish culpability in that conflict, the TUC supported Britain's war.[30] Tillett was a particularly virulent antisemite throughout his political life, spanning his trade union days to membership of the Fabians, the ILP and SDF, before two stints as a Labour MP.

OUT OF PLACE

Tillett blamed 'foreigners' for living and working conditions. His class concerns and 'immigration concerns' were indistinguishable: '[an] influx of continental pauperism aggravates and multiplies the number of ills which press so heavily on us'.[31] Beatrice Webb, driving force behind the Fabian Society, echoed the sentiments of many in Britain's workers movement, claiming Jews had 'neither the desire nor the capacity for labour combination'.[32] This despite the already significant organising among Jewish workers in Britain. Webb went further: 'the love of profit distinct from other forms of money earning' was 'the strongest impelling motive of the Jewish race'. For her, Jews were 'deficient in ... social morality'.[33] Here was an attempt to unify figurations of 'rich Jew' and 'poor Jew', concluding that proletarian Jews were against integration and worker solidarity. They were merely, *inherently*, capitalists-in-the-making. The TUC formally committed to a position against 'alien' immigration. Resolutions supporting controls were passed at 1894's Cardiff conference and a specially arranged congress on 'alien' control the year after. They even sent a delegation in 1896 to meet with the Tory Home Secretary and register their demand for controls.[34]

Poor Jewish migrants arriving in Victorian Britain had, like many migrants and refugees today, few options as to how they might reproduce their own existence and that of their families. Most drew on hometown or family connections to find accommodation and work as pedlars or down backstreets as:

> sweated labour: often outworkers in the clothing industry – sub-contracted by Savile Row tailors – employed for limitless hours either in their own cramped dwellings or on the fetid premises of some 'master' who earned little more than they, which, in 1890, was rarely as much as 1 pound a week.[35]

Super-exploitation existed before poor Jews arrived, much like finance has never been the sole preserve of Jews. Nevertheless, both were personified as 'Jewish problems', made clear by an 1888 *East London Advertiser* editorial:

> competition is ... at the bottom of all this evil – foreign competition *for the most part*. The swarms of foreign Jews who have invaded the East End labour market are chiefly responsible for the sweating system and the grave evils which are flowing from it ... If this foreign immigration can be checked half the battle against the sweating system will be over.[36]

Jewish workers came to personify the 'grave evils' of capitalist exploitation, in contrast to a national moral standard of respectability around work. The 'sweated' trades were once populated by women and children. Mechanisation of former craft trades coincided with the transition to a nationally formalised 'free labour contract', fought for by unions to supersede 'master and servant law', where employers could sue and jail workers for not honouring contracts. New Unionism's birth was determined by the parochial nature of industry and employment, composed of diverse forms of manufacture and local disputes between workers, magistrates and industrial bourgeoisie. Jewish migrants arrived at a transitional moment in British capitalist development. Trades unions appealed to concepts of equality and exchange in the market to finally defeat the legal bond between master and servant and generalise a labour identity.[37] Jewish workers were caught in the imperial grip of a national polity emergence. British antisemitism was centuries old, embodied in Protestant morality and liberal reformism. Proletarian Jews were subject to relations of production and forms of exploitation that a labour movement seeking moral enfranchisement and respectability sought to overcome. Imperialist competition, economic crisis and war were on the horizon, creating opportunities for *nationalised* workers prioritising the welfare of a 'race' of workers above the mass of the working class.

Popular support for purging Jewish workers followed. Anti-immigration movements emerged, with rich donors. The British Brothers League (BBL), formed in 1901, held rallies and protests demanding controls. Targeting the East End, it held packed meetings and demonstrations numbering in the thousands,[38] only ending its activity once the Aliens Act passed. A petition in Tower Hamlets demanding alien exclusion garnered 45,000 signatures,[39] giving voice to nativist concerns about the supposed effect of immigration on housing, wages and jobs. The BBL's prime mover was Tory MP for Stepney, Major William Evans Gordon, who referred to the East End's 'Hebrew colony' as a 'race apart',[40] drawing on abounding discourses of inassimilable Jews 'invading' and displacing 'natives'. The BBL had substantial cross-class support,[41] helped by the involvement of local newspaper owners.[42] Colin Holmes described 'an alliance of East End workers and backbench Tory MPs'.[43] Supporters carried banners declaring 'Britain for the British'[44] and chanted 'wipe them out, wipe them out!'[45]*

JEWISH SELF-ACTIVITY

Newly arrived Jews had to struggle on multiple fronts: pushing back against super-exploitation by employers, the racism of trade unions *and* the cynical paternalism of the settled Jewish elite. Most couldn't speak English so ended up working for other Jews as apprentices or 'hands'. Such precarious conditions of low pay and

---

* Jews were blamed for rising crime, including sex trafficking and the 'Jack the Ripper' murders. They became signifiers for hygiene discourses about disease or ableist discourses about 'lunacy' and 'idiocy'. The case for bordering was fortified as a racialised form of disease control.

isolation made existence extremely hard, and resistance even more so. And yet, this period saw the flourishing of a diverse and experimental radical Jewish scene. This has parallels with labour, housing and migrants rights organising in Britain today, including groups such as United Voices of the World and the IWGB. Jews established their own unions, organised strikes and protests, set up an Alien Defence League in Brick Lane to counter anti-immigrant racism.[46] Histories of autonomous anti-racist struggles such as these have always tended to be subterranean, typically relegated to minoritarian concerns, remembered usually by the racialised communities involved and their descendants, if at all.

Tracing the historical tensions and splits inside the SDF (later the British Socialist Party, BSP) shows Jewish socialists also forced change from *within the left*. Practically all consistent resistance to controls was led by Jews, including those struggling within existing unions and parties. Over more than a decade, Jewish members of the SDF/BSP exerted pressure on the leadership and party press, forcing consequences for their antisemitism. Figures like Theodore Rothstein, Zelda Kahan and Joe Fineberg all challenged the party over its antisemitism and militarism, achieving local and national leadership positions in the organisation, but facing hateful racism for their trouble. Workers' newspapers document rich testimonies of resistance. Yiddish-language anarchist paper, *Der Arbeter Fraynd* (Workers' Friend), was printed out of the Berners Street Club at the heart of the Radical Jewish East End. It castigated British workers for their nationalism and Jews for any religious conformity. When the TUC supported controls in 1895, a London meeting was organised by ten Jewish trade unions with Eleanor Marx and Peter Kropotkin speaking. A leaflet promoting the event announced:

Jews! The English anti-semites have come to the point where the English workers' organisation calls on the government to close England's doors to the poor alien, that is, in the main, to the Jew. You must no longer keep silent. You must come in your thousands to the meeting in the Great Assembly Hall.[47]

A Voice From The Aliens was printed and circulated in 1895, written by Joseph Finn, a Jewish worker in Leeds. This pamphlet chastised English workers:

> Surely we cannot blame the foreign working man, who is as much a victim of the industrial system as is the English working man. Neither can we blame the machine which displaces human labour. The only party at fault is the English working class itself, which has the power, but neither the sense nor courage, to make the machines serve and benefit the whole nation, instead of leaving them as a source of profit for one class ... In Germany the immigration is one-tenth of the emigration. In the United States it is vice versa. Still, the wages of a tailor in Germany is 15s, whilst in the United States it is 58s. What will our opponents say to this? If the English worker has reason to be dissatisfied with his lot, let him not blame his foreign fellow working man; let him rather study the social and labour question – he will then find out where the shoe pinches.[48]

Finn already saw the need for workers in Europe to find an answer to capital's outsourcing of production to sites overseas with access to cheaper labour-power:

> Whether, so far from being the enemies of the English workers, it is not rather the capitalist class (which is constantly engaged in taking trade abroad, in opening factories in China, Japan, and other countries) who is the enemy, and whether it is not rather their duty to combine against the common enemy than fight against us whose interests are identical with theirs.[49]

While many socialists today cannot, nineteenth-century 'alien voices' could differentiate the free movement of capital from the subordination of the global working class to these movements. A tiny minority of organisations took up anti-racist positions. William Morris and Eleanor Marx left the SDF to create the Socialist League, pursuing a more pluralist, internationalist socialism composed of a mixture of anarchists and Marxists in a handful of cities.[50] They opposed the SDF's chauvinism. Eleanor Marx, in an

1884 letter to Wilhelm Liebknicht, bemoaned the fact that 'whereas we wish to make this a really international movement, Mr Hyndman whenever he could do with impunity, has endeavoured to set English workmen against foreigners'.[51] The League's founding manifesto, written by Morris in 1885 and published in *Commonweal*, included a pointed passage that would have been anathema to Hyndman:

> The Socialist League therefore aims at the realisation of complete Revolutionary Socialism, and well knows that this can never happen in any one country without the help of the workers of all civilisation. For us neither geographical boundaries, political history, race, nor creed makes rivals or enemies; for us there are no nations, but only varied masses of workers and friends, whose mutual sympathies are checked or perverted by groups of masters and fleecers whose interest it is to stir up rivalries and hatreds between the dwellers in different lands.[52]

Solidarity that stretched to the inclusion of Jews was isolated compared to nationalist left currents. The Socialist League was always small and divided. By 1901, it had disbanded. As Virdee puts it: 'such politics proved incapable of generating the vocabulary required to hold the line against the rising tide of an aggressive, racialising nationalism to be found throughout society, including much of the working class'.[53]

Nor could Jewish workers rely on Anglo-Jewish elites, who were keen to disassociate themselves from newer, poorer Jews. The representative organ of the community, the Board of Deputies, was formed in 1760. The Board of Guardians, which issued charitable poor relief, in 1859. They were led by wealthier, more integrated Jews, descended from much earlier migrations. To protect their own positions and civil rights, they wouldn't allow anyone to cast aspersions on their allegiance to the nation.* The Anglo-Jewish establishment recognised working-class Jewish activism early on,

---

* Achieved over that century with legislation removing legal discriminations and 'disabilities' against Jews in Britain. Jews (mostly men) were enabled to attend certain universities, practice certain trades, and become Members of Parliament.

and the dangers it posed. They circled on Jewish radicals, trying to control Jewish labour. Sir Samuel Montagu, Jewish Liberal MP for Whitechapel, believed socialists posed the greatest threat to British Jewry. A constant thorn in their side, he sponsored conservative trade unionism, conciliated disputes between Jewish employers and workers, and convinced printers not to publish radical materials. Anglo-Jewish MPs like Harry Simon Samuel and Harry Marks spoke at BBL rallies. Sir Benjamin Cohen campaigned and voted for the Aliens Act.[54] He was made a baronet shortly afterwards.[55] The editorial position of the *Jewish Chronicle*, established in 1841, wavered between conformist pleas for integration and support for restriction and repatriation of Britain's 'Ostjuden'.*

Communal leaders and organisations even took it upon themselves to arrange for proletarian Jews to leave for America or return to Eastern European pogroms.[56] Communal philanthropic organisations, serving a quasi-state function, rationed and withheld aid to destitute immigrant Jews.[57] Operating through bourgeois relations of conditionality and moral improvement, charities encouraged recipients to ditch the Yiddish language. Such internalisation of British state interests for social control by appointed (or self-appointed) leaders of stratified 'communities' is characteristic of longue durée British race and class management in its colonies *and* on British soil right up to today.[58] The shaping of identities by state appointment erases the class antagonisms that have always existed within racialised communities, providing the racist common sense of sameness and alienness the far right weaponises.

BRITISH WELFARE

Following the passage of the 1905 Aliens Act, the number of Jewish refugees granted asylum takes a precipitous nosedive. Meanwhile, a limited architecture of social welfare is established.[59] It was expanded incrementally, before taking on a more systematic design after the Second World War. As Steve Cohen found, the twinned

---

* German for 'Jews of the East'. Used in nineteenth-century Germany and Austria to distinguish between more 'integrated' Jews of Central Europe and the poorer Jews of Eastern Europe.

birth of welfare and immigration controls was constructed around the racial exclusion of Jews and that was no coincidence: 'racism is not peripheral to the welfare state itself but is essential to it'.[60] While some workers became eligible for Old Age Pensions in 1908, National Insurance in 1911, and later other benefits, this was never available to *all* workers. This was a feature, not a bug. The twentieth-century interrelationship of welfare and exclusion is a central, if often obscured, aspect of British society and British racism. Cohen wrote that 'welfarism' was historically 'defined and constructed within the same ideology as immigration control, that is the ideology of race, eugenics and nation'. In 1898, TUC President James O'Grady was already envisaging proletarian social reproduction as part of a corporatist national project: 'if … national prosperity depends on the well-being of the worker, the necessary corollary is that the state should care for him in sickness'.[61] With the advent of 'formally free labour' came the moral constitution of the abstract, legally free citizen. Robbie Shilliam describes the 'strongly interventionist science of eugenics' as being 'deeply implicated in the movement from provincial poor relief towards a system of national insurance and welfare'.[62] This was demonstrated by the welfare state's chief architect, William Beveridge, a eugenicist keenly preoccupied with the health and propagation of the 'British race', which he feared was in inexorable decline.[63] The welfare state was a national system organised for the reproduction of labour-power, privileging a national-racial white population. The formal contradiction, El-Enany argues, is that welfare 'embodied the assertion of white entitlement to the spoils of colonial conquest'.[64] There was no 'spiritual' break from the eugenicist Edwardian-era and its interwar development. Early social security provisions excluded Jewish migrants; the new system retained informal and formal means to flexibly exploit labour and organise welfare provision accordingly. The post-war compact remains a powerful blueprint for liberals and socialists, because it was, in part, a concession to workers' struggle and emphasised citizen ideals that now seem distant from neoliberal crisis and the valorisation of private interest. Yet, 'welfare' was never an unconditional 'public good'. It was shaped through racialisation and exclusion at every stage of development. By essentialising it as a concession 'won by and for workers', we make it harder to see public institutions as exploitative workplaces, where institutional cultures exist that are hostile to the working class. A tension described in *The Heart of the Race*, from the viewpoint of workers:

> When Black women began arriving in Britain after the Second World War to provide the newly-established National Health Service with much-needed labour, we came into a service which regarded us not as potential clients but as workers. Our role was to become the nurses, cleaners and cooks who would supply and maintain the service for others. From the very beginning, the NHS had one purpose – to replenish this country's labour supply with fit, white, male workers.[65]

Not all at once, but sections of the Victorian working class became absorbed (often working hard to be so) into ruling definitions of 'white' and 'British' racial identity. Alastair Bonnett points to a 'shift in emphasis from whiteness as a bourgeois identity, connoting extraordinary qualities, to whiteness as a popularist identity connoting superiority but also ordinariness, nation and community'.[66] Most Left figures and organisations used eugenic frameworks and language, racial or 'civilisational' hierarchies, to think about the 'racial stock' of the population and the role of the state/Empire in breeding a strong and healthy workforce and citizenry. Eugenics was used to justify the rejection of other (or *othered*) workers and rationalise support for imperialism. Focus was also trained on the positive qualities of the British/English 'race' as perfectible and discrete populations, the health of which were anxiously monitored. Irish migrants were targeted as an inferior 'Celtic Race'. Popular cartoons depicted Irish people as simian, not fully evolved human beings. Similar language was used to describe impoverished East Enders, seen as comparable to or 'worse than' far away colonised populations. A bourgeois observer like wealthy shipowner-cum-social reformer, Charles Booth, conducting his influential study of poverty in London, described East End 'casual labourers of low character' as living 'the life of savages'.[67] His namesake, William Booth, founder of the Salvation Army, asked:

As there is a darkest Africa, is there not also a darkest England? Civilisation, which can breed its own barbarians ... Darkest England, like Darkest Africa, reeks with malaria. The foul and fetid breath of our slums is almost as poisonous as that of the African swamp.[68]*

Shilliam plots a course through the history of British ruling-class domination and its constant reformulation of racialising and moralising discourses and distinctions along the binary of the 'deserving' and 'undeserving' poor. He reminds us: 'Britain's division of labour has never been national in constitution or scope.'[69] Rather, 'the enslavement of Africans was a fundamental reference point for the initial racialization of deserving and undeserving characteristics, with the "slave" – and thereby the condition of blackness – exemplifying the latter.'[70] Through Shilliam's impeccable telling, this schema is developed through state restructures, from Victorian poor laws and workhouses to later national systems of insurance and welfare. Particular attention is paid throughout to a jealous protection of the nationalist, moral and fundamentally racialised concept of the 'English genus'. It is impossible to separate race and class in the story of social movements and struggles attempting to either reform or overthrow British capitalism. Ruling-class segmentations have continually been *taken on* by socialists, feminists and others as ways to identify themselves as more deserving than others.

Notions of a racially degraded working class were used to justify the SDF's approach, which prioritised hierarchical leadership by what tended to be middle class, formally educated members and focused on parliamentarism over industrial organising. Eugenic reasoning allowed Hyndman to blame SDF failings (its struggle to attract more members and make a wider impact on society) on the

---

* The bourgeois gaze cast upon the Victorian 'residuum', seen as under-evolved white detritus amidst imperial advancement, brings to mind more recent depictions of 'the English poor' seen through a lens of 'fallen' whiteness. The 1990s/2000s saw a cultural-political focus on working-class whites on council estates. Television characters like Wayne and Waynetta Slob from *The Fast Show* or Vicky Pollard on *Little Britain* were typical depictions of 'chavs' – whites who made themselves undeserving of the euphemism 'ordinary' when apprehending Britain's 'working class', viewed from above.

tools he was working with, that is, Britain's working class not being up to scratch. Daniel Edmonds writes:

It is perhaps a testament to Hyndman's arrogance that he understood his organisation's marginalisation ... and unpopularity in the era of rising labourism as an indicator not of their own flawed strategies or precepts, but of the physical and mental degeneration of British workers.[71]

The British Socialist Party maintained strong ties to 'race science'. The Eugenics Society delivered numerous talks at branches.[72] A fundraising calendar, edited by Dora Montefiore, contained quotes from notable supporters, including George Bernard Shaw calling for 'a eugenic revolution [to] save our civilisation'.[73] Karl Pearson appeared in the same calendar. He was a protégé of Francis Galton (cousin of Charles Darwin and the father of 'eugenics'.) Pearson was a self-described 'socialist', who applied eugenics to the terrain of a competition between nation-races and their levels of civilisation.[74] His 1925 report with Margaret Moul on 'The Problem of Alien Immigration into Great Britain', examined Eastern European Jewish children, judging them physically and mentally 'inferior' to children of the 'autochthonous race'. The rise of eugenics dovetailed with the establishment of national border technologies. The hierarchical ordering of the world into 'races' met with the desire of the 'civilised' to be protected from contamination by lower 'races'. The report concluded:

the whole problem of immigration is fundamental for the rational teaching of national eugenics. What purpose would there be in endeavouring to legislate for a superior breed of men, if at any moment it could be swamped by the influx of immigrants of an inferior race, hastening to profit by the higher civilisation of an improved humanity? To the eugenicist, permission for indiscriminate immigration is and must be destructive of all true progress.[75]

Immigration controls acted then, and act now, as the ultimate exclusion from national welfare, by preventing entrance and exercising deportation powers against 'aliens' within. The work of the border has always entailed a more banal, bureaucratic violence of internal controls and surveillance against target populations.* With early welfare provision, the primary target was Jews. Pensions and National Insurance came with conditions *designed* to exclude Jewish workers – a requirement of 20 years of citizenship and residency.[76] Many Jews sought naturalisation to escape these exclusions. While some achieved it, many struggled with the English language component or the process took so long that they gave up, were deported or died before receiving a decision. In an echo of people seeking naturalisation today, many Jews were simply priced out by prohibitive costs (£5 in 1907).[77]

The infrastructures and logics established by the 1905 Act set the foundations for further controls: the Alien Restrictions Act in 1914, another Aliens Act in 1919 and the 1920 Aliens Order. Legislation removed any recourse to an appeals process, gave the Home Secretary executive deportation powers and introduced identification requirements upon entry that we are now accustomed to. Jews felt under siege. Even the *Jewish Chronicle* spoke of a 'war on aliens', who were told to carry identity cards.[78] Draconian restrictions were placed on their movements and social lives. They had to sign special registers to use a hotel.[79] Restriction was not only enforced at the national level but also by local government. In 1919, London County Council refused scholarships to foreign-born children, even if they were naturalised. By 1925, foreigners were excluded from council housing.[80] For years, politicians debated giving preferential treatment to British nation-

---

* Today's 'Hostile Environment' intensifies existing logics with ramped up, more coordinated exclusion and state terror. Vans were driven around major cities telling 'illegal immigrants' to 'Go Home'. Expanded internal controls were introduced with Immigration Acts in 2014 and 2016 and 'a host of new rules, protocols, 'memoranda of understanding' between government departments' casting a social and technological dragnet across society. Britain's border regime now bears down on 'migrants' more than ever before. Policing and monitoring extends across state, private and third sectors, aided by eager members of the public. For decades this regime has been able to count on the cooperation of unionised public sector workforces. Normalised bordering aims to enlist the citizen-worker in the uncontroversial national duty of capturing fugitive 'illegals', making a border guard of every teacher, doctor, landlord and data analyst. See *The UK Border Regime: A Critical Guide* (Corporate Watch, 2018), https://corporatewatch.org/wp-content/uploads/2018/10/UK_border_regime.pdf.

als at labour exchanges. The plasticity of bordering as a flexible legal instrument means it can target and identify where expedient, redesigning citizen status and jurisdiction of exploitation where necessary. Protection of the deserving, patriotic citizen is one expedient crucial to shaping electoral politics. Some 'aliens' legislation was shelved because it wasn't enforceable, but in the depths of depression in 1930, Margaret Bondfield, Minister for Labour in an ill-fated Labour government, announced in Parliament:

it would obviously be impractical to ascertain the nationality of applicants in all cases. The exchanges are, however, instructed to do so if there is reason to believe that the applicant is not of British nationality and where in such cases the applicant is found to be an alien who has resided in the United Kingdom for less than six months he is not to be submitted for any vacancy if suitable British subjects are on the register.[81]

There is a misconception around formal politics that a progressive-reactionary spectrum from left to right operates as a guide to what side you are on. But the left has always facilitated racist and chauvinist factions. Ernest Belfort Bax, who joined William Morris and Eleanor Marx in splitting from the SDF and forming the Socialist League, was a prolific writer and thought of as a leading socialist thinker of his time. He was also a propagator of race science. While Bax believed each 'race' deserved democratic autonomy in their separation, his summation of racial division in America was premised upon notions of racial fixity and hierarchy. His preoccupation with innate social hierarchies also extended to gender. He used an example of natural difference between 'races' to ballast his argument against women's suffrage and feminism. That Bax could hold to such racist ideology despite being part of the *least* racist strand of British socialism at that time shows how deeply entrenched 'race-thinking' and imperialism had become. Bax, thinking of multiracial societies like the USA, saw total racial segregation as the only 'solution'. A position he shared with many white socialist contemporaries on both sides of the Atlantic.

BRITISH PROTO-FASCISM

Despite an intensification of industrial action in the lead up to the First World War, most of the labour movement leadership supported it. The Labour Party and TUC called, in the national interest, for a cessation of industrial disputes for the duration of the conflict.[82] The committed and principled did campaign against the war from pacifist, radical liberal, international socialist and anarchist perspectives. Jewish workers were especially active in protesting the draft. Meanwhile, pro-war labour factions (some of a proto-fascist character) gained traction. Study of parties and trade unions during this period reveal a 'geopolitical antisemitism' – where crises and world events are explained by Jewish interference. In 1900, referencing the Boer War, John Ward of the Navvies Union, complained about taxpayers' money being spent 'trying to secure the gold fields of South Africa for cosmopolitan Jews, most of whom had no patriotism and no country'.[83] *Labour Leader* barked: 'Wherever there is trouble in Europe, wherever rumours of war circulate and men's minds are distraught with fear and change and calamity, you may be sure that a hook-nosed Rothschild is at his games somewhere near the region.'[84] The conspiratorial structure of antisemitism evolved from 'anti-imperialist' critiques of earlier wars to pro-war rancour leading into the First World War. Edmonds notes,

the shift from anti-semitic anti-imperialism to a focussed attack on Jewish members for the crimes of 'anti-nationalism' and traitorous activities, coupled with a willingness to appeal to the security services to police Jewish members, marked a serious upturn in the tenor and ferocity of socialist anti-semitism.[85]

Earlier fixations on 'financial Jews' had erased working-class Jews, but Jewish workers increasingly came under direct conspiratorial attack. In 1916, the BSP split. Its nationalist right wing was forced out. Hyndman formed the National Socialist Party. Also launched was the British Workers League (BWL). These pro-war socialist groupings were later absorbed into the Labour Party.[86] The BWL began as the Socialist National Defence Committee, with famed author H.G. Wells and Robert Blatchford of *Clarion* as founding members. It was led by middle-class journalist, former Fabian and SDF member Victor Fisher, who provided the ideological framing:

[the] community of blood, of tradition, of glory and victory, of defeat and suffering, this common tie of language, of literature, of habit and institutions, this sense of a birth land ... this larger family divided from the other families of men by the very lines of national and racial life.[87][*]

Fisher claimed splits in the socialist movement were engineered by Jews 'with all the acuteness of their race'.[88] The BWL garnered establishment support and recruits from across the political spectrum. Its executive included 15 sitting Labour MPs. *The Times* anointed them 'the authentic voice of the working classes'.[89] Fanatically nationalistic and pro-Empire, the BWL only allowed British nationals as members and believed in the permanent militarisation of society. The organisation was partly funded by Viscount Lord Alfred Milner, a seasoned, high-ranking colonial administrator in South Africa, a race patriot[90] and a member of Lloyd George's war cabinet. Milner paid Fisher £5,000 for his services.[91] He and others wanted a counter-presence to anti-war street movements. Adam Hochschild says Milner,

did not mind working with trade unionists, for he had always been open to what some called 'gas and water socialism'. Public health? Better schools? Public Ownership of electric power? No problem: such things were entirely tolerable if they made the economy more efficient and the working class more enthusiastic for the empire – and the war.[92]

The BWL generated a brand image of working-class authenticity and pro-war 'social imperialism' by canvassing the streets and

---

[*] While this gets about as close to blood and soil fascism as anything emerging from Britain's workers movement, notions of racial and biological destiny were commonplace. This period saw European and US imperial expansion, accompanied by ubiquitous 'race-thinking', suffused in high and popular culture. The advent of universal primary education coincides with hardening racial ideology to explain and justify empire.

filling the broadsheets. By 1917, they had over 150 branches and a weekly newspaper with a circulation of 25,000–30,000 copies.[93] They combined calls for nationalisation of industries and higher wages with pro-war jingoism and vilification of 'shirkers'. They and their pro-war media allies[*] encouraged assaults on anti-war social-ists.[**] They worked with the authorities to persecute opponents who were foreign nationals, particularly Jews – a xenophobic, anti-socialist violence that anticipated the coming European fascism. Slogans and banners included 'All-British from the core'[94] and 'Britain for the British'.[95] In November 1916, a 1,500-strong pro-war mob of BWL and British Empire Union members, miners and veterans broke police lines to attack an anti-war meeting in Cardiff.[96]

Associations in mainstream discourse between immigration, 'race' and radical politics never reached the fever pitch of US Red Scares, but it was a tactic used by state, press *and* socialist nation-alists, to link anti-war elements to foreign origins, particularly Jewishness.[***] Milner even arranged for Fisher to advise Lloyd George on suppressing worker unrest after the Bolshevik revo-lution. Associating revolutionary politics with a racialised other goes back at least to Chartism, when press and authorities blamed activities on Black and Irish troublemakers.[97] An early attempt to introduce an Aliens Bill in 1894 had targeted 'destitute aliens and

---

[*] Lloyd George supplanted Asquith with the help of Milner and press barons Lord Northcliffe (owner of the *Times* and *Daily Mail*) and Lord Beaverbrook (owner of the *Daily Express*). The former was named Director of Propaganda in the new Government, the latter Minister of Information.

[**] Followers of seaman's union leader and BWL Vice-President, J. Havelock Wilson, set fire to the offices of an anti-war opponent. Another supporter of the BWL was, of course, Ben Tillett.

[***] The treatment of 'Alien Jews' mirrors the past three decades of hyperventilating Islamophobia in Britain. Muslims and Jews are often similarly racialised in traditionally Christian countries. While antisemitic conspiracy remains a bedrock of Euro-American reaction, Islamophobic conspiracies have grown in prominence. Invasion narratives and reverse-colonisation fantasies like 'Eurabia' and 'Creeping Sharia' have seeped into wider consciousness. Such declinist fears of civilisational degeneration have deep roots in Europe. Some, certain of Islamic takeover, raise the alarm about major cities being 'no-go zones' to national law and order. Fear spreads about reversing birthrates and demographic obliter-ation, a looming 'great replacement'. Muslims today and 'Alien Jews' of yesterday get cast as 'terrorists', 'radicals', traitors to the nation, uniquely sexually predatory and unable or unwilling to assimilate. Far right discourses cast national rulers and European elites as weak and supine in the face of foreign invasion by stealth.

anarchists'.[98] During Parliamentary debate over the 1919 Aliens Restrictions Bill, Manchester MP Rei Carter, announced himself as part of 'the movement called "Britain for the British"'. He deplored the weakness of the bill, stating it wouldn't 'carry behind it ... the will of the people'. Carter remarked: 'I believe that an alien never comes to this country for our good, but only for his own. If he comes here to live with us, there is no reason why he should come here to rule us.'[99] He added:

the unrest that is at present prevailing in this country has a very great deal to do with the alien enemy. You never hear of any disturbance, rioting or anything of that kind without a fair sprinkling of aliens. Bolshevism, of course, is introduced in England almost entirely by aliens.[100]

Justice printed unevidenced claims that East End anarchists (code for Jews) were agents provocateurs who engaged in 'propaganda of the deed' solely to discredit socialism. They called for Jewish anarchists' asylum to be repealed and claimed Jewish-American anarchist, Emma Goldman, was a Russian spy. There were 'deportations of communists and other revolutionaries',[101] many of them Jews, often with tenuous connections to radical politics.*

THE AGE OF ALIENS?

Historical attempts at social transformation have always involved a working class composed of various professions or unemployments, as well as lived multicultures. The militancy of bourgeois intellectuals and dissenters – Karl and Eleanor Marx, William Morris, Sylvia Pankhurst – have also made undeniable contributions to revolutionary activity in Britain. Equally, conservative reaction doesn't simply work top–down. It has emerged through alliances of aristocrats, entrepreneurs and opportunists, liberals, socialists, state appointees of racialised groups, nationalist recruits

---

* In 1925, a young Jewish man who had lived in England since he was five was deported. Because, said the *Jewish Chronicle*: 'of a charge made against him in connection with a Communist meeting in a public park'. Quoted in Steve Cohen, *No One is Illegal: Asylum and Immigration Control Past and Present* (Stoke-On-Trent: Trentham Books, 2003), 180.

from the working class. Many socialist currents in this period were actively working against socialist transformation. 'Socially mobile' workers were no guarantee of revolutionary solidarity. Ben Tillett was a bright, witty and militant strike leader-turned-parliamentarian, and also an inveterate racist. His conspiratorial antisemitism formed a far right discourse depicting a hobbled national bourgeoisie made powerless by the machinations of Jews.[102] The 'English working class', 'traditional working class' or 'white working class' have operated for over 150 years as signifiers of deservingness that *immiserate the working class as a whole.* Labour heroes helped invent the 'alien' in their wake. The ascription of Jews as 'aliens' was one way Britain's working class became white, incorporated into the polity of the national taxpayer.[103] While the 'making' of the English working class suggests a heterogeneous culture subjectively assembled by workers themselves, the *nationalisation of the British working class* as a specific polity coincided with the creation of modern bordering. In Chapter 3, we saw British Black feminists analyse a Marxist stagism that disregarded or undermined histories of migrant workers. 'Neoliberalism' named a stage of capital's reorganisation that has now led to social democracy being considered 'militant'. This has proven a functional substitute on the Anglophone Left for thornier questions about social imperialism and the role of labour representation in subordinating working-class agency and culture. Conservatives have their own attack rhetoric against 'multiculturalism' and 'anti-racism' but have been able to adapt their polemics to incorporate the 'socialist' positioning of the fed up 'ordinary man'.

Jewish workers provide an entry point to understand the reality of the working class in Britain at this transitional moment – its heterogeneity, divisions, discordances. Radical Jewish figures expressed and demonstrated expansive visions of solidarity. Working-class identities were composed through the various neighbourhoods, industries and multicultures of Britain's metropolises and manufacturing centres. The 'worker' identity became a point of controversy as working-class movements diversified. It included the unskilled, the migrant, the people who were both. There was no overarching unity in early British trade unionism. Moments of solidarity were precarious and historically contingent. There *was* some evident in the strike waves of New Unionism. Jewish workers took part in wider protests against unemployment in 1886–1887. In London, Jewish tailors struck in solidarity with the dockers in 1889.[104] The favour was returned when dockers and socialists lent Jewish tailors material support and attended their rallies.[105] Black dockers in London also refused to strike-break.[106] Jewish anarchists and labour leaders, often at odds with each other, drummed up support for strikes, building close ties with the Socialist League. Eleanor Marx, through these common struggles, began to identify with her Jewish roots.[107] Manchester saw strikes across racial lines as Jewish, Irish and English workers downed tools together in the tobacco and tailoring trades.[108] When a long strike in 1912 left Irish dockers' families on the point of starvation, lasting bonds were still visible. Jewish anarchists and unions organised for over 300 dockers' children to live in Jewish tailors' homes.[109] A generation later, many Irish, and many dockers, stood side-by-side with East London's Jews in defiance of police violence and Mosley's Blackshirts at the Battle of Cable Street.[110]

Are we in a new age of 'aliens'? If so, how will socialism adapt? Arguments made by Jewish workers could be reprinted today and feel just as fresh. Aaron Lieberman,* founder of the Hebrew Socialist Union, declared: 'while we Jews are a part of humanity, we cannot achieve personal liberation except through that of all men ... notwithstanding colour, race or creed'. Lieberman drew up the union's statutes in 1876, including the lines, 'as long as there is private ownership, economic misery will not cease. As long as men are divided into nations and classes, there will be no peace between them.'[111] You would seldom see such a perspective on the British left at the time, nor much more today. A decade later, *Der Arbeter Fraynd*, addressed Zionism in the Jewish community:

> from the pure socialist viewpoint ... We may say again that no colonisation, no land of one's own and no independent Government will help the Jewish nation. Jewish happiness will come

---

* Though only 35 when he took his own life in 1880, Lieberman's tireless writing and organising earned him the title of 'Father of Jewish Socialism' from Rudolf Rocker, among others.

with the happiness of all unhappy workers, and Jewish emancipation must come with the general emancipation of humanity.[112]

Jewish working-class diasporism rejected the nation-state as an artefact of colonialism, whether for Zionists or Brits. There was also non-Jewish solidarity with anti-deportation and anti-draft campaigners, including from Sylvia Pankhurst.[113] She told a 1917 rally: 'the fight of the Jews Protection Campaign on behalf of their compatriots [i]s a fight for the freedom of every section of the British people'.[114] Non-Jewish SDF/BSP members worked with Jewish members to pressurise the leadership, forcing occasional climb-downs over antisemitism. Such alliances eventually helped topple Hyndman from the party he founded.[115] British and US socialist traditions are deeply entangled with state immigration and polity formations that all serious emancipatory projects should find intolerable. These bordering practices were developed by the states of rich, white nations simultaneously. A generation before British whiteness attacked Jewish 'aliens', a cross-class US effort was determined to 'build a wall' against Chinese 'invasion'.

5

Storming the Ideal

Local and national politicians alike used race- and class-based economic arguments to nationalize the Chinese question ... the anti-Chinese movement in California was a 'building block of national trade-union politics' that 'transposed anti-capitalist feeling with anti-immigrant hostility.[1]

Erika Lee

Trump's promise to organise industries and markets for the benefit of (white) Americans reformulated nineteenth-century racial conspiracies. During the great swell of markets and people, from the 1850s onwards, those who identified as 'workingmen' began to secure zones of commercial activity. These early unions were not simply made up of proletarians with nothing to sell but their labour-power but white Americans who made or sold white American commodities (including white American labour-power). In the American West, workers sought land to settle and own, factory owners were pressured to hire white, and shopkeepers to sell only 'white-made' goods. Cultural signifiers of craft virtue were highly racialised then, as they are today, with certain manual trades being signifiers of working-class authenticity. Trump's revival of 'white-made' America as 'America first' felt like a throwback, but it wasn't a simple regression into myth either.

Bipartisan support for economic liberalism over the last four decades had galvanised a fragmented enterprise culture with hypermasculine traits. Small businesses tend to be low-margin enterprises, requiring a degree of ruthlessness to survive endless personal disputes with suppliers, employees, banks and the competition – all of which bear the aggressive features (and humiliations) of commodity exchange. Informal economies expanded through this period as have whole towns devoted to prisons, with local labour sinks recruited as guard labour, or into militia and survivalist projects.[2] Trumpian neoliberalism was able to penetrate this historical conjuncture from every angle: themes of economic and cultural decline were already rich vortices of right-wing radicalisation, which Trump nationalised. The idea of rolling back to a purer American economic prairie was the jouissance of the Trump rally. Local and state issues were spun around a racial signifier of economic redistribution – away from immigrants, to 'Americans' – that cut across a nation's classes and white hetero-patriarchal relations without any intent to materially transform anything. White supremacist master narratives of 'liberty' were evident in the storming of the Capitol – a building with no immediate strategic bearing on the economic structure of American capitalism, but symbolically rich for a movement operating within the historical riptide of deep state 'corruption' plots and other heavenly plains.

Many of his insurrectionist supporters struggled to repay debts and due to the Covid-19 pandemic lost control of both their workforces and their markets.[3] They needed Trump to 'open up' America, on one hand, and 'lock up' elites on the other. The participation of struggling entrepreneurs in the Capitol Insurrection was a reminder that hatred of capitalism manifests in very different ways. Having no overdraft to accrue debts is not the same as a small employer driving down your wages to serve their own and yet both workers and capitalists can have reason to hate those above them. These differences can be hard to grasp when class analyses come to depend on signifiers alone. The Trump supporter was often mistaken for working class because of a directness that rejects liberal passive aggressive methods of coercion. Yet, this exaggeration of the local manner can itself be highly refined – a way of managing class antagonism in depressed locales or forming cross-class, often racial, communitarian politics.

The post-2016 currency of blaming 'identity politics' for losing the working class fed into these misconceptions and new concepts developed out of them. After the Capitol Insurrection, *Jacobin* turned to centrist-styled focus groups to prove once and for all that the 'woke progressive' was a liability for low-income swing voters.[4] John and Barbara Ehrenreich's concept of 'the professional managerial class' ('PMC') was resurrected to this end. This theory was partly advanced in the 1970s to explore fractures on the New Left. In particular, the way socialists and radicals had become estranged from working-class people. Some found they could smooth over this contradiction by constructing simplistic ideas of the workers they championed.[5]* Academics and podcasters in the Sanders movement took this concept and shredded it of any introspective value. It was instead put back to work on the old enemies: liberals, anti-racists, anarchists, arty academics, or anyone, really, who exhibited the cosmopolitan signifiers working-class people were supposed to hate. Gabriel Winant wrote in 2019,

> Spend time in the forums of socialists who've long been loyal to Sanders and critical of 'Identity politics' – *Jacobin* readers, say, or in the listeners of *Chapo Trap House* – and you'll see 'PMC' everywhere, a sociological designation turned into an epithet and hurled like a missile.[6]

This was precisely what the Ehrenreichs' cautioned against: 'the search for a "pure" proletarian line to an ever more rarefied sectarianism'.[7]

This obsession on the left with the most visible metropolitan fraction of the middle class (or the 'alt right' as the most visible fraction of US fascism) ignored how fragmentation and identity-thinking cut across the whole of society. Trumpism was never taken seriously as a movement with its own so called 'professional managerial class' articulated through the activism of local elites. Yet, he had already proven it was possible to look across electoral compositions to organise a broader movement of suburbanites, entrepreneurs, survivalists, paleoconservatives, evangelicals and patriot groups, who might secure the election by unlawful means. It is understanding of these movements, not adaptation to them,

---

* 'If the left is to grow, it must come to an objective understanding of its own class origins and to comprehend objectively the barriers that have isolated it from the working class.' Barbara and John Ehrenreich, 'The Professional-Managerial Class', in Pat Walker (eds), *Between Labour and Capital* (Boston, MA: South End Press, 1979), 6.

that is desperately needed.* The policies of Trump's war on immigrants – the so-called 'Muslim Ban', the building of a wall along the US–Mexico border – also demonstrated the potential for historical forms of immigration legislation to be rehabilitated and adapted to new racialised threats. Trumpism revived the racial conspiracism of the white workingmen – not to be mistaken with that section of the working class racialised white – via the cross-class identity of the American patriarch, which in these chaotic circumstances, reverted to vigilantism in a bid to vanquish the enemy.

THE PRODUCERS

Just over 170 years ago, US settler-colonial outposts in the 'West' discovered gold, precipitating a rapid migration of (disproportionately male) prospectors and labourers hoping to strike it rich in something of a lawless free-for-all. Capital quickly concentrated, meaning the expansion of wage-labour. The search for fortunes (or employers) continued across the region, as private railroad contractors competed to track the rail. While most labourers were first or second generation Irish and German immigrants, there were also migrants from South America, Mexico and China. Chinese labour was fundamental to the rapid development of the American West. By the early 1870s around a *quarter of all wage-labourers in California were Chinese.*[8] Most were male, and from the poorest strata of the Pearl River Delta region on China's Southern coast. The treacherous journey by boat was one many did not survive.

At the same time, there was a political contest between the two main parties to define American nationalism. The Republicans could claim to be the progressive party of national unity after victory in the Civil War, while the Democrats remained an untidy coalition of Southern whites and Northern artisans. Considering their compositional problem, the Democrats tried to modernise

---

* We limit ourselves to a summative history of the nineteenth-century US border to explore constitutive identities of race and racism that have form in the US colonial context. For a fuller analysis of contemporary US political economy and its ideological currents, we recommend Phil A. Neel, *Hinterland: America's New Landscape of Class and Conflict* (London: Reaktion Books, 2018).

Jacksonian Democracy. The Democrat-supporting *San Francisco Examiner* summarised this aim neatly in 1867:

> The self-styled Union or Mongrel party [referring to the Republicans] have but one principle ... and that is the doctrine of universal equality for all races, in all things. Take away the Chinese, negro-suffrage, and negro-brotherhood plank from their platform, and they become simply a plunder-league, banded together to rob the government and use its powers for the aggrandizement of special interests and favored classes ... The Democracy are, and ever have been, the party of the Constitution, the party of the people. They are for a white man's government, constitutionally administered, against a great Mongrel military despotism, upheld by a union of the purse and the sword, and sought to be perpetuated through negro and Chinese votes.[9]

This polemic against the Republican Party is reversed today. Democrats are painted as 'corrupt' elites – most recently and explosively via 'Qanon' conspiracies about child sexual exploitation. Elite Democrats have long been perceived as getting fat off the votes of 'minorities' – constructing the 'minority' as a pliant tool of elites has always been a formative instrument in building cross-class power bases in US politics. It is used to ratchet up white resentment and it has also been used historically to expand the electoral identity groups assimilated into whiteness. This was the strategy of the Democrats in the 1860s. Growing urban populations provided a mass base of poor European immigrants, who could be *made* white. For a limited demographic, then, *whiteness was democratised.**

Enmity towards Chinese immigrants and their descendants contributed to this. White American men proudly cherished their constitutional rights within a political system they had a stake in.

---

*   Early waves of Irish Catholic immigrants were welcomed into the Democratic Party and organised by the 'producerist' tendency. The entry of Catholics into the democratic realm was a particularly important innovation. The votes of enfranchised European migrant communities were controlled through tightly marshalled political machines like New York's Tammany Hall.

The 'producer' was a labour identity that reflected the unique status of democratically enfranchised white Americans. It rotated with the identity of the 'workingmen', which could be conceived of capaciously as wage-labourer, shop-owner, artisan, or small farmer. In antebellum times, it included a substantial pro-slavery support base of artisans and master craftsmen who saw abolitionism as a means to degrade their conditions by allowing emancipated slaves to flood the labour market. Postbellum 'producerism' in the West was able to establish itself by jettisoning nativism against European migrant populations. Nativism, ethnic chauvinism and anti-Catholicism remained salient into the twentieth century, but less so in areas where 'white' unity acted as a political ballast against Chinese immigrants or concentrated Black populations.*

WHITE MADE

Chinese workers who migrated to the Pacific West had a general lack of spoken or written English and even less access to the minimal legal protections other workers had. This made them more vulnerable to violence and super-exploitation. Subjugated to the bottom rung of a racial division of labour from the start, they were forbidden from holding mining claims and labelled 'coolies'.[10] After California's gold ran dry in the 1870s, railways, agriculture, construction, and other extractive industries became the main recruiters of Chinese workers. Persistent, large-scale unemployment worsened once the ripple effects of the 1873 depression reached the West. Joblessness was concentrated in towns, particularly San Francisco, where a movement formed among unemployed whites. Their demands were focused against Chinese migrants. They showed up in numbers demanding large employers 'immediately discharge their Mongolians and give [jobless whites] employment'. The movement was endorsed by the *San Francisco*

---

* Mid-century Irish immigrants, particularly in the industrialising zones of New England and later the Midwest, were met with furious Nativist backlash by cross-class Protestants who felt 'their' native land was being invaded. The Know-Nothing Party became home to a virulent anti-Catholic Nativism, while the Whigs declined precipitously. It would be the remnants of these parties and the 'Free Soil' splitters from the Democrats, that would merge in the lead-up to Civil War to become the Republican Party of Abraham Lincoln.

Examiner: 'every country owes its first duty to its own race and citizens. This duty properly observed on this Coast will cause much riddance of the Chinese pest'.[11] Mainstream politicians engaged in similarly violent, racist rhetoric. There were targeted taxes, regulations and bans levied by California's legislature ever since the state came into existence. Most were later ruled unconstitutional and overturned. Restrictionists knew that federal legislation had to be the real target. But tensions and contradictions existed between local and national interests, as well as different fractions of capital, as Adam M. McKeown describes:

> Beginning in the 1850s, white settlers around the Pacific worked to keep Chinese at the margins of their communities, if not entirely excluded. They sometimes discriminated against resident Chinese through the venerable methods of special licenses, taxes, and residential segregation. They also tried to limit the entry of Chinese through quarantines, head taxes, bonding, and passenger-per-ship limits ... Struggles over these laws generated debates around the Pacific over the relationship of local, state, national, and colonial laws, imperial interests, international treaties ... Parties and legislatures rooted in local popular politics were more willing to infringe on rights of Asians than were the elites and elite institutions who focused on international relations and protection of property. Objections from the latter group, based in international obligations, laissez-faire ideology, and jurisdictional struggles ultimately led to the repeal of many early laws.[12]

Early on, debates about Chinese immigration reached the national level only sporadically, though a consensus around anti-Chinese racism did exist, strengthened by Radical Reconstruction's decline. Nebraska congressman and Republican Edward K. Valentine said: 'In order to protect our laboring classes, the gate must be closed.'[13] The *New York Times* bemoaned Chinese people's 'heathenish souls and heathenish propensities'. The *New York Herald*, then the most read paper nationally, wrote: 'Chinese people remain as barbarous as ever. Their pagan savageness appears to be impregnable to the mild influences of Christian civilization.'[14]

For decades leading up to the 1882 Chinese Exclusion Act and in the years after it, groups of workingmen formed multiple organisations, pushing for the abatement of Chinese immigration. This took the form of political parties, trade unions, boycotts, lobbying, rallies, demonstrations and anti-Chinese pogroms. The embryonic form of anti-Chinese organising was the Anti-Coolie Club. This was sometimes used to organise vigilante violence against Chinese immigrants, but trod a thin line between legal and illegal activity. Their legal activities largely consisted of consumer boycotts. Chinese-made goods were targeted as early as 1859.[15] The 'white label' became a common sight. Cigar boxes had labels stating: 'The cigars herein contained are made by WHITE MEN. This label is issued by authority of the White Cigar Makers' Association of the Pacific Coast.'[16] Campaigners pressured businesses to pledge to the 'Anti-Coolie' boycott and demanded shopkeepers put signs in their windows confirming their participation. Campaigns could turn against white businessesmen employing or renting properties to anyone Chinese. Anti-Coolie Clubs and unions were so entwined that 'union-made' and 'white-made' became all but synonymous.[17] Anti-Coolie Clubs operated like nineteenth-century enterprise zones for white workingmen. The objective was to redistribute privileged market access through a union-regulated business environment. British socialist nationalists looked to US Chinese Exclusion as a model for British labour to replicate, but on their own national basis.

According to Alexander Saxton, since 'the earliest encounters of Chinese and non-Chinese in California, groupings appeared which undertook systematic anti-Chinese activities.'[18] Many formed through mining camps and among white railway workers. They overlapped with new postbellum unions like the National Labour Union (NLU) and the Knights of Labor.* Cornelius Hickey of the

---

* The Knights of Labor grew rapidly but collapsed precipitously. They combined craft, industrial and community forms of organising – hosting assemblies and social clubs, making newspapers, forming a militia and developing internal dispute resolution systems. They recruited from across 'white' ethnic communities with more success than most, and made efforts to integrate and organise with Black/women workers. They also supported the passage of the 1882 Chinese Exclusion Act. See Mike Davis, *Prisoners of the American Dream: Politics and Economy in the History of the US Working Class* (New York: Verso,

Stonecutters Union demanded worker representation in the two main parties in 1867, railing against capital's conspiracy to block the eight-hour movement by importing 'the lowest caste of the human race in China'.[19] Beth Lew-Williams writes that 'tens of thousands of white Californians joined anti-Chinese rallies'.[20] This included a 20,000-strong rally in April 1876 – the largest gathering in the region to that point.[21] The *Daily Alta* newspaper reported on every speech, including those by San Francisco's Mayor and California's Governor, and listed the slogans of banners held by workingmen: 'Our Cause is Just, and Conquer We Must', 'Let Us Preserve Our City From Invaders', 'We Are a Unit on This Subject', and 'We Require White Labor Only'.[22] Anti-Coolie Clubs enjoyed cross-class appeal. White businessmen became actively involved, fearing the relative growth of a Chinese petit bourgeoisie. White workers resented Chinese workers entering forms of work that custom had previously excluded them from.

The Trades Assembly and the extravagantly named League of Deliverance scaled-up agitation. The Assembly organised boycotts and 'white label' campaigns, aiming to defend not only the skills and social position of their members but 'white civilisation' itself. The League was a network organising boycotts and pledges stretching the length of the West Coast – a kind of interstate expansion of the Anti-Coolie Club model, but with stronger executive functions, including two of the only full-time salaried union organisers in the country at that time.[23] Membership, open only to citizens, provided white replacement labour for employers pressured into firing Chinese workers. They inspected workplaces and shops to see that they upheld their pledges. There was a threat of explicit violence written into the modus operandi of members and branches. Their rulebook spoke of warning Chinese workers to leave town and then conducting 'abatement by violence' in 'every district until no Chinese remains on our shores'.[24] While the written principles of many unions spoke of non-discrimination, they excluded Chinese workers, as they did Black workers across the country. Mike Davis has pointed to the ease with which individual workingmen could

2018), 70–116; and Beth Lew-Williams, *The Chinese Must Go: Violence, Exclusion and the Making of the Alien in America* (Cambridge, MA: Harvard University Press, 2018), 97–150.

advance into positions of political power as being a significant drag historically on the formation of working-class organising.[25] Pools of white workingmen were politically organised into religio-ethnic groupings. Emerging leaders ascended via the favours, spoils, greasy poles and deal-brokering of machine politics. Voting bases that built up through new parties were routinely incorporated into the ruling parties and a late nineteenth-century California dominated by railway corporations. Anti-Chinese platforms offered a window of opportunity for labour struggles to become electoral forces, with electoral messages that combined worker resentment with racist polemic.

'RACE' AS CONSPIRACY

The most popular solution proposed for California's economic crisis and working-class division can be summed up by the motto of the Workingmen's Party: 'The Chinese Must Go!' The party was formed in 1877 during the 'July Days' worker uprising that spread across the country.* In San Francisco, strike action combined with anti-Chinese violence, including murder and arson.[26] The Workingmen's Party's brief success came from its ability to mobilise and channel discontent and racism among proletarian and petit bourgeois whites into an assault on the two-party consensus. The militancy of nineteenth-century US unionism had no coherent imperialist identity to organise pliantly around, as did British socialist nationalists. This was a different kind of historical ensemble. Workers' demands like the 'eight-hour day' could be radically and militantly posed. Republican visions could be utopian in their imagery. Racism could also be intertwined with utopias of radical republicanism. Resistance to mainstream politics could be reconciled with a vigilantism of the border. It is tempting to remove ideas of republicanism from the colonial setting or separate the racism of unions from their successes and militancy, but these

---

* Miners, railway labourers and factory hands joined a strike wave which matured into the US labour movement's first ever general strikes in St. Louis and Chicago. Militias fired on crowds as state, private and volunteer forces crushed the strike. The federal state's willingness to use force to 'restore order' was in stark contrast to its lapsed appetite for intervening in Reconstruction, which it withdrew from months before.

ideas formed around a peculiar historical conjuncture. US unions showed *potential* to develop in an internationalist direction but were also positioned within the racial ideologies of the colonial context. US monopoly capitalists were also willing to violently destroy them, as Davis argues,

> The precocity of working-class suffrage as an integrative force in America must be balanced against the great difficulty of Yankee trade unions in achieving durable organization ... if American workmen possessed an unrestricted vote over half a century earlier than their English counterparts, they also had to struggle a generation longer in the face of hostile courts and intransigent employers to consolidate their first craft union. American labor may never have had to face the carnage of a Paris Commune or defeated revolution, but it has been bled in countless 'Peterloos' at the hands of Pinkertons or the mlitia.[27]

Whether the advent of the first 'craft union' marks significant progress in the English case is questionable, given that the lowest working-class strata of these unions could also be thrown into jail for breaches of contract, up until the 1870s. But Davis' point stands that US workers, despite suffrage rights, were subjected to exceptional violence. The settler-colonial setting and monopoly violence of US capitalism could not provide more hostile circumstances for solidarity, as even successful union resistance showed.

At the height of the 'July Days', the Workingmen's Party gave California's political establishment a real scare, winning state senate by-elections and gaining the support of the *San Francisco Chronicle*. But constructing solidarities in this space was entangled within mutating universalist paradigms that drew on racism as the most durable basis from which to compose the class struggle. Denis Kearney, a naturalised Irishman, exemplifies this. A rousing stump speaker, he gained a following among workers and unemployed men. His polemics inveighed against corrupt politicians and Chinese 'heathens'. 'The rich have ruled us until they have ruined us,' said Kearney in October 1877. 'We will take our own affairs into our own hands. The republic must and shall be preserved, and only workingmen will do it.'[28] The Party mobilised large crowds, demanding an eight-hour day. At one rally, Kearney demanded workingmen put a stop to the judiciary and railway magnates blocking the abatement of Chinese immigration and turn instead to the law of 'Judge Lynch'.* Kearney is reported as saying, 'the dignity of labor must be sustained, even if we have to kill every wretch that opposes it'.[29] Some workingmen tried to identify their anti-Chinese violence with the political violence being deployed against states and ruling classes by radicals in Europe. In the USA, similar weapons – arson, dynamite – were used to target China-town, or washhouses employing Chinese workers.

Racism, for a time, concentrated and drove workingmen to a form of militancy that ran itself into the ground with greater force as a result. The main advocacy for Chinese immigration was from sections of the national bourgeoisie invested in exploiting Chinese labour-power. The restrictionist consensus was advocated for by parties, unions and politicians, who competed for democratic leverage in a perpetual race to the bottom. The steer of public opinion is illustrated vividly by an 1878 referendum when Califor-nia's new constitution was drafted. Of those who voted, 150,000 to 900 favoured total exclusion.[30] California had produced a graphic media culture of racist conspiracism. The most common accusa-tion was that 'the Chinese' were 'unassimilable'. Their customs, habits, 'paganism' and lack of English meant they could never inte-grate and be loyal Americans. And such non-citizen-like traits made them a threat to republican values. Workingmen argued 'big business' was using Chinese immigrants as pawns to undermine *their* rights as Americans. Producerist tendencies were deeply infused with American exceptionalism, venerating national mythologies of Founding Fathers and American Dreams. US labour was identified with individual enterprise and the virtuosity of craftsmanship, while Chinese workers were denounced as hope-lessly meek, homogenous, robotic. They were deemed unable or unwilling to organise against employers. These stereotypes were shared by workingmen and the laissez-faire capitalist elites they despised. The racialising stereotypes ascribed to Chinese workers (pliable, hard-working) were what this part of the national bour-

---

* A well-known euphemism for the practice of lynching.

geoisie valued in them and what white workers and petit bourgeois reviled.

Cartoons from *The Wasp*, newspaper of the Workingmen's Party, depicted Chinese people as pigs and locusts, sub-human creatures surrounded by filth, scavenging and swarming all over the nation.[31] Others portrayed them as inordinately powerful, scheming and crafty. This racialisation corresponds strongly with that of Jewish 'Aliens'. In both cases, we see workers movements identifying with and becoming integrated into the nation, then racialising the class antagonism. As well as 'positive' identification with the nation, there was a self-identification by negation. The nation's 'workers' were *not*-Chinese, *not*-Jewish, *not*-Black. These prejudices could only be rationalised as defences of the working class if the capitalist logic of exploitation was accepted as a regulative norm and foreign penetration the basis for its corruption. Chinese immigration coincided with ongoing colonial wars against Native Americans and Mexico, not to mention a civil war over slavery. This was a society permeated by racist discourses and violence. Anti-Chinese racism combined European Orientalism with modern 'race science', much of it mapping onto existing narratives of anti-Blackness: ideas of 'civilisational' fixity, natural servility, even an integration of anti-Chinese representation into minstrel shows. As Erika Lee puts it: 'both the "bought" Chinese prostitute and the "enslaved" Chinese coolie were conflated with African American slaves'.[32] For workingmen, whiteness became inseparable from their vision of the nation. It was the foundation stone for their peoplehood and the basis to externalise the logic of capital through conspiracies of 'race'.

BUILDING THE BORDER

Widespread conceptions about racial hierarchy, and a need to protect white civilisation from contamination, developed on this basis. Isaac S. Kalloch, formerly a Baptist minister, was elected as Mayor of San Francisco on the Workingmen's Party ticket in 1879. On 4 July 1878, Pastor Kalloch recited a prayer distilling the basic tenets of the social compact desired by workingmen: 'we pray that our rules may all be righteous; that our people may be peaceable; that capital may respect the rights of labor, and that labor may honor capital; that the Chinese must go. Miners' unions of Virginia City and Gold Hill put out a statement in 1869 illustrating their enthusiastic embrace of this vision for a workingmen's democracy:

> Every branch of industry in the State of California swarms with Chinese ... Can we compete with a barbarous race, devoid of energy and careless of the State's weal? Sunk in their own debasement, having no voice in government, how long would it be ere ruin would swamp the capitalist and the poor together? ... Here, then, upon the threshold of a conflict which, if persevered in, will plunge the State into anarchy and ruin, we appeal to the working men to step to the front and hurl back the tide of barbarous invaders.[33]

Influential ideologue and publisher of the labour journal *Truth*, Burnette Haskell, saw the situation facing the white man in America, against the connivance of 'corporate powers', as nothing less than an apocalyptic race war,

> There are corporate powers that do not care, so long as they can fill their coffers with extravagant profits at the expense of the blood of the Caucasian race ... In order to fortify ourselves against this menacing migration of the savage, vicious, idol-worshipping and barbarous race, every man in America should be at work ... This is a war of races and should be conducted on the same principles that have brought success in other wars.[34]

Trumpism peddled similar nativist narratives of an America of forgotten whites sold out by a corrupted Washington 'swamp'. The narrative was supported by conspiracies of competitor nations (such as 'Chinnaa') and 'globalists' who made trade deals with them that 'ripped off' the United States.* The upside of these conspiracies is that they allow neoliberal centrists to maintain the image

---

* Anti-Chinese conspiracies intensified after Covid-19 hit the USA and Trump blamed China for what he called the 'China Virus'. This complemented antisemitic conspiracies, particularly around the figure of George Soros, about Jews facilitating 'white genocide'. These conspiracies animate much of the US far right from nativists to the alt-right to neo-Nazis

of a progressive party and coerce the protest vote, when in fact they have been significant innovators of this racial regime. The 1965 Hart-Celler Act immigration act was part of Civil-Rights-era momentum and did away with the 1920s quotas which explicitly restricted immigration from everywhere, barring Northern Europe. It led to increased labour migration from Asia and Africa.[35] Targeting skilled workers, Hart-Celler equalised the number of migrants accepted across various nations, setting limits on Latin American countries for the first time. This is when liberal America's 'Nation of Immigrants' identity was popularised. Not only does this liberal catchphrase erase the Indigenous people colonised and the African people (and their descendants) enslaved and transported, it also serves to differentiate *between* migrations. Past migrations were retrospectively legitimated, while those in the present became 'illegal'. New restrictions were imposed upon Mexican entry and settlement. Border crossings were increasingly criminalised, with a gradual build-up of fencing, guards and patrols. This was coterminous with an intensification of racialised carceral systems, and an explosion in the prison population. Both Blackness and the figure of 'the immigrant' (strongly attached to Latinx communities) came to personify discourses around criminality and disorder in neoliberal America – particularly from the perspective of white suburbia and border towns, from which many racist movements draw their base. Mass shootings in recent years have directly targeted Latinx communities.[36] The Manichean logic of 'legal' versus 'illegal' hardened. Undocumented people were immigrants who hadn't 'played by the rules' or 'come the right way', unlike white (or *whitened*) forebears. Trump even threatened to eliminate birthright citizenship, constitutionally guaranteed by the 14th Amendment, a legislative gain from Radical Reconstruction.[37]

'Build The Wall' was Trump's brashest signifier, even set against predecessor presidents who ramped up border militarisation. But while a powerful symbol, the site of most border violence is not at crossing points but in ICE raids and the multi-faceted precarity of being undocumented. The promise of Trump's wall was as real-

and the Klan to militias ranged against a 'New World Order'. It inspired the massacre at the Tree of Life Synagogue in Pittsburgh.

isable as a revolution 'storming' the Capitol. This is what Daniel Denvir calls 'security theater': the huge populist, electoral component to immigration politics whereby racist ressentiment and coalition-building are prioritised over nativist 'results', many of which aren't achievable.[38] While the Wall is more spectacular, it is an open question how much more violence Trumpism added to Bush and Obama's regimes. It is also an open question as to what improved under Biden.[39] Families separated in detention facilities, and the increase of unaccompanied children, rightly provoked outrage against Trump. But breaking up families has always been part of the violence of 'race' and borders.[40] Many Chinese immigrants in the late nineteenth century did not see family members for decades. Some never did again.

CHINESE SELF-ACTIVITY

Huie Kin wrote a memoir of his life in America, having arrived in 1868 aged 14. He wrote of the violence he remembered facing: 'we were simply terrified; we kept indoors after dark for fear of being shot in the back. Children spit on us as we passed by and called us rats'.[41] The edited collection *Chinese American Voices* states:

> While assaults against individual Chinese became commonplace throughout the West, one of the worst cases of mob violence was the 1871 attack on the Chinese community in Los Angeles that took the lives of some twenty or more Chinese, with over a dozen lynched in the streets while their homes were looted ...[42]
> ... Throughout the West in the 1870s and 1880s, murderous mobs regularly stormed Chinese settlements, looting, lynching, burning, and expelling the Chinese.[43]

The conditions Chinese workers experienced left little room for rebellion or self-organisation. Throughout this period, however, they were involved in significant class struggles. In 1867, Chinese workers on the Central Pacific Railroad held a massive strike. Mostly Irish and Chinese labourers worked punishing hours in all weathers, digging tunnels and laying tracks over and through the Sierra Nevada mountains. Chinese workers did so for longer

hours and lower pay than whites and were given the most dangerous jobs. Strike action was sparked by an explosion which killed
five Chinese and one white worker. Along 30 miles of track nearly
3,000 Chinese workers downed tools, demanding pay parity with
whites and a shorter working day.[44] The *Sacramento Daily Union*
newspaper reported that they also took action against 'the right of
overseers ... to either whip them or restrain them from leaving the
road when they desire to seek other employment.'[45] The strikers'
demands were not met. The railroad company and Chinese labour
contractors withheld their food, starving them back to work.[46]

A victory for Chinese crewmen on the Pacific Mail Line
steamers came in 1873. Though the employers were white, the
labour contractors were Chinese, showing a willingness from
Chinese workers to struggle against their exploitation *and* against
the vertical structure of the Chinese-American community.* In
1876, Chinese workers in a shoe factory walked out after a dispute
over stolen deposits. Remaining unpaid, the workers 'finally armed
themselves and attempted settlement by direct action.'[47] A similar
situation played out just over the Canadian border in 1881 when
'several hundred' Chinese railway labourers in British Columbia
'arrived with shovels, sticks and crowbars' and 'marched into Yale
and broke into the Railroad company's storehouse, badly wrecking
the building.' The *Daily Alta* reported that '[m]eeting a policeman,
the rioters stoned him. The Chinese left town in the afternoon, but
threaten to return and burn Yale down.' The newspaper gathered
that the workers' grievance was 'against a Chinese firm at San
Francisco, who impose a tax of two per cent a month of each lab-
orer's wages.'[48] There was also a successful strike for higher pay by
Chinese cigar makers in San Francisco in 1884.[49] The *Daily Alta*
claimed Chinese workers formed a union and drove up the piece-

---

* The social and class order of the Californian Chinese community was part-devolved to
a bourgeois benevolent association known as 'The Six Companies'. Based in San Francisco's Chinatown, it offered welfare provision, helped immigrants acclimatise and arbitrated
disputes within the community. It defended the community and spoke on its behalf. Its
responses to racism were channelled through liberal means: publishing articles in US
newspapers offering factual correctives to racial stereotyping, petitioning both governments, and seeking justice through the courts. Like Anglo-Jewish elites, California's Chinese
leaders bristled at racialisation that recognised no social distinction between them and poor
migrants.

work rate, explaining that 'to prevent any further increase, and also to curb the demands of their Chinese workmen, who were getting insolent and independent in their prosperity, the white manufacturers recently formed a union to govern trade matters'.[50] This manufacturers' association:

> resolved that all factories controlled by it should be shut down at 3 o'clock on Monday next, and the Chinese should be laid off until they submitted to just discipline ... it was further resolved that if any member of the Association employ Chinese until the labour difficulty was settled he must pay a fine of $5 a head per week for each Chinaman.[51]

Angel Island immigration station in San Francisco Bay was part of the infrastructure introduced to enforce Chinese Exclusion. It was a former army barracks where hundreds of thousands of immigrants, mainly Chinese and Japanese, were detained and interrogated. A riot by Chinese inmates in 1919, protesting the food, meant 'troops had to be called in to restore order'.[52] The authorities were forced to bring in Chinese chefs. Unsanitary and unsafe conditions were protested too. Suicides were commonplace. Hundreds of poems and messages were later found, carved into the walls by Chinese detainees, saying things like:

> 'America has power, but not justice. In prison, we were victimized as if we were guilty. Given no opportunity to explain, it was really brutal.'
>
> 'Even while they are tyrannical they still claim to be humanitarian.'[53]

While solidarity with Chinese immigrants was thin on the ground, we can at least point to two individuals to glimpse the potential for anti-racist solidarity.[54] In 1869, at the height of Radical Reconstruction, Frederick Douglass made a speech in Boston addressing anti-Chinese discrimination:

> Already has California assumed a bitterly unfriendly attitude toward the Chinamen. Already has she driven them from her

altars of justice. Already has she stamped them as outcasts and handed them over to popular contempt and vulgar jest. Already are they the constant victims of cruel harshness and brutal violence. Already have our Celtic brothers, never slow to execute the behests of popular prejudice against the weak and defenseless, recognized in the heads of these people, fit targets for their shilalahs. Already, too, are their associations formed in avowed hostility to the Chinese.[55]

Against the tide, Douglass tried, as ever, to carve out space for a humanist anti-racism, in common with his vision for Black freedom:

I have said that the Chinese will come, and have given some reasons why we may expect them in very large numbers in no very distant future. Do you ask, if I favor such immigration, I answer I would. Would you have them naturalized, and have them invested with all the rights of American citizenship? I would. Would you allow them to vote? I would. Would you allow them to hold office? I would ...
... I submit that this question of Chinese immigration should be settled upon higher principles than those of a cold and selfish expediency. There are such things in the world as human rights. They rest upon no conventional foundation, but are external, universal, and indestructible. Among these, is the right of locomotion; the right of migration; the right which belongs to no particular race, but belongs alike to all and to all alike. It is the right you assert by staying here, and your fathers asserted by coming here. It is this great right that I assert for the Chinese and Japanese, and for all other varieties of men equally with yourselves, now and forever.[56]

Douglass' virtue of rights of movement was kept alive while 'Revolutionary Time' was in spring. Yet it could not compete with the 'cold and selfish expediency' of restrictionism, practiced across political constituencies of capital and labour. For the latter, this tied 'worker' autonomy to controlling the immigration status of *other workers*. Sigismund Danielewicz, a Jewish immigrant from Poland, a 'San Francisco barber turned seaman', attended an 1885 congress of white labour organisations to argue over this very point.[57] As a member of the Coast Seamen's Union, he argued socialists should stand for class solidarity and internationalism, and focus on the struggle against capitalism. The *Daily Report* cites:

> [Danielewicz spoke of how] he belonged to a race which had been persecuted for hundreds of years and was still persecuted – the Jews; and he called upon all of his people [fellow union members] to consider whether 'the persecution of the Chinese' was more justifiable than theirs had been. And he left it upon the Irish to say whether it was more justifiable than their persecutions in New York had been; upon the Germans to make a similar comparison.[58]

Danielewicz's intervention was met with howls of laughter. The chair, Frank Roney, ruled him out of order. His contribution possibly led to little more than a preamble in that congress' final statement admitting Chinese immigration wasn't the 'cause of hard times', nor would expulsion 'settle the labor question'. This was followed by the kind of screed typical of the movement:

> considering their bad moral habits, their low grades of development, their filth, their vice, their race differences from the Caucasians, and their willing status as slaves ... we demand their complete removal from all parts of the Pacific Coast.[59]

AMERICAN STANDARDS

Historian Mae Ngai has noted that: 'President Trump's executive order "Protecting the Nation from Foreign Terrorist Entry into the United States", the so-called "Muslim Ban", eerily recalls Chinese exclusion.' Ngai argues: 'The comparison is apt not just in the palpable animus it displays toward an entire group, but also because much of the legal basis of Chinese Exclusion still stands.'[60] Trump's executive order, announced weeks into his presidency, banned all travellers hailing from Iraq, Syria, Iran, Libya, Somalia, Sudan and Yemen from entering the USA for at least 90 days. It also further cut the number of refugees allowed into the country. Trump was more explicit on the campaign trail, pledging a 'total and complete shutdown of Muslims entering the United States until our country's representatives can figure out what the hell is going on!'[61] Protests at multiple airports greeted the ban, as did a strike by New York taxi drivers, many of whom are Muslim.[62] The policy received domestic and international condemnation, and a litany of legal challenges.* The terms of the ban were continually reformulated throughout Trump's presidency with banned countries and religious discriminations added, removed and finessed in response to litigation. The Supreme Court upheld most restrictions in 2017 and 2018 rulings which followed a near identical national security logic to its Chinese Exclusion judgement in 1889.[63]

'The fundamental question of our time is whether the West has the will to survive,' Trump said in a 2017 speech in Warsaw.

> Do we have the confidence in our values to defend them at any cost? Do we have enough respect for our citizens to protect our borders? Do we have the desire and the courage to preserve our civilization in the face of those who would subvert and destroy it?[64]

Note the similarities between Trump and the restrictionists at *Truth* in 1882:

> The supreme moment has arrived from which shall date either the decadence of our civilization and our country, or the unimpeded glory of the one and unrestricted prosperity and happiness of the other ... The Chinese restriction bill is a weak and sickly invention designed to lull us into security while this silent invasion proceeds. Let us all, men and women, unite for the common purposes of race and national preservation. Let not an inch of land or habitation be leased, rented or sold to these people.[65]

This was in reaction to a bill that watered down the absolutism of exclusion as both movement principle and goal. President Chester

---

* Not from the British government.

A. Arthur initially vetoed a restriction bill proposing 20 years of exclusion. 'Workingmen' and the West Coast press fulminated that 20 years *wasn't enough*, some burning effigies of Arthur. He eventually settled on ten years, signing the Chinese Exclusion Act in 1882.* The League of Deliverance and Trades Assembly didn't know how to react to the passage of federal legislation. Eventually the organisations, so steeped in anti-Chinese obsession as the all-consuming content of their politics, doubled down on their claim to be the only *real* force against Chinese immigration, dismissing the legislation as a sham.**

A wave of anti-Chinese expulsions spread up the West Coast in 1885. Exclusion may have become law but violence and rhetoric remained primed against its perceived ineffectiveness *and* against the Chinese-American population that remained. Massacres took place at Rock Springs in Wyoming Territory and Eureka, California. In Rock Springs, Knights of Labor members took the lead. Several buildings were set on fire, leaving 28 Chinese people dead and 15 injured – actions defended by newspapers, local government and law enforcement.[66] Any censure was reserved for foreigners on 'both sides' for bringing an 'alien' violence to American life. No charges were brought and no compensation went to survivors, nor the families of those killed. The riot wave reached Seattle and Tacoma in Washington, as white mobs drove Chinese workers from their homes.[67] The Governor declared martial law and President Grover Cleveland sent federal troops as pogroms raged across Oregon and California. Chinese refugees fled over the border into Canada. 'More than a hundred and fifty communities' on the West Coast joined the anti-Chinese purges from 1885 to 1887.[68] A mass exodus of thousands of starving Chinese internal refugees converged upon San Francisco in search of safety.

The organisations that made Chinese exclusion the mantle of their politics folded quickly, with large chunks of their base presumably satisfied with federal reforms. Racism was a durability of

---

* It was renewed in 1892 and in 1902, and then exclusion was enforced in 1904 without time limit.
** There's division among nativist constituencies today too. 'Real' nativists, nationalists, fascists want to see an assault on *legal* immigration. Some want an ethno-state. Trump only gestured towards these.

organisation that blew hot through moments of reaction but threatened to run aground once the state answered some demands. The Geary Act of 1893 added internal controls, though early efforts at immigration control were often ineffective. The borders of large territories remained highly porous, but the logics of national bordering had coalesced, laying the basis for today's common sense. As Adam M. McKeown writes:

> By the end of the century ... the enormous legal, political, and administrative effort put into enforcing these laws would gradually shift the momentum in favor of borders, thus establishing the basic principles and practices of border control as an integral part of modern, liberal polities.[69]

Anti-Chinese violence persisted alongside legislation that provided a 'rational' basis for racist moral panics. In 1900, a bubonic plague scare hit San Francisco with the initial victim alleged to have been Chinese. City authorities quarantined Chinatown, with officials sent in to carry out inspections and fumigation. The journal *Organized Labor* wanted *more* draconian measures, claiming borders were still too lax. 'The almond-eyed Mongolian is watching for his opportunity, waiting to assassinate you and your children with one of his maladies,' said one editorial. Adding that 'the Chinese' had 'long since outlived their usefulness in the world's history'.[70] Anti-Chinese racism had become an ingrained, fundamental part of Pacific West politics, with border violence established as part of a nascent, uneasy compact between local and national state, sections of capital and organised labour. Such logics proved insatiable. From the viewpoint of organised labour, Saxton summed it up succinctly:

> The Chinese question became for them an indispensable professional asset. The only real danger was that the Chinese might finally leave or die out; but happily the Exclusion Act had been written only against Chinese, and there remained a parade of Asian menaces – Hindoos, Filipinos, Japanese – waiting in the wings to provide employment for subsequent generations of craft union officials and labor politicians.[71]

Obsessive anti-Chinese racism did *nothing* long term to resolve the tensions and contradictions between industrial and craft unionism, nor the organisational dilemmas posed by a cross-class movement. Denver's socialist newspaper, *The Labor Enquirer*, argued in favour of an anti-Chinese position on the basis that struggle and 'evolution' bred solidarity. Its correspondent wrote: 'I regard it as the adding of a fresh ring to the tree of solidarity whenever men are roused to the self-sacrifice of putting aside their selfish private interests for the sake of a common cause.'*

By 1893, Denis Kearney had new targets in his sights, throwing in some conspiratorial antisemitism for good measure:

foreign Shylocks [who] are rushing another breed of Asiatic slave to fill up the gap made vacant by the Chinese who are shut out by our laws ... Japs ... are being brought here now in countless numbers to demoralize and discourage our domestic labour market.[72]

Kearney's adjusted slogan? '*The Japs Must Go!*' There was anti-Japanese violence in 1906. A Japanese and Korean Exclusion League had been founded the previous year by workers who organised conventions and meetings, following the blueprint set by the anti-Chinese movement. Part of the white aggression in pushing for Japanese exclusion was because some Japanese-Americans

---

* The correspondent further explains:

   The workingman may not be able to explain his motives with scientific precision, but when he beats a scab, I believe that if we could see into his mind, we should discover that he is prompted to his action by an instinctive sense that the scab is false to the cause of labor, that he is a traitor to the principle of solidarity by which alone the proletariat can hope to win. So it is with the anti-Chinese crusade; a great part of the repugnance felt to them upon this coast is that they do not act as citizens, that they have no concern in the solidarity of the nation. A precisely similar sentiment has dictated the persecutions of the Jews in Germany, Austria and Russia, persecutions which have been justified precisely on this ground.

Quoted in Alexander Saxton, *The Indispensable Enemy: Labor and the Anti-Chinese Movement in California* (Berkeley, CA: University of California Press, 1971), 268.

   This reification of the 'workers instinct' has been retained as the soft sell of contemporary apologia for immigration control. It is a conspiratorial motivation which spreads into other projections about what 'workers' think, that is, they hate 'cosmopolitanism', they resent 'educated language' etc.

were setting up homesteads, trying to live American settler lives, to escape the racial division of labour. Racialisation itself was coded through this tiering of labour.* Head of the League was Olaf Tveitmoe, Norwegian-born union leader and editor of the afore-mentioned *Organized Labor*. Tveitmoe was an ally of legendary trade union leader, Samuel Gompers, of the American Federation of Labour (AFL). Gompers' nearly 40 years at the helm oversaw a solidification of craft unions as the dominant form of labour politics. Accommodationist and nationalist in politics, bureau-cratic and hierarchical in form, the AFL saw huge increases in full-time staff. They occasionally condemned racism officially but practiced de facto exclusion or segregation towards Black and Asian workers. An AFL convention agreed 'Orientals' brought 'nothing but filth, vice and disease', that 'efforts to elevate them to a higher standard [had] proven futile' and that white Americans would be justified in 'righteous anger' to 'sweep them from the face of the earth'.[73] Gompers and the AFL** came to support more generalised border controls, including against newer waves from Southern and Eastern Europe. They backed literacy tests as part of the federal border regime.[74] Such an expansion of bordering was becoming increasingly popular.[75] The *Los Angeles Times* suggested in 1893:

> If we can keep out the Chinese, there is no reason why we cannot exclude the lower classes of Poles, Hungarians, Italians and some other European nations, which people possess most of the vices of the Chinese and fewer of their good qualities.[76]

Gompers, like Trump, felt the nation should bring more immigrants from places like Norway and fewer from 'shithole' countries.[77] Such a shift of racial coordinates challenged previous formulations of whiteness, particularly within the working class. Gompers and others, including the Socialist Party who also backed the eugenic

---

* Legislation in 1913 limited land ownership rights for Japanese people. Exclusion was introduced in 1924.
** The AFL's official journal also advocated the Colonization of Black Americans to Liberia or Cuba in 1898, claiming Black workers lacked 'patriotism, sympathy, sacrifice', which apparently made them ill-suited to trade unionism.

restrictions of the 1920s, had to persuade some members that literacy tests were not a class barrier to immigration but a national-racial protection against invaders from inferior civilisations.[78] Here was a racial ideology capacious enough to encompass the so-called 'Negro question' and all manner of immigrants. 'Caucasians', according to Gompers (born into a Jewish family in London's East End) were 'not going to let their standard of living be destroyed by negroes, Chinamen, Japs, or any others'.

WORKERS EMIGRATE ...

Anti-immigrant arguments mobilised by organised labour about foreign workers lowering wages and conditions have generally progressed from the explicit racial conspiracism of Ben Tillett and Denis Kearney in the late nineteenth century. Conservative, nationalist social democrats like Angela Nagle, Wolfgang Streeck and Paul Embery now provide colourblind technical cases for border control that suspend the reality of racialisation at the border. The neoliberal centre speaks to immigration dreams in opposition and falls back on this same defence in power. Kamala Harris told Guatemalan migrants, who formed a caravan for self-defense and safety in 2021, 'do not come ... if you come to our border, you will be turned back'.[79] Immigrant labour, or sections of it, are figured as 'tools' of the capitalist class or dysfunctional nations in these explanations. We have seen the origins of such formulas, which resulted in groundbreaking legislation. The Chinese Exclusion Act was an early blueprint for the modern logistics of 'race'. Technological integration of the world market has today produced a stickleback regime of national and supra-national controls over the movement of labour. Regardless of risk, labour will keep moving, driven by changes in climate, automation and inter-imperialist violence. As Marx quipped: 'workers emigrate; in fact they are merely following capital, which has itself emigrated'.[80] The logic of borders is never settled. It merely expands in scale, technology and targets. The targeting of other racialised groups of migrants followed Chinese Exclusion, as did specific forms of labour, including sex work. The Page Act of 1875 actually *preceded* more general restrictions, targeting Chinese 'prostitutes', essentially spelling the end of Chinese women's migration into the USA as through its implementation all Chinese women were assumed to be prostitutes. In Britain, anti-Alien legislation laid the groundwork for a century of immigration controls attacking Black and Asian citizens, migrants and asylum seekers. Anti-Chinese and anti-Alien campaigns were mobilised through combinations of labourism, nationalist populism and a racism borne of colonial histories, structured by racial divisions of labour and citizenship laws. Campaigns were transformed into policy and modes of governance through interventions at local and national levels of state power.

Workingmen of the nineteenth century generally conformed to and renovated the national-colonial project for an expanded electoral composition. Yet, the proletariat these organisations were trying to control was far from coherent or unified. Parts of the working class have been able and, to some degree, have chosen to *become* white. In California, the composition of movements of 'workingmen' was constituted through a process of 'whitening' for European Catholic, and to an extent Jewish, workers. A whitening that in the Pacific West was defined in opposition to Chinese immigration. Overall, this process was rooted in the longer term construction of Black unfreedom and inferiority, upon colonised Native lands, amidst the ongoing elimination of Indigenous people. Immigration has always been a racial politics of population in settler America – whether in the filling up of colonised territory with Europeans or the expulsion of 'illegals' who do not belong. The 'working class' category is no guide to class politics if the workers you defend are confused with a defence of the national interest. Trump managed to build a coalition of oligarchs and the suburban middle class, entrepreneurs and workers of various ethnicities – democratised white through their identification with a flexible and creative innovation of whiteness. He had the same instinct to democratise whiteness for a US class composition that has further fragmented, twisted by indebtedness, property and stock acquisition, the rise of 'self-employment', social media conspiracism, vigilantism, plus legions of 'guard labour' in the form of police, prisons, borders and military.

6

Whiteness Riots

It was bad enough to have the consequences of [racist] thought
fall upon colored people the world over; but in the end it was
even worse when one considers what this attitude did to the
European worker. His aim and ideal was distorted ... He began
to want not comfort for all men but power over other men ... He
did not love humanity and he hated 'niggers'.[1]

W.E.B. Du Bois

Conservative reactions to anti-racist movements are sensitive to
temporal shifts in street protests and uprisings. The most dangerous point in a movement cycle is when things quiet down. State
functionaries and journalists work hard to alienate the integrity of
the utopian moment by generating debates that trivialise its political nucleus, while police move in to make arrests. Conservatives
are aware of this and choose their moments carefully. The conservative claim that anti-racism *causes* racism (or makes racism worse)
can be convincing because the state and the press personalise its
causes. The pitting of opinions about 'race' at the national level
creates hypervisibility for racialised people in schools, workplaces
and streets. Those who 'innocently' identify with Britishness are
painted as victims of anti-racist 'race-baiting', with many people of
colour alienated by the direction this discourse takes, and the
dangers it presents. State racism cannot proceed without this kind
of maintenance, the ultimate goal being to enhance state powers
over the organisation of workers and working-class communities
more generally.

After Colston, we saw precisely how this happened. Within days,
thousands of white supremacists gathered to protect a Churchill
statue. Similar marches engulfed memorial squares across the
country. In Coventry, a viral video showed a mass of white male

and female football fans mobbing two young Black men. Dozens approached them, hurling glass bottles and racist epithets. When police arrived, the crowd accused one of the Black men of having a knife, even as weapons were visible in the hands of those crowding them. Cops moved in to arrest the two men. As part of the fans' celebrations, BLM placards, left behind in the town centre from two recent multiracial anti-racist marches, were destroyed. Police later announced the incident wasn't 'racially motivated'.[2] Two weeks later, 'WHITE LIVES MATTER' was scratched onto a hill in huge letters in a Coventry park, a video showed someone wearing a KKK hood next to it.[3]

One year on, the government commissioned a race report to find out if there was really a racism problem in Britain: 'In many areas of investigation, including educational failure and crime, we were led upstream to family breakdown as one of the main reasons for poor outcomes.'[4] The report found prejudice had statistically declined and that a 'highly subjective dimension' entered into 'references to "systemic", "institutional" or "structural racism"'.[5] The *Daily Mail* heralded the report: 'Britain's Race Revolution: Landmark report says UK "a model to the world" on diversity – and finds NO evidence of institutional racism.'[6] Other threats were detected, however,

> a strident form of anti-racism … reinforced by a rise of identity politics, as old class divisions have lost traction … tend to stress the 'lived experience' of the groups they seek to protect with less emphasis on objective data.[7]

The same oppositions between 'identity politics' and class, inculcated on the left for decades, were used as part of a government offensive. If anything was systemic, it was 'anti-racism', and with exclusionary effects: 'the UK is open to all its communities. But we are acutely aware that the door may be only half open to some, including the White working class.'[8] Whereas data on various ethnicities were compared, horizontally, and related to cultural or familial explanations, the 'White working class' was the only identity where systemic injustice could be explained. The report was launched with an almost trollish smirk from politicians. They searched and searched but no structural racism could be found in the data (except for a disregarded White working class). All this commotion and yet Britain was more inclusive than ever? 'BLM' was wrong to make British people feel otherwise. The report was immediately repudiated and discredited, even by some falsely credited as authors.[9] But the government just pushed through the media cycle and pressed harder.

That same month, the Police, Crime, Sentencing and Courts Bill was proposed. This was an opportunity to rubberstamp the far right reaction to 'wokeness' with concrete legislation that could suppress future protest waves and direct action tactics. The bill had a broader outlook, however, threatening the very existence of Gypsy, Roma and Traveller communities, by awarding police – and landowners – new powers to criminalise trespass and seize transport, that is, homes. Digital surveillance powers were enhanced, stop and search, as well as legal barriers to protest, including ten-year sentences for vandalising statues. 'Back to the 80s,' wrote Liz Fekete, 'into the kind of territory that led to ... the 1981 and 1985 inner city rebellions, the 1984–85 miners' strike, and the mass unrest that followed the introduction of the Poll Tax'.[10] The Nationality and Borders Bill followed. It presented a heinous broadening of deportation powers. *Clause 9* would allow the state to deport any of six million naturalised or dual national British citizens, 'without notice', if the decision corresponded with the 'public interest'.[11] Nisha Kapoor predicts, 'disqualification from voting rights, the withdrawal of access to services and provisions – bank accounts, passports, driving lessons – already administered ... in counterterrorism cases, may become more routine. And should citizenship deprivation come, offshore detention centres will be waiting'.[12] The verticalisation of far-right social media trends and mainstream policymaking deserves proper attention. Undoubtedly, fascism and electoral politics are aligning. The ramping up of state powers to police, prosecute, deport and brutalise, depends on money and media pressure organised through liberal, conservative and fascist elites. That being said, reasoning around these authoritarian turns can also be underwhelming when the charisma of authoritarians, or fascism more broadly, is isolated as the cause. Racist anti-immigration legislation has been built piece by piece, over time, by politicians of every stripe.

In his writing on the Notting Hill riots of 1958, Peter Fryer describes 'thousands' of whites storming migrant neighbourhoods.[13] Rioters surrounded Black people's cars, shouting 'let's lynch them!' Tory and Labour MPs joined the press (and a returned Oswald Mosley) in calling on the government to halt 'coloured' immigration and demanding deportations.[14] The Tory government's solution to the unrest was the 1962 Commonwealth Immigrants Act, ending automatic right of entry and settlement in Britain for Commonwealth subjects. Labour initially opposed the broadening of controls, though largely based on a colonial sentimentality about 'Mother Country' duties and maintaining good trade relations with Commonwealth states. Harold Wilson embraced controls once in government,* further restricting 'coloured' immigration with a 1965 white paper.[15] Labour's 1968 Commonwealth Immigrants Act built on this precedent. It was rushed through amidst government fears Britain would have to accept all Kenyan Asians made stateless by an independent Kenya's 'Africanisation' policy.[16] Restrictions didn't apply to white Commonwealth settlers, because these 'patrials', as they were called, could trace their family lineage back to British blood and soil. Jim Callaghan, future Labour Prime Minister, told Tony Benn: 'We don't want any more blacks in Britain.'[17] The TUC supported Labour policy throughout.[18]

In this chapter and in Chapter 7 that follows, we examine the relationship between street racism and the modernisation of policing and immigration controls. The historical mutability of 'whiteness' is concretely determined by the peculiarity of the given racial regime and the stresses of the historical conjuncture. However, over time, best practises and rules of thumb are distinguished and generalised. What we refer to as 'whiteness riots' are 'sparks' of violence, routinely followed by 'race reports' and legislative reactions, designed to impart control through indirect means:

---

* Labour's argument was that 'the economy', framed benignly as a mutually beneficial national abstract, should determine how many immigrants come and go. Broadly speaking, the same argument has been made by different wings of the party ever since.

the market, but also courts, social care, schools, border forces, policing. Through these instruments of the liberal democratic state, in the name of equality, racism is not only preserved, but also formalised, nationalised and modernised. It is important therefore to apprehend racist street violence – and the infantilising, innocent register used to explain it – as structural, indeed, *as bordering*, an action that seeks to incite and lobby for state violence further up the chain. This is why Sivanandan made racism central to his analysis of fascism, rather than isolating the fascist as an egregious extremist: 'We have fought the idea that racism was an aspect of fascism – our take was that racism was fascism's breeding ground.'[19] We look now at the relationship between state and popular racism, starting with the significance of racist violence to the neoliberal transition. This is followed by a case study, the 1919 whiteness riots, which we also look at in the USA in Chapter 7. These riots blew up across British ports and represent a distinctive moment in the constitution of the identity, *white British*. What gave form to this identity? How has it come under regular challenge and what problems for *Britishness* evolved from it?

TOO MUCH MIXING, NOT ENOUGH INTEGRATION

Enoch Powell personifies the psychodrama of Britishness. He was an early adopter of post-war immigration as a minister, who later mourned an English race contaminated and in decline. The post-war moment has ever since remained the freezing point for British imaginaries of the migrant – as nation-builder, or nation-destroyer. Powell framed the colonial anxieties of post-war liberal democracy in his 1968 'Rivers of Blood' speech. It infamously depicted a foreboding future of racial role-reversal, of who would soon hold the 'whip hand'. He referenced the murder of Martin Luther King Jr. and the riots that followed in the USA, warning similar would befall Britain unless immigration was halted. Powell's dismissal from the Tory front bench for his speech was met with solidarity strikes by East End dockers. In an era when strike action was invariably economistic, a 'political' strike in support of a Tory politician was extraordinary. Over a thousand dockers and several hundred meat-porters from Smithfield Market marched to Westminster with signs saying: 'We back Enoch!' and 'Back Britain, not Black Britain'.[20] Harry Pearman led the strike, demanding a 'total ban on immigration because there were enough already here'.[21] After meeting Powell, he declared: 'It made me feel proud to be an Englishman ... We are representatives of the working man. We are not racialists.' Powell's popularity with a section of the working class, as Shilliam explains, is due to a perennial 'defence of the ordinary, deserving working class as the *white* working class'.[22] Tory legislation in 1971 and 1981,[23] as well as its 1972 accession to what would become the EU, cemented Britain's racist immigration policy.[24]

Uprisings in Brixton, Bristol and elsewhere in the 1980s, developed in resistance to racist violence that had been building for generations. The insecure contracts most racialised workers survived on during the post-war era expanded as the empire broke down. Post-war racialised super-exploitation foreshadowed what has become a more generalised, if uneven, condition today. The turn towards less stable conditions of work and home life, and the growing replacement of Britain's industrial base with outsourced production, and of human labour-power by machine, left the state in need of new social control strategies. Modernisations of border control dovetailed with modernisations in policing. British policing absorbed practices and personnel from its colonial model in Ireland and Palestine. Counter-insurgency techniques developed against anti-colonial and communist struggles in Malaya and Kenya were used on Black communities in Britain, who came to view police as occupying armies.[25] Countless cases of police victimising people of colour pepper the records.[26]

Race Today expressed succinctly how young residents of Brixton or Toxteth experienced the state in 1981: 'Thousands of black youth have grown into their teens aware of no other social force but the Special Patrol Group, the Vice Squad, the Regional Crime Squad and now the riot police'.[27] Orgreave miners, brutalised by police in 1984, their villages raided and occupied, were subjected to a brutality that shocked Britain's labour movement, but would have been no surprise to racialised communities. The separation of white industrial workers, occupied Ireland, and racially excluded labour kept these struggles apart, materially and historically, even as the state moved on each, learning from one, to brutalise the other.* These insurrections were as grave a threat to Thatcherism as organised labour, especially with the latter left weakened, isolated and unprepared by years of incorporation into a state now prepared to eviscerate it. As with riots that raged across England in 2011, there was frenzied discourse in 1981 about arming the police or deploying the army.[28] Despite the mixed-raced anti-state nature of the uprisings, media speculated on dysfunctional Black families or 'political correctness' and 'over-sensitivity' as possible causes. From the 'Alien Jews' onwards, assimilation panics about 'racial mixing' have been the touchpaper for a British century of racial violence. Either there's excessive mixing – too much living and loving between 'races' – or communities aren't mixing enough. 'Racism is as racism does,' wrote Sivanandan,

> Powell changed the parameters of the race debate in Britain both in Parliament and in the country at large, and gave a fillip to popular racism that made the lives of black people hell. He brought scholarship and reason to white working-class fears and prejudices and, by stirring up the basest emotions with messianic oratory, drove London dockers and meat porters to march on Parliament to demand the immediate repatriation of 'the coloureds', who were taking their jobs, their homes, their daughters … He took the shame out of middle-class racism … and to the genteel racism of the haute bourgeoisie, he brought the comforting message that … there were still the lesser breeds.[29]

Powell provided the polemical impetus for Thatcherism, which forced through the breakdown of the teetering post-war compact via a growing consensus for authoritarian nationalism, individualism and racist policing. The state's only answer to working-class dissent and racialised surplus populations was parodied in crime reporting that legitimised a terrified 'public' desiring stronger policing.[30] The last decade of centrist reaction and far right pandering has further established the importance of Sivanandan as a

---

* This discordance continues to do damage as white left institutions continually refuse to recognise uprisings as sites of working-class resistance, pointing instead to unlawful acts, or 'strategic' errors.

guide to Britain. His now infamous quip seems to ring in the ears, the more time goes on: 'What Enoch Powell says today, the Tories say tomorrow, and Labour legislates on the day after.'[31] The New Labour era crystallised this theorem, with Starmer's Labour now the farcical rerun. New Labour is rightly remembered for imperialist wars, but they also helped modernise Powellist doctrine. The so-called 'Northern town riots' of 2001, taking place in towns and cities with large South Asian communities – Oldham, Bradford, Burnley, Leeds – were some of the most significant Britain has ever seen. They were met with frantic racist reactions from politicians, media and courts. When football firms and fascists left a pub and marched on the Asian neighbourhood of Glodwick in Oldham, 'shop and house windows were smashed and bricks thrown'. One family told *CARF*:

> About seven racists were outside attempting to kick in the door, shouting 'fucking Paki, I'm going to kill you, black bastard'. Realising the door would not last the battering, they retreated behind a second door and barricaded it with furniture. Luckily, the second door held off the attackers. 'God knows what they would have done if they smashed through the second door' ... 'If things got worse, we would have been hurt. And they would have been hurt as well.' Outside Abdul's house, eight police vans were parked, their occupants apparently unwilling to intervene to halt the rampage.[32]

Local press portrayed Oldham's Asian communities as 'insular', creating 'no-go areas for whites', with 'fears growing over plague of racist attacks by Asian gangs'.[33] This alerted the BNP to local electoral opportunities, while national papers fanned the flames, warning 'Whites Beware'. Rioting spread as police began 'pre-emptively' flooding 'Asian areas', antagonising long standing tensions. In Bradford, massive anti-police violence erupted and the charge of riot was brutally enforced. New Labour fully backed the police. Blair and Blunkett reduced the uprisings of Asian youths against white supremacists and police to 'thuggery'.* The racists who

---

* The term 'thug' entered the English language via colonial rule in India. The British categorised and repressed 'Thugs' as a 'tribe' or 'caste' or 'gang', whose criminality they characterised as hereditary.

attacked Glodwick were charged with public order offences or affray. Riot charges were dropped, Judge Geake ruling the defendants were not responsible for the rioting.[34] In Bradford, the number of convictions for riot was unprecedented. Hundreds of years of convictions were distributed among Asian men.[35] 'Community cohesion' became the new watchword for Labour, a term borrowed from British colonial policing in Northern Ireland. 'Forced integration' was one proposed solution. The 'self-segregation' of 'failing communities' was elevated to the insidious realm of 'public concern' in an era of fever pitch Islamophobia. The far right could grow its appeal by shadowing the rhetoric of the centre. The riots came just months before 9/11, super-catalyst for a new age of violence and surveillance against anyone coded as Muslim. Whiteness riots have familiar features: police partisanship, local and national media fomentation, moral panics about crime and 'race-mixing', followed by calls for new criminal and immigration legislation.[*] They have also operated as significant flash points for constituting the *public interest as white*. As Darcus Howe once said:

> Every single government, during our presence here, has been able to mobilise white workers on the basis of the little petty privileges that they get over blacks ... We would have loved some help from white workers. Didn't get it.[36]

THE SELF-SEGREGATION OF BRITISH LABOUR

The case of 'coloured seamen' in 1919 is a significant prehistory to Notting Hill and Glodwick. Britain long had a cosmopolitan working class, which imperial administrators struggled to regulate. This was not a country that 'invited' Commonwealth migrants to rebuild after the Second World War.[37] This was an empire constantly having to respond to the mixed character of the working class it had differentiated and subordinated over centuries. Twenty thousand Black people already lived in Britain by the end of the

---

[*] Labour passed a flurry of laws in the 2000s. Help for asylum seekers was cut. New detention centres were built to buttress a new 'biometric' regime. Deportations, including charter flights, accelerated with claimants having no right to appeal until they had been 'returned home'.

First World War, the majority being younger men.[38] During wartime, as white seamen were drafted to serve at the Western front, there was greater demand for 'colonial' labour in shipping. Wages began to rise and some 'coloured seamen' prospered, at least compared to the pre-war years.[39] A minority bought small property, some built up savings. Significantly, some married white British women. In large cities, a small Black middle class of students, lawyers and doctors developed, as did a nascent Black press. But most Black people lived in slums, especially in the ports through which many arrived and from which seamen frequently set sail. Those not in shipping worked as servants and nurses, in factories or theatres. There were Black miners in the coalfields of South Wales and Black 'hands' in munitions factories in Manchester. In 1919, genuine labour militancy was interfacing with racist purges of colonial seamen from Britain's coastal towns. This racist violence set off solidarity strikes in several British colonies. The state responded to the whiteness riots and anti-colonial insurrections abroad by creating flexible immigration controls, which could play fast and loose with the status of racialised British subjects, just as Priti Patel aims to do today.

Between the November 1918 armistice and March 1919, over 2 million service personnel were demobilised in Britain. Traumatised servicemen returned to a Britain racked by economic downturn and growing unemployment. Many felt aggrieved, like their sacrifices hadn't been appreciated or had been futile. Joblessness was something many were less willing to bear.* Lloyd George had promised 'a land fit for heroes' – the reality was a Britain scarred by grief and poverty. Wage cuts were seen as one solution, escalating the class war in the most important empire industry: shipping. As white veterans returned, bosses implemented wage cuts alongside the replacement of Black workers with white. This complex of race and class antagonisms manifested in pitched

---

* There was broader social unrest in Britain in 1919. Around 2.4 million workers went on strike. Police did too. Violence involving demobilised British, US and white Commonwealth soldiers sometimes ended with them fighting the authorities, not just attacking Black and Asian people. Luton's 'Peace Day Riots' saw ex-servicemen, angry about unemployment and a lack of recognition for their service, riot and burn down the town hall. Social fractures were gaping and guns were more widely accessible than ever before.

battles on the streets and efforts to self-segregate white from Black labour.

Glasgow Harbour, 23 January 1919, saw the first whiteness riot. White and Black seamen fought each other with fists, knives and revolvers. Outnumbered, Black sailors – British subjects from Sierra Leone – retreated to their lodgings, pursued by a growing crowd of whites. Police arrested 30 Black men; 3 were convicted. This took place in the context of a wider struggle that is today remembered as one of Britain's most militant examples of trade union resistance. Just four days after the racist attacks at the harbour, 70,000 proletarians stopped working in and around the docks as part of a huge strike. This part of Glasgow, nicknamed 'Red Clydeside', had a reputation for working-class militancy. Its strong shop steward movement and socialist contingents led a powerful anti-war tendency, mobilising wildcat walkouts and successful rent strikes. Joined by workers throughout Scotland, Belfast and Tyneside, strikers demanded a 40-hour week. Unions mobilised 100,000 in George Square. The government feared what Scotland Secretary, Robert Munro, termed a 'Bolshevist uprising' – it had been just over a year since the Russian Revolution.[40*] The rally was met with brutal baton charges. Lengthy battles spread into surrounding areas. Strike leaders were arrested as 12,000 troops, 100 lorries and 6 tanks were deployed but violence died down before the army was required. Instead, they occupied the city for weeks. Union leaders were jailed, the strike defeated.

The racist riot and the huge strike involved the same leaders, suggesting a complex idiosyncrasy to this period of British labour militancy. As Jacqueline Jenkinson writes, 'two of the Glasgow

---

* The year 1919 could rival any other year for the global scope of its social upheaval. 'Spanish' flu continued to wreak havoc. British imperial forces intervened across the globe. They sent troops to aid the White Army in the Russian Civil War, attempting to crush the Revolution. In Egypt, they imposed martial law, cracking down on rebellions across the country. 1919 saw emergency measures in India and a series of massacres by British forces. At Amritsar, over 1,000 people were killed. The Rowlatt Act (or 'Anarchical and Revolutionary Crimes Act') allowed the state to detain anyone suspected of being a 'terrorist', without trial or limit. In South Africa, the ANC mobilised passive resistance against the 'Pass Laws'. Central Europe saw failed socialist revolutions in Germany, Hungary, Czechoslovakia and Austria. British imperialism benefited from the post-war carve-up of defeated powers' territories and colonial possessions, becoming a major power in the Middle East. This marked its apogee. But it faced resistance on all fronts.

labour leaders [Emanuel Shinwell and Willie Gallacher] who sought to marginalise black and Chinese colonial workers were subsequently mythologised under the banner of "Red Clydeside" and later played prominent roles in national politics'.[41] 'Manny' Shinwell, head of the British Seafarers' Union (BSU) in Glasgow, the son of Jewish immigrants, often called for the exclusion of Chinese and Black sailors. The National Sailors' and Firemen's Union (NSFU) under Joseph Havelock Wilson had been accusing 'alien workers' of undercutting British wages since the 1890s. Its Glasgow branch, led by Shinwell until he was part of a BSU breakaway from Wilson's leadership in 1911, called for a 'post-war ban on the employment of Black sailors from the port'.[42] Though the Glasgow branch had an acrimonious split from the NSFU and an ongoing rivalry, they agreed on exclusion. The BSU barred Black sailors from membership entirely. Seamen's unions at times proved themselves militant, but their leaderships were laser-focused on national-racial exclusion. These unions were launch pads for their leaders to leap into Parliament. Wilson was a long-time Liberal MP, while Shinwell represented Labour in Parliament for over four decades, eventually becoming a Baron. Ben Tillett, the dockers' leader, was a trailblazer for this kind of aspirational social mobility. By May 1919, he was MP for Salford and asking a question in Parliament of War Secretary, Winston Churchill: 'What steps are being taken to deport Chinese, Asiatic, and coloured labour being employed for war purposes; and what restrictions are proposed to prevent such cheap labour being employed in home industries of the United Kingdom?'[43]

The cosmopolitanism of seafaring labour presented possibilities for multiracial solidarity, with workers of the world united by circumstances. Yet, unions continually demonstrated the fierceness with which they would maintain unity through division. In March 1919, populist magazine *John Bull* published a petition and letter, signed and handed into the Colonial Office by 132 Black sailors in Glasgow protesting against union colour bars. The seamen knew that total exclusion was the union's aim but pointed to massive social ruptures brought about by the war:

[white seamen's unions were] working to have coloured men abolished not only from British ships but expelled altogether out of Britain … the great European war have brought the aspirations of every race to the forefront. We are not living in the stone and iron age.[44]

Part of the prejudice directed at Black men was a spurious 'common knowledge' that they had avoided military service, instead 'making good' in Britain while white men were away fighting. In fact, close to 2 million Black and Asian people – three-quarters of them from India – served the Empire in the First World War.[45] Some Black veterans living in post-war Britain – many disabled by lasting wounds – took to wearing their uniforms, hoping it might spare them from racist abuse and accusations of shirking. Black men's demands for recognition as British subjects were present in the class antagonisms of wartime service. Volunteers of the British West Indies Regiment (BWIR), having served in combat in the Middle East, were stationed in Italy following the armistice. Facilities at Taranto were segregated. Only white troops were given a pay rise and BWIR troops alone had to carry out servile duties, including cleaning whites' latrines. Black soldiers launched a strike in December 1918. Not only this, they rose up and attacked officers, demanding an immediate pay rise and an end to racial discrimination; 49 Caribbean soldiers were convicted of mutiny – one was executed by firing squad.[46]

In sympathy, writers at *John Bull* provisionally stretched their nationalism to demand the inclusion of Black veterans as a secondary tier of union entitlement, arguing they should at least not be left to starve. 'Apology is due from the National Sailors' and Firemen's Union which took the disgraceful step of refusing them,' *John Bull* argued, '[coloured seamen] are modest enough to say – "first place for white Britishers; after that coloured Britishers". Yet they are ordered to "clear out" from ships at Glasgow, while they see Norwegians, Swedes and Spaniards taken on.'[47] Returning to the back of the queue, after being slung out of work and boards in the post-war restructure, was the best Black workers could hope for, even from 'allies'.

HORROR ON THE RHINE

The wartime increase in Black labour was met with great anxiety in the British socialist press. Some saw it as a harbinger of 'race suicide', similar to far right panics today about 'white genocide'. Tom Quelch wrote against Black workers in *The Call*, journal of the BSP, in 1917.* He claimed migrant workers – whom he referred to as 'fifty thousand jolly coons' – would scab, undercut wages, and pose a sexual threat to white women.[48] Internal discussions in the BSP exhibit fears of a racial order being overturned. One pamphlet felt 'the Great War convinced the people of Europe and America that recurrence of the struggle must result in the destruction of the white race'. They feared violent Black people would seek revenge for colonial wrongs and 'take reparation for the crimes of slavery', rehearsing common fears of whites in slave societies.[49]

As well as stories about Black men dodging service, rumour also circulated about France's deployment of colonial troops as part of the Treaty of Versailles terms imposing French rule in Alsace-Lorraine.** The so-called 'Black Horror on the Rhine' moral panic that followed was, in part, birthed through the organs of the British left. E.D. Morel, a French-born British journalist and respected figure on the left, penned an article for Britain's leading left-wing newspaper, *The Daily Herald*, which spoke of France 'thrusting her black savages ... into the heart of Germany'.*** A central focus, as in Britain's whiteness riots, was an overwhelming fear and disgust about interracial sex and an obsession with the 'violence' of Black masculinity. Morel attempted to drum up European solidarity around the protection of white womanhood by pitting white workers against the manipulative ruling classes setting Black mercenaries against them. 'The workers alike of Britain, France, and

---

* Son of Harry Quelch, long-time editor of *Justice*.

** Among a French occupying force of nearly 100,000 troops was a small contingent of colonial troops – Moroccan, Tunisian, Algerian, Vietnamese, Senegalese and Malagasy soldiers.

*** *The Herald* has an interesting history. Set up in 1911 as a syndicalist strike bulletin by, among others, Ben Tillett. By 1919, it was a daily, edited by Labour politician, George Lansbury. The paper went through periods of being run by the TUC and Labour Party, before finally being renamed *The Sun* in the 1960s and then being acquired by Rupert Murdoch.

Italy,' Morel warned, 'will be ill advised if they allow it to pass in silence because today the victims happen to be German.' Ethel Snowden – leading suffragist and Labour official – said African troops didn't have 'the same powers of sexual control as more developed races' and were a 'menace to ... white women'.[50] Resolutions were passed in local Labour branches, women's groups and trade unions. The ILP condemned the use of African troops. Labour's National Executive bemoaned the 'degrading and dangerous practice'.[51] By September 1920's TUC conference, every delegate received a copy of Morel's pamphlet 'Horror on the Rhine'.[52] This aggressive policing of the colour line in socialist movements showed a clear desire for part of the working class to be alienated, outlawed, even deported, from the British workers movement altogether. It is for this reason important to reserve doubt around the true 'strength' of labour in a period where memberships were growing. By arousing class resentment via the state patronage of racist cruelty, unions were weakened, *even if* their memberships grew. This provided capital with one section of labour-power weakened by racism and another alienated from the fullest formation of its power. The whiteness riots of 1919 gave the British state room to manoeuvre against 'British labour' while also presenting itself as the legal guardian of its future.

One of the few countering voices against Morel's campaign was Jamaican-born poet and communist revolutionary, Claude McKay, living in London at the time. His reply to Morel's *Herald* screed was published in Sylvia Pankhurst's *Worker's Dreadnought* for whom he was a correspondent.[53] Under the heading, 'A Black Man Replies', McKay took Morel's sordid campaign apart, asking simply: 'Why all this obscene maniacal outburst about the sex vitality of black men in a proletarian paper?' McKay brings us back to 1919, warning, 'the ultimate result of your propaganda will be further strife and blood-spilling between whites and the many members of my race ... who have been dumped down on the English docks since the ending of the European war'. He had been 'told in Limehouse by white men ... that this summer will see a recrudescence of the outbreaks that occurred last year'.[54] In 1922, McKay would call on white women comrades to recognise their 'duty ... to overturn the malicious assertion that their relations with colored comrades must necessarily be immoral and to show that this is a vile lie and slander'. He advanced a more capacious vision of the multilayered fight for liberation, stating simply: 'The Negro question is inseparably connected with the question of woman's liberation'.[55]

THE RACIST DEMAND

The assumption that Britain was not, and could not be, the 'homeland' of Black people, was structuring a modern vernacular of popular racism. Following Glasgow, Black sailors were attacked on London's Cable Street. In April 1919, scuffles between Black and white seamen saw gunfire exchanged. The Times reported 'a number of coloured seamen ... injured', with several 'detained by the police'.[56] In May, white mobs attacked Black sailors' hostels in Limehouse. Fights broke out again on 16 May, with more Black men arrested. The next night, the Eastern Post and City Chronicle described a 'sequel' that 'developed from a rough and tumble into a pitched battle' on Commercial Road, ending in 'a rout of the black men'.[57] Sylvia Pankhurst wrote her Dreadnought article 'Stabbing Negroes in the London Dock Area' in early June, challenging white dockers who attacked Black workers: 'Do you think that the British should rule the world or do you want to live on peaceable terms with all peoples?' Pankhurst inverted the restrictionism of trade unions, turning it into a critique of British imperialism, asking:

> those who have been Negro hunting: – 'Do you wish to exclude all blacks from England?' If so, do you not think that blacks might justly ask that the British should at the same time keep out of their countries? ... Do you not know that capitalists, and especially British capitalists, have seized, by force of arms, the countries inhabited by black people and are ruling those countries and the black inhabitants for their own profit?[58]

In South Shields, violence first sparked off at the shipping office – where sailors went to find work and where the racial division of labour was administered. On the mouth of the River Tyne, Muslim seamen, mostly from present-day Yemen or Somalia, were attacked by white mobs after John Fye of the Cooks' and Stewards' Union shouted: 'Don't let these Arabs sign on the ship. Come on you black Bastards, you are not going to join the ship!' James Gilroy of the NSFU also warned the ship not to take on any 'Arabs'.[59] The ship hired all whites (including one Swede). The excluded sailors beat Fye and Gilroy. Later in court, an arrestee, San Bin Salah, claimed there were 200 whites and only 9 Muslims.[60] Fighting continued in the East Holborn neighbourhood as the homes and lodging houses of people of colour were attacked with stones. Police intervened only when the attacked sailors fought back, reinforced by 'a naval detachment, while the Durham Light Infantry was held in reserve'.[61] Every local context featured panics about interracial relationships. In South Shields, Arab men and white women were under the microscope. Some Arab men who owned boarding houses or cafés employed white women as waitresses or cleaners. This was seen by many as demeaning to white womanhood, transgressive of racial and sexual norms. Local press had long complained of a troublesome 'Arab colony' and continued to centre the racialised population in their coverage of the violence, which they termed an 'Arab riot'.[62]

The workers' movement supported seamen's unions in their quest to exclude 'coloured seamen' and 'aliens' – categories the state differentiated, but were collapsing into the same rhetorical vent against 'foreign' labour. At a TUC conference in 1916, Havelock Wilson demanded an end to Chinese immigration, the exclusion of Chinese sailors from British ships and expulsion of Chinese people from the country. This motion was supported by Joe Cotter of the National Union of Ship's Stewards:

> So far as the British seamen are concerned, the Chinese question in this country is almost as important a consideration as the war itself. It is not a bit of use trying to keep the Germans out of the country if we allow Chinamen to take the place of the boys who are fighting for us.[63]

Cotter added, 'these Chinese are not only a menace to the seamen on board ship, they are also a distinct danger to society in general'.

He argued the movement had been lax on Chinese immigration because it was mainly confined to shipping but warned that Chinese people were beginning to settle, taking up other trades, and their 'evil will spread beyond our ships, and every other trade will be affected'. He was cheered after ending with a rousing call: 'We want you to vote for the resolution, and to ask the Parliamentary Committee to do something to see that these people are cleared right out of the country.'[64] The Cardiff branch of the National Union of Railwaymen passed a resolution during the 1919 pogroms, calling on the government to 'do their duty by the coloured men in this country and send them back to their homeland.'[65] In September 1919, the TUC passed a further resolution condemning wage undercutting by 'Asiatic labour', and demanding priority be given to white British labour. James Henson of the NSFU, who put forward the motion, reassured Congress he had

no objection to a Chinaman as such. He is a very nice man so long as he remains in China, but when he is made use of by shipowners ... to undercut the British seaman I am up against him on economic grounds.[66]

The resolution was carried.*

David Olusoga writes that violence in Liverpool 'was orchestrated by well-organized gangs, hundreds and sometimes thousands strong, who hunted black men on the street.'[67] Liverpool's Black population by war's end was Britain's largest outside London. Peter Fryer, in his seminal history of Black people in Britain, *Staying Power*, showed that the 'hate strike', common tactic of white workers in postbellum America, was deployed by white British workers too:

In one week alone, in the spring of 1919, about 120 black workers employed for years in the big Liverpool sugar refineries and oilcake mills were sacked because white workers now refused to

---

* Havelock Wilson eventually proved too right wing even for the TUC. He and the NSFU were expelled for not supporting the 1926 General Strike. Even after his death in 1929, when the union was readmitted, its politics and strategy remained the same: collaborating with bosses, railing against 'Communists' and displacing the class struggle with obsessive attacks on 'coloured seamen'.

work with them. Unemployed black workers, living on credit from day to day, were being turned out of their lodging.[68]

On 4 June, a Black man, John Johnson, was stabbed by two Scandinavians 'when he refused to give them a cigarette'. Another fight broke out the next night when Johnson's friends found the same men and attacked them 'with sticks, knives, razors, and pieces of iron taken from lamp-posts, knocking unconscious a policeman who tried to stop them'. Police raided several Black lodging houses seeking the perpetrators. Residents 'defended themselves, one with a poker, others with revolvers, knives and razors. One policeman was shot in the mouth, another in the neck, a third was slashed on face and neck, and a fourth had his wrist broken.'[69] Living at one lodging house was 24-year-old Charles Wootton, a Royal Navy veteran from Bermuda.[70] Police attempted to take Wootton into custody but he ran away. Upon escaping, he found himself being chased by a lynch mob of hundreds, before being pushed into the Mersey river. Onlookers cheered, shouting 'LET HIM DROWN',[71] throwing objects into the water until Wootton had drowned at the Queen's Dock.[72] No arrests were made.[73]

Black people were repatriated before the month was out. There was talk of detaining them in camps pending deportation but it was decided this would be too hard to implement. Those who remained were left to starve, pawn off belongings or live on credit until it ran out. Salford saw smaller scale violence that year. Its tiny Black community, mostly sailors from Sierra Leone, were confined to a ghettoised neighbourhood called Greengate, characterised by locals as a 'Black colony'. The *Manchester Evening News* used racial epithets gleaned from a Southern US context to caricature West Africans threatened with repatriation: ' "Few home-sick coons" – Salford negroes not keen on free passage. The dusky denizens of the Greengate colony have not "cottoned on" to the offer of a free trip back to "Dixie" and only about ten have volunteered.'[74]

THE GLOBAL LABOUR PROBLEM

Cardiff's pogroms in June were the worst of all. The city has a long history of migrant settlement, being one of the key imperial ports from the mid-nineteenth century onwards. It had seen racial violence before. When the NSFU embarked on strike action for union recognition and higher wages in 1911, a central plank of its platform was a refusal to work with Chinese sailors. White workers showed their willingness to enforce exclusion by their own hand as all thirty of Cardiff's Chinese-owned laundries were ransacked and set on fire.[75] Butetown, the mixed immigrant neighbourhood of South Cardiff, was home to people from West Africa, the Caribbean, Yemen, China, Somalia and more. It was also home to opium dens, brothels and illicit gambling. Butetown was nicknamed 'Nigger Town' by whites – including the *Times* newspaper. Similarities with Liverpool are clear in the territorial form of the pogrom – a naked desire to clear Black people, encroaching into 'white' areas. Three people lost their lives with dozens more injured amid beatings, gunfights and stabbings. The touchpaper was initially lit in familiar fashion: a white mob accosted Black men and their white wives. The rampage spread as 'a crowd of around 2000 people gathered outside the Labour Exchange offices in Cardiff's Canal Parade and began attacking non-white seamen'.[76] A house was 'set alight with the Blacks still inside'. Mobs were often led by uniformed veterans, serving troops were deployed to stop them. Mohamed Ali and Mohamed Khaid were imprisoned for shooting at policemen as rioters invaded their home. The judge said of Ali: 'the prisoner and his race should realise that the police were their friends'. The historical record shows this to be anything but the case – tragically underlined by the fact that Khaid died in a Cardiff prison in May 1920.[77*]

Cardiff saw Black people fight back, even when heavily outnumbered. Ron Ramdin describes 'besieged black men us[ing] razor blades and a revolver to defend themselves'.[78] *The Monmouthshire Evening Post* reported from Newport that 'it was shortly before midnight when the Blacks, armed with sticks and iron bars, charged

---

* Mohammed Khaid's death in custody is part of a long history of deaths in police and state custody. British police have disproportionately killed racialised people, with impunity, from Khaid to David Oluwale 50 years later, to Rashan Charles nearly 50 years after that. See Harmit Atwhal and Jenny Bourne, *Dying For Justice* (London: Institute of Race Relations, 2015); and 'BME Deaths in Custody (1991–2014)', *Institute of Race Relations*, www.irr.org.uk/research/statistics/bame-deaths-in-custody/.

169

the crowd'.[79] The sensationalising of Black aggression was typical, but the growth of militant Black self-defence was bound up, as we shall see, with sharpening, cross-pollinating Black struggles from the Caribbean to the USA. Migrant labour and decolonisation struggles were exploring the contradictions of 'identity' exposed by the colonial reach of the 'British subject' – an identity that supported the fluid deployment of labour across British territories, but also a problem Britain was uniquely 'burdened' with and used racial differentiation to manage. The *South Wales Echo* reported on different communities in Cardiff joining together to counter white violence:

> A meeting was held at Cardiff docks yesterday of Arabs, Somalis, Egyptians, West Indians and other coloured races, to protest against the treatment to which they are being subjected. It was pointed out that they had done nothing to originate the disturbances ... They claim that as British subjects they are entitled to protection, and a resolution was passed calling upon the Government to take measures with this end.[80]

The riots were international in scope, with waves on either side of the Atlantic. Violent ripples continued in Hull, Newport, Barry, London and Salford in subsequent years, as repatriations continued. Black resistance in Britain extended to the working class of the empire as colonies saw acts of retribution. As feared by colonial administrators and imperialist onlookers, counter-riots and outcry greeted news of British pogroms. Sierra Leone saw attacks against white residents, 'Disturbances ... directly influenced by the treatment of blacks in Britain.'[81] An uprising in Trinidad was part of a wider dock strike, which won union recognition and a 25 per cent pay increase.[82] In Belize, repatriated seamen and veterans attacked whites with sticks, chanting: 'We want to get the white man out' and 'the white man has no right here'.[83] There was fighting between white and Black seamen in Guyana, as there was in Jamaica in July and October. In July, Black sailors in Kingston attacked white men, chanting 'kill the whites!'[84] This mirrored resistance put up by West Indians in Liverpool where 'a black man taking vigorous action on the streets was heard to shout: "Down with the white race." '[85] In October, upon arrival in Jamaica, Black men repatriated from Britain beat up white seamen.[86] Colonial authorities knew the violence related directly to 'the treatment which had been received by coloured sailors at Cardiff and Liverpool'.[87] There were even uprisings on boats taking repatriated seamen from Cardiff to the Caribbean.[88]

Colonial Secretary Lord Alfred Milner – key funder of the British Workers League – worried about the impact of the 'race riots' in the colonies:

> I am seriously concerned at the continued disturbances due to racial ill-feeling against coloured men in our large sea ports. These riots are serious enough from the point of view of the maintenance of order in this country, but they are even more serious in regard to their possible effect in the colonies.[89]

The experience of war, of Black men's service on behalf of Empire, and the racist violence that followed its end, opened the path for an expanding Black resistance to white domination crossing borders and oceans. Officials sought to blame the rise of Black resistance on manipulation by communists, Japan and Marcus Garvey.[90] One US intelligence official communicated from the Versailles Conference that he'd spoken to Sir Basil Thompson of Scotland Yard:

> [he] told me of the strikes and political disturbances in Sierra Leone, Jamaica and other British colonies where Blacks far outnumber the Whites. The British seem very apprehensive of a united movement on the part of the coloured race and are making special enquiries into any racial cohesion or unity among the coloured races generally.[91]

A protest meeting was held by a coalition of groups in Hyde Park on 14 June, organised by the Society of Peoples of African Origin. General secretary, F.E.M. Hercules, was one of the speakers. He demanded an official inquiry into the death of Charles Wootton but one never materialised. Political community among colonised peoples in Britain was spurred on further by the anger felt by veterans when African, Asian and West Indian troops were excluded from the victory parade in London on 19 May. *The African Telegraph* – the largest Black newspaper in Britain, edited by Hercules – announced with disappointment: 'we can only conclude that it is the policy of His Majesty's Ministers to ignore the services of the black subjects of the Empire'. The editorial continued beyond disappointment, expressing righteous anger, a realisation of what their colonial rulers expected from Black subjects who escaped war service with their lives:

> Every ounce of strength was put into the struggle by the black man ... He fought with the white man to save the white man's home and the war was won. Black men all the world over are asking to-day: 'What have we got? What are we going to get out of it all?' The answer, in effect, comes clear, convincing and conclusive: 'Get back to your kennel you damned dog of a nigger!'[92]

Racist violence, including that which never became a full-on riot nor was it always reported and logged for posterity, was constant in these towns both before and after 1919.

DIVISION BEFORE UNITY

Whiteness riots were followed by state repatriation schemes. The government collected data on Britain's Black population and offered repatriation as their best 'option'. Public bodies coordinating the schemes included local government officials and trade union leaders, many of whom had encouraged the violence.[93] By August 1921, around 2,000 had been deported.[94] Small amounts of money plus free passage were offered to those willing to leave but the paltry £6 on offer was barely enough to get most people's belongings out of pawn.[95] Some Black seamen left willingly. Little distinction was made between those of long residence (including those born in Britain) and more recent migrants for work and war service. As British shipping began falling behind, and unemployment worsened, Black seamen suffered most as life below the colour bar stretched long into the distance. Many more were repatriated, some taken to countries, even continents, they had never been to before.[96] More struggled and stayed, unwilling to leave their families, asserting their right to live and work in Britain. Many people in Britain today can trace their descendants back to them.

As Jacqueline Jenkinson argues, the substantial repatriation of racialised workers must be seen as a success for the white rioters. Direct action, taken by a cross-section of the 'white community', was about inflicting direct violence based on racial hatred. But clear demands were also being made to the state: to institute stricter border controls and an even more stringent racial division of labour. The entanglement of popular racist demands, revolutionary feeling, class struggle and imperialist foment, complicates conventional rationales for riots. Riot, according to Marxist historian Eric Hobsbawm, is rooted in class antagonisms between workers and capitalist elites. His theory is based on eighteenth-century bread riots and nineteenth-century machine-breaking, which he argued were forms of 'collective bargaining by riot'.[97] Hobsbawm read these riots against a liberal view of 'the mob', noting an intelligent collectivity, an intent to force change. A specialist on Britain's 1919 'race riots', Jenkinson, whose excellent scholarship we have relied upon, builds on Hobsbawm, while stressing how 'race' distorted the aims of the rioters, 'which, although targeted at Black seamen and other Black economic competitors, were in essence, protests against the shipowners'.[98] But how watertight is the claim that 'in essence' the 'riots' were protests against the shipowners, a case of misdirected class hatred?

This more passive framing of 'division within the seagoing population' leaves us to understand racism as merely a form of irrationality. Irrational it may be, but racist societies lend this irrationality an objectivity. If 'divisions' in the working class are explained as superimpositions or distortions of elites alone, racism is understandable only as 'ideology', a garish expression of fallible human passions. Racism is *historically constituted* and so possesses an attractive power for the divisions it can *speak to*. 'Creating division' isn't simply about 'splitting' – 'division' from one perspective is a basis for 'unity' from another. Trade unions were organising labour in conformity with racial lines before 1919, so the idea that the heat of the riots triangulated the passions of class hatred doesn't hold. The imperialist stress and the barbarities of war provided hostile conditions for solidarity. 'Racial unity' offered some labour organisations and leaders a working model for 'class unity' that could negotiate the threat from capital and lend these struggles a vision of national prosperity. Shipping magnates could balance wage cuts with concessions to a more limited employ of white workers without directly engaging trade unions in antagonistic disputes. The state wanted negotiations that could prevent more strikes. Propagating 'racial unity' leads to paranoid conspiracies and panics, while offering class societies a reliable means to organise peaceably across classes. This sort of strategic compromise is never controlled, yet it is not totally irrational to a racist society either.

Criticisms of capital's 'excess' can also be accommodated by racist frames. In 1919, criticism of capitalism was not limited to labour movements. Welfare fixes were being prospected by reformers, with white unity in mind. The failures of capitalism to generalise prosperity demanded nationalist solutions to popular 'anti-capitalist' feeling. White shipping workers and the most firebrand, nativist union leaders were genuinely motivated by hatred for some employers. This militancy is not necessarily in contradiction with imperialist paths to organisation. Imperialism makes it possible to hate your employer but love your nation; to show solidarity for some workers, hatred for others. Were the 1919 'riots' *in essence* a class struggle, which lost this essential character due to racial division? Or was racism essential to organising a struggle limited to white workers? The nationalisation of 'whiteness' allows for collaboration even where antagonists are pitted against one another. State repatriation and racialisation of 'coloured seamen' was an explicit focus for white rioters, expressed in a *racist demand* to deport them. The state was invested in regulating and differentiating British from 'colonial' labour because its own interests demanded it. Bordering mechanisms were introduced to regulate the deployment of colonial labour at home and manage the seditious potential of it abroad. What the whiteness riots provided, with union collaboration, was the seam of a racial consensus at home. Imperial Britain had to balance an antagonised and mobile colonial labour force with insurgencies at its ports and factories. British whiteness developed through this compressed moment of imperial crisis as a speculative 'bond' as well as an 'identity' – a funnel for strategic investments in the nation – that the state, capital and workers movements could together, even if as icy collaborators, unify the partial interests of each. If Hobsbawm could speak of earlier proletarian uprisings as 'collective bargaining by riot', then perhaps we can look at British workers whiteness riots in 1919 as 'lobbying for tighter border controls by racist pogrom'?

Legislation and convictions followed. Where authorities and newspapers sought leniency for whites, it was out of sympathy for a 'just cause'. Fears of 'miscegenation' translated as clear provocation – a *good reason* for violence. A judge in Newport 'could understand and sympathise with the feeling of the white men when they saw white women associating with black men'.[99] With the 1920 Aliens Order and the Special Restriction (Coloured Alien Seamen) Order of 1925, the state attacked the rights of work and abode of 'alien' seamen. Continuing in the traditions of the Aliens Act, both 'owed much to union lobbying'.[100] The new laws, though, tied bordering directly to skin colour, placing in jeopardy the citizenship or residency claims of *all* Black people, even those born in Britain.[101] Immigration controls offered Britain a more flexible form of labour deployment, dependent as it was on the global transportation of labour and commodities. Marx wrote on the transport of commodities, 'what the transport industry sells is the actual change of place itself'.[102] For the British Empire, 'race' designated a 'change of place' for the commodity labour-power. 'Black' identities were flexible, capturing people from across the world. New modalities and stratifications of 'race' were invented and managed by a system that calculated and balanced the time colonial labour could 'stay' and assume British sovereignty. The deployment of 'identities' *followed* the racist deployment of labour. Neil Evans explains,

> coloured sailors were required to have an identity card complete with a thumb print (because they all looked the same!) in order to go about their business. They were only excused this proviso if they could prove that they were British subjects.[103]

In short, 'being black and British had become almost impossible'.[104] Since many never owned a passport, they were constantly harassed by police, pressured into registering as 'aliens', and denied work upon arrival. British subjects had their citizenship reversed, arbitrarily and continuously. Shipping employers, unions and police worked together, withholding wages until Black workers accepted Aliens Cards. Such innovations foreshadowed the colour-coded bordering to come between 1962–1971 that so deeply defined skin colour as a marker of Britishness, designating people of colour as suspect, leading Sivanandan to remark: 'we wear our passports on our faces'.[105] As Luke de Noronha has documented, Black British people continue to be deported because this colonial flexibility is internalised within the 'grey areas' of Britain's 'multi-status' border regime.[106] For years after 1919, in various towns, moral panics and white bourgeois vigilance were trained on small, segregated, super-exploited, racialised populations. Police, Christian groups and local authorities obsessed over the degenerative effects of Butetown. Labour MP for Cardiff South, Arthur Henderson Jr., referred to the growth of a 'half-caste' population as 'a social menace'. Anxieties around hygiene, sexual threat, disease, idleness, ill-discipline and crime mingled into terrifying visions of Black folk devils in their midst. These were attempts by white supremacy to deal with an ongoing 'problem' Patrick Wolfe named so accurately. 'Racialisation,' Wolfe advanced, was a 'response to the crisis occasioned when colonisers are threatened with the requirement to share social space with the colonised.'[107]

7

The Mad and Hungry Dogs

If we must die, let it be not like hogs
Hunted and penned in an inglorious spot,
While round us bark the mad and hungry dogs,
Making their mock at our accursed lot.
If we must die, O let us nobly die,
So that our precious blood may not be shed
In vain; then even the monsters we defy
Shall be constrained to honor us though dead!
O kinsmen! we must meet the common foe!
Though far outnumbered let us show us brave
And for their thousand blows deal one deathblow!
What though before us lies the open grave?
Like men we'll face the murderous, cowardly pack,
Pressed to the wall, dying, but fighting back![1]

'If We Must Die', *Claude McKay*

One of the first recorded uses of 'woke' goes back to the 1930s. Folk singer, Lead Belly, says it on a recording of his 1938 song 'Scottsboro Boys', about the 1931 case of nine Black teenagers accused of raping two white women on a freight train in Alabama. This is one of the more notorious tales of miscarried justice, wrongful imprisonment and extra-judicial murder of Black men and boys, falsely accused of violence against white women. On the recording, Lead Belly warns other Black people to avoid Alabama: 'I advise everybody, be a little careful when they go along through there – best stay woke, keep their eyes open.'[2] An estimated 6 million Black Americans fled the South over six decades, escaping mob violence and grinding poverty.[3] Around half a million between 1914–1918 alone left the rural South for Northern cities, meeting growing demand for labour and stimulated by preparations for war. More recent appropriation of 'woke' came after the first BLM wave. It retained its original meaning before becoming generalised in pop culture and liberal media activism to signify a multi-issue ethically motivated youth politics. The right became accustomed to it as liberal 'anti-racism'. The significance of 'wokeness' as Black working class savviness to racist violence was turned on its head. Trump's team pounced on the trend. A memo from the National Budget Office, in the autumn of Trump's presidency, began,

It has come to the President's attention that Executive Branch agencies have spent millions of taxpayer dollars to date 'training' government workers to believe divisive, anti-American propaganda.

… all agencies are directed to begin to identify all contracts or other agency spending related to any training on 'critical race theory', 'white privilege', or any other training or propaganda effort that teaches or suggests either (1) that the United States is an inherently racist or evil country or (2) that any race or ethnicity is inherently racist or evil … cancel any such contracts and/or to divert Federal dollars away from these un-American propaganda training sessions.[4]

The reaction against 'Critical Race Theory' was escalated after the publication of the *New York Times'* '1619 project' – a compendium of essays on slavery in America that could be used in school curriculums. With his directive Trump initiated a sequence of McCarthyite hunts across GOP-controlled states that would outlast his presidency. The GOP needed to keep its base watered and 'CRT' provided the perfect opportunity to create an 'anti-woke' wedge issue to last until Trump, or another 'anti-woke' candidate, ran in 2024. Christopher Rufo, a fellow at the Manhattan Institute, admitted as much,

We have successfully frozen their brand – 'critical race theory' – into the public conversation and are steadily driving up negative perceptions. We will eventually turn it toxic, as we put all of the various cultural insanities under the brand category. The goal is to have the public read something crazy in the newspaper and immediately think 'critical race theory'.[5]

It can come as no surprise that conservative think-tanks help foment racist moral panics. It is less clear why some on the left propagate them. When Vivek Chibber, author of the *ABCs of Socialism*, was asked for his opinion on 'Trump famously [declaring] war on critical race theory', he joked it was 'one of his better moments, actually'. Chibber continued, 'take over the school, rewrite the text-books ... this is bullshit and profoundly reactionary'.[6] There is plenty to criticise in the 1619 project, but we are also mindful that teachers assess the strengths and weaknesses of source material. How the working conditions of teachers might be impacted by this moral panic never entered into the discussion. The aim was to prove that: 'Marxism is Way Better Than Critical Race Theory'.[7] For Chibber, like the anti-communist right, 'wokeness' became ad hominem to attack any political argument asserting the centrality of race in history.[8] Meanwhile, reactionaries were organising to stop histories of slavery being taught at all. Attacks on Critical Race Theory provided the GOP with the race-baiting plank of a 'parental rights' front that included 'state by state' purges of LGBTQ+ and abortion rights.[9]

The reification of 'CRT' from the left is conservative pivoting. It also provides no alternative to the nationalist character of liberal anti-racist historiography. Making race central to histories of capitalism does not mean reducing everything to slavery. It is merely the first step to exploring how forms of exploitation and oppression are historically differentiated. Claude McKay travelled between Europe, the Soviet Union, the Caribbean and the USA, before, during and after 1919, offering insight into how white supremacist reactions were being met with determined resistance under very different historical conditions: by sharecroppers in Arkansas and unemployed veterans in Chicago, by Sierra Leonean, Yemeni and Jamaican sailors in Cardiff and Freetown, South Shields and Kingston. These different circumstances were also brought together through the literature and analyses of communist and anti-colonial traditions. McKay's poem, 'If We Must Die', was a transnational call to arms. First published in *The Lib-*

erator, the poem was quickly republished in *The Messenger, The Crisis* and *The Crusader,* as well as the *Workers' Dreadnought* in London. Working-class struggles against racism *are labour histories.* Racism is the product of a colonial setting and a reaction to massive upheavals and displacement.

In the USA, self-emancipated former slaves, their children, their grandchildren, journeyed North, fleeing violence and in search of a better life. The 'Great Migration' has clear parallels to colonial migration to Britain. The difference being that the USA could not 'repatriate' its colonised subjects, whose labour-power was assimilated into American society with one hand, while Black people themselves were harassed, pursued and purged into foreignness with the other. Governor of Illinois during the 1919 Chicago riot, Frank Lowden, mused: 'in earlier days the colonization of the Negro, as in Liberia, was put forward as a solution. That idea was abandoned long ago. It is now recognised generally that the two races are here in America to stay.'[10] While there are no general analogies to be made between historical phases of capitalism, there are no total breaks either. If there are continuities, they need to be determined and considered. In this final chapter, we recognise generational throughlines in the way resistance is remembered and elite power is conglomerated. Archaic forms of racism, like lynching, have developed in conjunction with liberal forms of capitalist exploitation, policing and incarceration. Whiteness riots happen under different circumstances but are also relentless, foundational features of US nation-building.[11] Militias formed from the first genocides of Indigenous people. White vigilantes have acted to prevent Black people from working, voting, owning property or guns, sharing public transport and public space. They stopped Black people from living where they lived, expelling Black populations entirely from neighbourhoods, towns and counties. Vigilantes and lobby groups are now returning to the streets and government offices to organise alongside GOP senators. They return to old right 'red scare' racial conspiracies to roll back rights. North and South, the whiteness riots of 1919 helped draw lasting colour lines and demographic shifts. What historical questions can be raised by these events without reducing present circumstances to them, or alternatively, denying their relevance?

'RED SUMMER'

The 'Red Summer' of 1919 was preceded by war and an atmosphere of febrile racism and anti-communism. 1915 saw the ground-breaking cinematic celebration of Ku Klux Klan mob violence in D.W. Griffith's *Birth of a Nation*. The hit movie was much loved by sitting US President, Woodrow Wilson,* based as it was on a bestselling novel by his college friend.[12] The spectacular depiction of heroic Klansmen on horseback protecting the honour of Southern belles against sexually aggressive Black men (played by white men in blackface) was blown up for the big screen and distributed nationwide. One of the film's captions reads: 'the former enemies of North and South are united again in common defense of their Aryan birthright.'[13] The film helped spur the founding of a second Klan. African Americans organised boycotts, protesting outside theatres in several cities, leading to bans in some.

In the summer of 1917, there was a grotesque anti-Black riot. In East St. Louis, 'a mob of white men, women and children … drove 6,000 Negroes out of their homes; and deliberately murdered, by shooting, burning and hanging, between one and two hundred human beings who were black.'[14] The *St. Louis Post-Dispatch* described the sometimes carnivalesque character of the whiteness riots: '[it] was a man hunt, conducted on a sporting basis … there was a horribly cool deliberateness and a spirit of fun about it. "Get a nigger", was the slogan.'[15] Black residents saw children and elders casually thrown into burning buildings. Beatrice Deshong witnessed the complicity of police and military:

> I saw the mob robbing the homes of Negroes and then set fire to them. The soldiers stood with folded arms and looked on as the houses burned. I saw a Negro man killed instantly by a member of the mob, men, small boys, and women and little girls all were trying to do something to injure Negroes.[16]

---

* The film used text from Wilson's own 'History of the American People' in its captions. Wilson hosted viewings at the White House for prestigious guests, including Chief Justice of the Supreme Court, Edward White, a member of the original Klan. Wilson also introduced Jim Crow to DC under his presidency.

She continued:

> The police and the soldiers were assisting the mob to kill Negroes
> and to destroy their homes ... I saw the mob hang a colored man
> to a telegraph pole and riddle him with bullets. I saw the mob
> chasing a colored man who had a baby in his arms. The mob
> shooting at him all of the time.[17]

The whiteness riots coincided with an uptick in working-class
militancy. There was revolution in Russia and a rash of anarchist
bombs targeting ruling-class figures in America. Radicals came
under severe state repression. War had produced an atmosphere
of heightened nationalism with members of the Socialist Party
and the Industrial Workers of the World (IWW) imprisoned for
opposing it. The height of the 'Red Scare' saw the federal government respond with the 'Palmer Raids'. Named after Attorney
General, A. Mitchell Palmer, who had a bomb explode outside his
own house, the raids targeted 'suspected' radicals (often conflated
with 'aliens'). In December, 249 people were deported to Russia,
including anarchists Emma Goldman and Alexander Berkman.*
The next month, a further 4,000 were detained, given closed
hearings and deported. Though the Constitution gave no powers
for summary deportations, the government could call on the precedent of the Chinese Exclusion Act.[18] The IWW – one of the first
and only US unions to organise across every occupational and
colour line – was especially targeted. Michael Cohen writes,

> In the violent, '100% American' climate of World War I and the
> Red Scare, vigilante organizations like the American Protective
> League, the American Legion, and, to a lesser extent, the second
> Ku Klux Klan, not only earned a measure of state legitimacy by
> participating in nationally orchestrated antiradical purges, but
> they became the vanguard of a reactionary social movement and
> played a critical role in the creation of the modern American
> political intelligence system.[19]

---

* Black radicals like Marcus Garvey and Cyril Briggs were also targeted in the Palmer Raids.

Just as Black-led rebellions today are means for escalating anti-communist discourses, Black resistance in 1919 was blamed on 'Bolshevik' interference. The racist trope of the white (often Jewish) 'outside agitator' riling up previously contented African Americans is a longstanding one.[20] Such conspiracy theories were peddled from on high by a young graduate, newly hired by Palmer, named J. Edgar Hoover.[21] July brought the *New York Times* headline: 'REDS TRY TO STIR NEGROES TO REVOLT',[22] speculating about 'Soviet influence'.[23] A cartoon in the *New York World* depicted Lenin as a king, grinning, reading about the Omaha 'race riot', the caption read: 'They're Learning'.[24] White supremacist mass media helped instigate and spread the violence as well as obfuscate the causes. Local newspapers egged on white mobs, warning of Black rapists and approaching 'race war'.

As we visit the riot-zones, patterns begin to crystallise. Most saw active support or passive acquiescence from law enforcement, white labour unions and newspapers. Rioters were animated by myths of 'black rapists' and violence manifested in indiscriminate beatings of Black people in public spaces and attacks on Black-owned property. The composition of the whiteness riot was always cross-class, to one degree or another, from bankers to shopkeepers to manual labourers to policemen. White gangs marshalled colour lines between white neighbourhoods and so-called 'black belts'. What appears a libidinal yet senseless violence also had an objective character that cannot be reduced to labour competition or 'misguided' resentments.

FAMILIES FIRST

There were 28 lynchings in the first six months of 1919. Seven victims were Black war veterans, murdered while wearing their uniforms.[25] Institutional support for lynching went right to the top of state and federal power structures. Towards the tail-end of the 1919 wave, Mississippi Senator John Sharp Williams said:

> I go as far in the pathways of peace as any man who was ever born. I am willing to arbitrate nearly everything in this world, except one thing, and that is the attempt to outrage a white

woman by any man, either white, black, or red. I surrender him at once as being beyond the pale of the law, to the first crowd that can get to him. I believe in law. I believe in law and order. I believe that there is no justification for taking the law into one's own hands. But I believe that there are now and then provocation and excuse enough for it ... Not only is blood thicker than water, but race is greater than law, now and then; and if race be not greater than law, about which there might be a dispute, the protection of a woman transcends all law of every description, human or divine.[26]

Ritual murder, lynching, public whippings were long standing practices of racial rule. As slavery was phased out in northern states but expanded in the South, mob violence tended to happen up North. After emancipation, it defined the South.[27] There was rarely a clear separation between mob and state. Police and troops were usually part of or sympathetic to the mob. The political activity of whiteness and patriarchal reasoning incited and legitimised the violence. America's settler-colonial context over-determined the identity of the 'American family' as a unit of political economy. Through the white patriarch and family, a common interest of 'free' property rights could be identified. In Britain, 'demands-based' racism secured, from the state, special provisions for 'British nationals'. America's entrepreneurial populism, its relationship to land and slavery, spawned a more proactive communitarian vigilantism, to secure the reproduction and economic advantages of the 'white race' in perpetuity. The figure of the hypersexualised 'black rapist' was a pretext for whiteness riots in both societies, but the agency of this trope was differently extended in each context. The focus of each 'riot' developed upon race and class antagonisms latent to each locality, though often conscious of being part of a larger wave.

In Washington DC, on 19 July, violence was sparked by rumours of a Black man raping the wife of a white Navy veteran. A mob of 400 whites formed, soldiers and sailors from local bars. They headed, armed, towards the Black neighbourhoods in the southwest of the city, assaulting any Black person they happened to encounter. DC had the largest Black population of any US city at the time.[28] Newspapers had for weeks been running sensationalist stories about an anonymous (but Black) serial molester of white women. The NAACP sent letters to the four biggest papers, warning that they were 'sowing the seeds of a race riot by their inflammatory headlines'.[29] Violence spread throughout the city. Black people were seen being beaten in front of the White House.[30] 'A mob of sailors and soldiers jumped on the [street]car and pulled me off, beating me unmercifully from head to foot, leaving me in such a condition that I could hardly crawl back home,' teenager Francis Thomas recounted. He saw others beaten, two of them women. 'Before I became unconscious, I could hear them pleading with the Lord to keep them from being killed.'[31]

Riots in Omaha began as a community manhunt. A Black man, Will Brown, was accused of raping a white woman. Mob spirit was urged on by the *Omaha Bee* newspaper, who 'made a majority of the people in Omaha believe that all Negro men were disposed to commit the crime of rape on white women'.[32] The newspaper called Will Brown a 'Black Beast' on their front page, two days before violence erupted. It carried stories along this same theme through-out 1919.[33] In four consecutive editions in March, the story of an assault 'by a negro of huge stature' on a 44-year-old white mother of seven was covered. Mrs Glassman, described as 'sick' and 'frail', was also claimed to have given 'terrific battle to the intruder for half an hour' while her children slept upstairs, her husband at work. Mrs Glassman told police she was 'struck by a club' and robbed of her money by two Black burglars who had threatened to kill her children before using chloroform to knock her unconscious. By the third day of coverage, the paper announced that 'thirty-five negroes were in custody',[34] but Mrs Glassman couldn't identify any as her assailant. *The Bee* lamented that 'two other like cases have occurred, and the efforts of the police to capture the lust-mad negro has failed in every case'.[35] Paranoid white women all over town began calling the police, terrified about home invasions. *The Bee* named and printed the addresses of Black men dressed in army uniforms being arrested and questioned. In the very next day's edition – tucked away on page five when the previous coverage was splashed across the front – it was announced that all 35 Black men were no longer suspects, though the opportunity was taken to charge some under vagrancy laws. At the end of four days of breathless coverage came the lines: 'Dr Elizabeth Lyman, physician called on the case, said Mrs Glassman had not been chloroformed or criminally assaulted. Dr Lyman attributes Mrs Glassman's dazed and semi-conscious condition to nervous shock.'[36]

Similar moral panics were filed through the paper as an organising funnel for white supremacist vigilantism. A letter dated 28 September, the day rioting began, was printed in the 1 October edition. Signed 'Citizens', it warned of what was to come:

> When an infuriated mob marches through the streets of Omaha to participate in a race riot to avenge the white race against the deperdations [sic.] of the black, there will be no one to blame but the authorities, who have repeatedly come to the assistance and protection of negroes who have committed grave assaults upon white girls.[37]

The authors expressed frustration at 'black beasts' being let off the hook, suggesting more funding for the police was needed. They end by saying, 'we hope that the man Brown, if guilty, is punished in a manner that will be a warning to all that the people of Omaha intend to protect their women and girls.'[38] Nicolas Swiercek has noted that 'by late summer, one Omaha newspaper, *The Mediator*, advocated the formation of "vigilance committees" to administer justice if the police "could not end the crime wave"'.[39] Once Will Brown was in custody, the *Omaha World-Herald* warned of the threat of imminent mob violence. Its editorial was unequivocal: 'Our women must be protected at all costs.'[40] A 10,000-strong white mob attempted to get to Brown, held in jail at the city courthouse. Intense fighting occurred between mob and police. Hundreds of firearms were looted as seven policemen were shot and the courthouse burned down. Will Brown was handed over to the lynch mob as he pled his innocence. He was hanged from a telephone pole. His lifeless body was showered with bullets and dragged around town tied to a car before the mob burned him at the stake. A horrifying photograph captured Will Brown's body set alight. His smiling murderers posed for it, no fear of repercussion. The lasting image of 'Red Summer'.

THE MAD AND HUNGRY DOGS

Figures of 'black rapists' are never 'hallucinations' of the mind but of the social context and its product. A colonial paradigm of white innocence gave these social reproductions a concrete imagery, and this imagery returned again and again to ratchet up popular racism, get a conviction, incarcerate, clear the streets, condemn to death. The experience of the Scottsboro Boys – Lead Belly's cautionary tale for African Americans needing to 'stay woke' – has been repeated for countless Black boys and men, before and since. The Harlem Six, another group of teenage Black boys, were convicted of murdering a white woman in 1965, while the Central Park Five, all teenage boys of colour, were wrongfully accused of raping a white woman in 1989.[41] Donald Trump had broadcast his desire to see the boys executed without trial, paying for full-page newspaper advertisements demanding: 'BRING BACK THE DEATH PENALTY! BRING BACK OUR POLICE!' The five were not released and exonerated until 2002. Like the Harlem Six, they were beaten mercilessly and tortured into giving false confessions, the only evidence used to convict them. According to the Innocence Project,

> Today, Black men [in the US] are twice as likely to be arrested for a sex offense and three times more likely to be accused of rape than white men ... not because they are committing such crimes at higher rates than people of other races or ethnicities, but because they are more often suspected and accused of such crimes ... innocent Black people are seven times more likely to be wrongfully convicted of murder than innocent white people. And studies show that Black men are sentenced to death far more often when accused of committing a crime against a white person.[42]

Cases like the Central Park Five point to an 'archaic' racism, thought to be anachronistic but systemically reproduced through liberal democratic institutions, alongside white vigilantism. This 'older' racism was *never* 'overcome' or relinquished, however much it was struggled against.

POLICING BOUNDARIES

The spark in Chicago came on 23 July 1919, when a Black boy, Eugene Williams, accidentally drifted into what was informally understood to be the 'white' part of the water at the beach. The 17-year-old, like Charles Wootton in Liverpool, was stoned by whites and drowned. A white policeman refused to arrest the principal culprit, George Stauber, and prevented a Black policeman from doing so, as agitated Black beachgoers demanded justice. Violence spread throughout the city for two weeks, with over 500 serious injuries. Knives, pistols, rifles, even machine guns, were used. Twenty-three Black people and 15 whites lost their lives, among them 'a colored woman with a baby in her arms'.[43]

Chicago's Black population more than doubled between 1915 and 1919. Black settlement had overflowed its informally established boundaries. White tension around proximity was expressed in the policing of racial and gender boundaries. *The Crisis** and *The Messenger* reported several Black homes being bombed in the year leading up to the riots.[44] Walter White provided an analysis of the Chicago riots in *The Crisis*, detailing the press' role in constantly linking Black people to crime. He also explained that white gangs had committed regular acts of violence against Black people, including children. Ethnically divided white gangs policed neighbourhood lines against Black 'invasion' and were involved in escalating the violence. In these 'Athletic clubs', members drank and played baseball. Many were of Irish descent but also Anglo-, Italian-, Lithuanian- and Polish-Americans. Some clubs were recruitment vehicles for labour unions and Democratic politics, with similar cultural forms and outward personae as 'Proud Boy' type gangs active today. Real estate agents also responded to the movement of Black people into 'white areas' by marking prices down and refusing residence. Popular and state violence maintained the colour line, tying 'race' to place. Space was cleared and 'made white again' in keeping with modern forms of gentrification,

---

* *The Crisis* is the house journal of the NAACP. Its founding editor was W.E.B. Du Bois in 1910, a role he continued in until his resignation in 1934. By the time of the pogroms of 1919, which it covered in great depth, the influential monthly had a circulation of over 100,000.

which builds on this process through indirect market relations and racialised policing. Whiteness riots in Chicago were struggles for segregation from below.

Similar dynamics of voluntarist and state policing of 'race' and space featured in struggles over 'busing', and in recent murders of Black Americans. Post-Second World War, the US federal government subsidised the entry of a large portion of white working-class veterans and their families onto the private housing ladder, into new suburbs, into college and steady jobs. Protagonists of the post-war consumer boom, the American 'middle class' was born, differentiated and separated from a racialised subproletariat.[45] By the 1960s, powered by the Civil Rights Movement, 'busing' children over longer distances to racially integrate schools[46] was one attempt to overturn the de facto and de jure segregation in education that had always operated. It was often implemented off the back of court rulings but remained contested and controversial. 'Busing' hastened white flight and the establishment of new private schools for white kids. White self-activity by parents and children exploded. Protests reached into the thousands as boycotts were attempted. The reaction against busing in Congress was led by a young politician named Joe Biden.[47] In Boston, a bus safety monitor recalls taking Black children[48] to their new school in 1974:

> I remember riding the buses to protect the kids going up to South Boston High School. And the bricks through the window. Signs hanging out those buildings, 'Nigger Go Home'. Pictures of monkeys. The words. The spit. People just felt it was all right to attack children.[49]

The white nuclear family is as much an economic unit of social reproduction and consumption as a means of regulating legitimate/ illegitimate forms of free association amid instability and unrest. Violence from white parents and students led Boston's mayor to implement a curfew. Such whiteness rioting shares common roots with the pogroms clearing Black people from 'white' neighbourhoods in 1919. Levels of de facto racial segregation in education have since moved back towards 1960s levels, pushed back by a tide of 'colourblind' arguments against 'affirmative action'.[50]

The murder of Trayvon Martin in a Florida suburb became a key spark to the initial Movement for Black Lives. As Dianne Harris argues, 'Trayvon Martin died on February 26, 2012, because he was a black youth wearing a hooded sweatshirt in a gated community in a United States that remains characterized by high levels of racism and housing segregation.' Harris continues, 'the man who shot and killed him, George Zimmerman, decided that a 17-year-old black youth was literally and suspiciously out of place.'[51] Other recent murders have followed the same logic. Teenager Renisha McBride was shot dead on a porch by a white homeowner in 2013 when she sought help following an accident in a Detroit suburb.[52] Ahmaud Arbery was chased down and shot dead by white residents while jogging in a Georgia suburb in 2020. All these white shooters, like many before them, have explained the fear *they* felt, causing them to shoot unarmed Black victims. An ex-policeman and his son were not charged for Arbery's killing for over two months, until a video of it went viral. Prosecutors initially invoked Georgia's 'citizen's arrest' law, drafted in 1863 to justify white vigilante powers to capture fugitive slaves, as the basis for not charging Arbery's murderers.[53]

BLACK RESISTANCE

In his important counter-history of the Civil Rights Movement, *This Nonviolent Stuff'll Get You Killed,* Charles E. Cobb Jr. places great emphasis on Black men and women of the First World War generation moving straight into the Black freedom struggle at home.[54] According to Cobb Jr., the spirit of what came to be called the 'New Negro' was not a top–down phenomenon. A study of radical Black publications bears this out. There was a clear sense in 1919 that Black resistance was more present than it had been during previous attacks. Significantly, *The Messenger* broadened the scope of its analysis, pointing to an emerging *diaspora* of Black resistance. 'The new spirit animating Negroes is not confined to the United States, where it is most acutely manifested,' they claimed, 'but is simmering beneath the surface in every country where the race is oppressed.'[55] Some of this can be put down to Black men's war experiences, their training and access to firearms, and a new context which sanctioned their shooting and killing white men. The contradiction between representing the nation in battle, and experiencing different racial regimes in Europe, before returning home to state oppression and popular violence was being stretched to breaking point for African Americans, North and South. One editorial in *The Messenger* stated: 'everybody overseas was better to the Negro soldier than the white American ... the Negro returned with vengeance and hatred for the white American in his breast'.[56] Du Bois and the NAACP were considered too moderate by some younger Black writers and leaders, particularly because they, like most of the Black middle class, supported the war and advocated Black service. Du Bois did, however, unequivocally support armed self-defence.

> For three centuries we have suffered and cowered. No race ever gave Passive Resistance and Submissions to Evil longer, more piteous trial. Today we raise the terrible weapon of Self-Defense. When the murderer comes, he shall not longer strike us in the back. When the armed lynchers gather, we too must gather armed. When the mob moves, we propose to meet it with bricks and clubs and guns.[57]

Walter White was another key player in the NAACP. Due to his light skin, blonde hair and blue eyes he could often 'pass' as white, making him an effective field reporter at riot scenes, reporting back to the pages of *The Crisis*. He relayed from Chicago:

> the new spirit aroused in Negroes by their war experiences enters into the problem ... These men, with their new outlook on life, injected the same spirit of independence into their companions ... One of the greatest surprises to many of those who came down to 'clean out the niggers' is that these same 'niggers' fought back. Colored men saw their own being killed, heard of many more and believed that their lives and liberty were at stake. In such a spirit most of the fight was done.[58]

Among Du Bois' sterner Black critics were A. Philip Randolph and his comrade, Chandler Owen, editors of *The Messenger* – a Black socialist publication defining itself as 'the only radical negro magazine in America.* *The Messenger* was keen to challenge existing Black leaders, disdaining the accommodationism of Booker T. Washington, but also Du Bois' war stance and Marcus Garvey's 'back to Africa' movement. They sought instead to bring an improved consciousness of racism into socialist and trade union movements and to build alliances. During 'Red Summer', *The Messenger*'s August editorial urged: 'Negroes and other oppressed groups confronted with lynching and mob violence to act upon the recognized and accepted law of self-defense. Always regard your own life as more important than the life of the person about to take yours.' They celebrated the rise of 'the New Negro' who, according to them, had been 'in the front ranks of strikes' and 'taken his place in Socialist politics' as 'an integral part of nearly every great social movement'.[59] *The Messenger* invoked Claude McKay's talismanic verse in speaking about the 'New Negro': 'If they must die they are determined that they shall not travel through the valley of the shadow of death alone, but that some of their oppressors shall be their companions'.[60] The magazine set out its own solutions to the violence, including: mixed trade unions, worker's control, universal suffrage, equal pay, the abolition of segregation, new school curriculums, popular control of the media and, ultimately, revolution.[61]

Black armed self-defence was particularly prominent in DC and Chicago. *The Messenger* hailed the emergence of the 'New Negro' in DC, willing to fight back against *his* oppressors (though the figure was certainly gendered, the resistance was not).

Here in the nation's capital he has thrown down the gauntlet to his country. The gaping wounds of would-be lynchers in the city morgue and hospitals speak an eloquent warning that the time of timidity is gone … when policemen failed to protect the Negroes, the latter shot them down.[62]

Counter-attacks reversed the tide against white mobs. *Black groups shot at whites*, pulled whites at random off streetcars and assaulted them. A 17-year-old Black girl shot and killed a cop trying to enter

* Randolph later founded the Brotherhood of Sleeping Car Porters, one of the largest Black labour unions in US history. He had become a more conservative voice by the era of Civil Rights.

192

her home.[63] Federal troops had to quell the rioting, as businesses shut down across the city.[64]

In Chicago, eyewitness reports again illustrated armed Black self-defence:

> A colored woman is said to have stood on the corner of 35th Street and Wabash Avenue and to have incited colored boys to throw stones at the white passersby. Two colored women, Emma Jackson and Katie Elder have both been indicted for the murder of a white man named Harold Dragnatello.[65]

The witness continued: 'One colored man, incensed by their cowardly action [white cops shooting Black people indiscriminately], walked out into the street with an automatic and shot several of the white officers.' Adding, 'in the colored sections, policemen were seized and beaten.'[66] Veteran and communist, Harry Haywood, was in Chicago that summer and later wrote about it in his memoir, *Black Bolshevik*:

> The Black veterans set up their ambush at 35th and State, waiting in a car with the engine running. When the whites on the truck came through, they pulled in behind and opened up with a machine gun. The truck crashed into a telephone pole at 39th Street; most of the men in the truck had been shot down and the others fled. Among them were several Chicago police officers – 'off duty', of course![67]

Haywood channelled the change in consciousness many Black veterans were undergoing: 'I had been fighting the wrong war. The Germans weren't the enemy – the enemy was right here at home.'[68]

Liberal historical narratives of slavery as 'original sin' provide a limited portrait of Black agency within a wider musical score of American 'progress'. Haywood and others refused this assimilationist frame. There was never any formal coherence to Black liberation movements. Forms overlapped between cultural or constitutional nationalism, classical abolitionism, spiritual renewal and other radical impulses. The struggles of the 'New Negro' in 1919 were as multi-tendency as Black Power in 1969 and every other struggle against racism since. Positions and strategies changed as others failed. The conflict some socialists have today with historical retellings of 'Black agency' is that they can encourage redemptive, 'heroic' narratives as a substitute for complex, collective histories.[69] The transnational view of Black liberation problematises both socialist *and* liberal perspectives on history, often united by competing claims to a 'national history' skewed one way or the other. In 1919, the violence transcended the old Mason/Dixon line and Black resistance took different forms under different conditions.

INSIDE AGITATORS

While most 'Red Summer' riot-zones were in cities, there was also extreme violence in rural areas. Near the tiny town of Elaine, on 30 September–1 October, in Arkansas Delta cotton country, one of the most catastrophic massacres of Black people in US history took place. Here white violence was mobilised, more explicitly than elsewhere, against Black labour organising. Black farmers tried to challenge their exploitative landlords, in a county controlled entirely by whites growing rich off Black labour. All within living memory of the slave plantation. Unlike the urban riot sites, whites here were strongly outnumbered. Nearly 80 per cent of inhabitants were Black but 'all the political power [wa]s in the hands of the 4,000 white voters'.[70] Here, Black agency took the form of a local sharecroppers union aiming to raise the price farmers received for their cotton. The Progressive Farmers' Household Union was imbued with the post-war spirit of resistance and raised expectations. Its leading members were veterans.

White locals and newspapers saw only conspiracy – long rooted in the collective psyche of Southern white rule and the ever-present fear of slave rebellion. Rumour abounded that local Black people, led by the union, were out to 'kill whites' on an indiscriminate rampage. When rumour spread that outside a union meeting a policeman was shot dead, a mob was quickly mobilised. Whites flooded in from neighbouring counties – even across state lines from Tennessee and Mississippi. Ida B. Wells-Barnett later went to Arkansas to conduct an investigation. Her findings tell a very different story. That union meeting in the Black church at nearby Hoop Spur – filled with Black men, women and children – was fired upon at around 11pm. It was burned to the ground. Black people were gunned down throughout the area, women and children murdered at point blank range. While there's no conclusive death toll, more than 200 Black people were killed by mobs, police and soldiers.[71]

Of the 122 Black people indicted, 66 were tried and convicted. No whites were arrested. 'The trials averaged from five to ten minutes each; no witnesses for the defense were called; no Negroes were on the juries; no change of venue was asked,' *The Crisis* reported.[72] Many were scared by others' sentences or tortured into taking plea bargains and making false confessions, receiving lengthy prison terms. *The Argus* newspaper from nearby Brinkley reported that the riot was quelled by '500 soldiers', sent in from the state capital, Little Rock.[73] The troops, dispatched by direct order of the White House, arrested over a thousand Black people, holding them in squalor. Hundreds more were detained by police. Twelve Black men were sentenced to death, though campaigners eventually got the charges overturned in the Supreme Court. Wells-Barnett visited the defendants, publishing interviews in a 1920 pamphlet revealing how the accused were beaten and tortured to extract false confessions and denunciations of others. Ed Ware, secretary of the Progressive Farmers' Household Union, told her:

> about 11 o'clock that night, some automobiles were heard to stop north of the church and in just a few minutes they began shooting in the church and did kill some people in the church (which they set afire and burned them up in it the next morning). Then about 150 armed men came over to my place and before they got over there the news reached us stating that they were coming over there to kill me and all of the other Negroes that belonged to that union.[74]

John Martin was 'put in jail and whipped near to death and was put in an electric chair to make [him] lie on other Negroes'. He went on:

It was not the union that brought this trouble; it was our crops. They took everything I had, twenty-two acres of cotton, three acres of corn. All my hogs, chickens and everything my people had ... These white people know that they started this trouble.[75]

Black tenants had to purchase all supplies from landowners' commissaries at a massive mark-up, leaving them spiralling into debt. Landowners then drove them off the land. Crops done for the year, a poor one due to bad weather, meant many had their whole year's crop and livestock stolen by landowners. Some sharecroppers planned legal action against planters for money owed. Their white lawyers were targeted for encouraging 'social equality' – indicative of the atmosphere of anti-communism and widespread paranoia about 'outside agitators'.

Raising the spectre of 'social equality' was incredibly effective for mobilising racial violence in the South. In his totemic study, *Hammer and Hoe: Alabama Communists During The Great Depression*, Robin D.G. Kelley writes of a 'popular perception of Communists as "foreigners" and "nigger lovers" whose sole purpose was to wage a race war in the South'.[76] This was often bolstered by conspiracy theories about racialised 'Jews' being the hidden force behind Communism, manipulating Black people into action. As Kelley shows, Black farmers/workers were a large majority in Alabama's Communist Party in the early 1930s – becoming, for a time, powerful enough to shape its character and activity. White supremacist ideology could not countenance Black agency or intelligence. Pervasive anti-communist discourses were so racialised as to make interracial organising a constant uphill battle.[77] In *Black Reconstruction*, Du Bois connected white skin privilege to the failure to build worker solidarity across the colour line: 'so long as the Southern white laborers could be induced to prefer poverty to equality with the Negro, just so long was a labor movement in the South made impossible'.[78] He described the changing nature of white violence as chattel slavery was briefly and tenuously under 'reconstruction', before being 'redeemed' by white violence and moulded into Jim Crow's image. The value and function of Black labour shifted. Du Bois sums up, with characteristic clarity, the white mob's role in the new landscape: 'instead of driving the negroes to work, bands of poor whites began to drive them from work.'[79]

A committee of seven white men was established to determine the causes of the violence in Elaine.* They concluded that the share-croppers union had 'deliberately planned insurrection' against whites. The committee rehashed the old racist canard that union leaders used the 'ignorance and superstition of a race of children for monetary gains.'[80] The Governor of Arkansas vowed to suppress Black publications. The town sheriff, with the support of a white citizens committee, was clearly keen to return to business as usual. He addressed an extraordinary proclamation, on 7 October, 'TO THE NEGROES OF PHILLIPS COUNTY':

The trouble at Hoop Spur and Elaine has been settled. Soldiers now here to preserve order will return to Little Rock within a short time. No innocent negro has been arrested, and those of you who are at home and at work have no occasion to worry. All you have to do is remain at work just as if nothing had happened. Phillips County has always been a peaceful, law-abiding community, and normal conditions must be restored right away. STOP TALKING!

Stay at home – Go to work – Don't worry![81]

OUTSIDE AGITATORS?

Despite Northern and Southern racism both settling on causal narratives of radical white 'outside agitators', appearances of an organised white left in riot scene accounts are more likely as aggressors. As Foner tells us: 'The year 1919 was one of the most militant in United States labor history ... 3,630 strikes were called involving 4,160,000 workers.'[82] The left were themselves subject to mob violence in the fever pitch of militarism and 'Red Scare' nativism.[83] Surging labour militancy was often put down to radical immigrant 'outsiders' seeking to overthrow democracy. Accounts of interracial solidarity in the riot-zones would be welcome – but we have

* Two large planters, a cotton factory owner, a merchant, a banker, the sheriff of the county and the mayor of a nearby town.

struggled to find them. *The Messenger*, in particular, who explicitly sought greater interracial worker solidarity, did not source any examples in 1919.[84] By then, the IWW was critically wounded by state repression. The Socialist Party, wracked by division, would soon split, resulting in a new Communist Party. As for the AFL, proud 'Red Scare' collaborators and opposed to all things radical, 1919 was the year they first granted charters to police unions, some of whom went on strike.[85] Unionised cops, killing Black workers on the streets, received more material union solidarity than their victims.

In East St. Louis, the Black population nearly doubled from 1910 to 1917. New arrivals were seen by white workers, above all, as labour competition but *all* Black people were targeted in the pogrom. September 1917's issue of *The Crisis* directly blamed the violence on labour unions:

despite this pogrom, engineered by Gompers and his Trade Unions, the demand for Negro labor continues and will continue. Negro labour continues to come North and ought to come North. It will find work at higher wages than the slave South ever paid and ever will pay, and, despite the Trade Unions and the murderers whom they cover and defend, economic freedom for the American Negro is written in the stars. East St. Louis, Chester and Youngstown are simply the pools of blood through which we must march, but march we will.[86]

That issue published a letter by Edward Mason, secretary of the Central Trades and Labor Union, and sent out to union delegates. It bolsters their claim that union leaders and members helped bring about the violence. Mason wrote: 'The immigration of the Southern Negro into our city for the past eight months has reached the point where drastic action must be taken if we intend to work and live peaceably in this community.' This 'influx of undesirable Negroes,' he claimed, was 'being used to the detriment of our white citizens by some of the capitalists and ... real estate owners.' Mason rallied his members to 'call upon the Mayor and City Council and demand that they take some action to retard this growing menace and also devise a way to get rid of a certain portion of those who are already here'.[87] White workers and unions bemoaned 'black scabs' to justify their opposition to Black migration and their calls for the state to halt it but made no effort to organise with Black workers – they 'did not include blacks in their union'.[88] As was so often the case, whites blamed Black workers for being strikebreakers while helping to maintain a status quo in which 'scabbing' was the only work they could get. East St. Louis unions had

won the support of the unorganized white unskilled workers by spreading the rumour that local manufacturers planned to bring in 10,000 to 15,000 more black laborers as part of an elaborate scheme to make East St. Louis a Negro town.[89]

Reminiscent of anti-Chinese movements of California 'workingmen', the city were warned by unions that 'if no official action was taken against the blacks, "violence" would be used to accomplish the objective'.[90] In Chicago, attempts at biracial unionism in meatpacking foundered due to white worker racism and manipulation by employers, and some Black community leaders in their pockets.[91] While it cannot be said that white unions led Chicago's whiteness riots, a charge laid at their door at the time, more than half the violence 'had taken place in the stockyards district'.[92]

Chicago congregated varied forms of reaction and Black workers were caught in a multipolar vice. White supremacist clubs and gangs, real estate magnates, white labour unions, Black businessmen and church leaders of different stripes, police and bosses, mayors and gangsters, shaped intuitional cross-class alliances that were bedded into the regional infrastructure for years to come. Harry Haywood, who took up his gun in self-defence against the white rioters, critiqued all these elements. It was the Bolsheviks and the IWW, who most perked Haywood's revolutionary interest. Black communists like Haywood were testing the waters, from sharecroppers to packers to autoworkers. Ideas formulating around working-class Black self-determination would later develop into some of the most radical working class organising efforts like the League of Revolutionary Black Workers, and the Dodge Revolutionary Union Movement (DRUM), which drew its charge from the Black insurrection of 1967.[93] Detroit's Black industrial proletariat were at the cutting edge of capital's latest automation and deskilling drives and faced the continued marshalling of racist white labour unions. Haywood took his fight there, 40 years after the whiteness riots, 20 years after fighting Franco and 10 years after he was expelled by the Communist Party. Read through Haywood's memoir and it is difficult not to look at the latest polemics being pumped out of mainstream US socialist platforms – 'woke!', 'identity politics!', 'PMC!' – and be struck with bewilderment. Histories of segregation in labour movements reflect badly on those impresarios of the political left who have devoted exhaustive time and energy into decrying the 'Identitarian Left' for indulging in marginality.

NO FUTURE, NO WAY PAST

In this history, one is continually confronted by generational throughlines. In most US metropolises, you can find dynastic local elites with years of accumulated interests in power-brokering arrangements. Richard J. Daley was 17 in 1919. He belonged to the 'Hamburg Athletic Club' on Chicago's South Side who were active in the riots, though his personal involvement is unclear.[94] These clubs offered routes into local Democratic Party politics. Forty years later, Daley was Mayor.* Responding to the uprising after the murder of Martin Luther King Jr. in 1968, Daley told a press conference he had ordered police 'to shoot to kill any arsonist or anyone with a Molotov cocktail in his hand, because they're potential murderers, and to shoot to maim or cripple anyone looting.'[95] Social forms and discourses that developed through colonialism and nationalism have become reconstituted in new ways, but in a more straightforward way, some people just wield amassed power and wealth, which can be traced back through centuries of white supremacy, or more recent 'nouveau riche' arrangements. The Daley family has several members still marshalling significant political power right up to today. Bobby Vanecko, Daley's great-

* Daley dominated Chicago's Democratic political machine for decades. His son, Richard M. Daley, later had his own long stint as mayor.

nephew, wrote a 'Letter to my cousins' in the *Southside Weekly*, in 2020, illuminating this throughline:

> Many people in our family are still committed to white suprem-
> acy today, even if they are not racist interpersonally, because
> they support racist politics and policies like mass criminaliza-
> tion, privatization, and austerity ... these policies are responsible
> for the thirty-year life expectancy gap between white and Black
> Chicago neighborhoods, and a nine-year racial gap in life expec-
> tancy on average.
>
> At this historic moment, instead of using his power to stand
> with Black Chicagoans by working to enact the transforma-
> tive change that our city needs, our parents' cousin, Patrick D.
> Thompson – the current alderman of Chicago's 11th Ward – has
> been blaming 'outside antagonists and criminals' for looting and
> instead 'standing with' police officers 'everyday'.
>
> That is because he, like almost everyone else in our family,
> idolizes our great-grandfather Richard J. Daley, who was the
> horribly racist mayor of Chicago from 1955 to 1976 ... roughly
> around the time he was mayor, 'Chicago's Black population grew
> from about 8.2 percent to 32.7 percent. At the same time, from
> 1945 to 1970, the city's police budget grew 900 percent and the
> CPD doubled the number of cops on the streets.' These police
> killed, tortured, brutalized, arrested and incarcerated Black Chi-
> cagoans without cause and with impunity throughout these
> years ... When Black and brown Chicagoans protested police
> brutality, segregation, and racial inequality, he denied that there
> was any problem, instead always emphasizing 'law and order',
> much like the current mayor and both candidates for president
> in 2020.[96]

Vanecko brings helpful context to the kind of 'family loyalties' organising white supremacy. These oligarchal-type arrangements of capital are part of the current conjuncture and problematise one-sided reasoning and theories of causation. Left populist mes-saging against 'elites' and liberal fetishisation of GOP baddies has failed to get into the grain of the problem of 'elites', especially the localised communitarianism of power-brokers. There are generational throughlines for elites and also generational memories of resistance. More diverse features and power imbalances locally are becoming obvious, and require the knowledge of 'folk' or 'community' politics derided as symptomatic of neoliberalism in recent years.[97] Indeed, some of the most striking successes in union organising, such as the first Amazon Union, succeeded because of the empathetic reasoning of reps, building knowledge between friendship groups, not the kind of aggressive pitching we get from left media outlets.[98] That's not a new thing. Nobody starts a conversation about workplace or housing issues or any other class issues by hurling epithets.

Such arguments typically turn on calls for the 'unities' of unspecified pasts, contrasted against today's betrayals of class universalism. If only it was this simple. There has to be left open the hypothesis that capitalism is one long movement *and* one long standing still. We are not moving towards anything in particular, not revolutionary redemption, nor any *universal* catastrophe. Identity is subject to historical change and circumstances. It is not the product of an 'age' of capitalism or a susceptible generation. There have been no great 'breaks' in the differentiated forms of state power we live under or the forms of capital this power mediates. Even where there have been great shifts in the mediation of these forms – historically, legally, technologically – there's also great potential for corrections. How we make connections between 'then and now' becomes increasingly important as echoes from the past shape new discourses and organisational forms. There are formal features to today's barbarism that repeat in uncanny ways. Adorno's analogy of the 'self-righting toy' is one way of approaching this problem of repetition. 'Philosophical questions,' he wrote, 'are always a bit like those self-righting toys, seeming to be knocked over but reappearing in changed historical-philosophical constellations, demanding an answer.'[99] Our emphasis on 'archaic forms' of racism is an attempt to move away from the polarisation of 'stages' to try to grasp the historical rupture Ferguson produced. That social relations have not qualitatively progressed is why brutal solutions are found again and progressive causes are rolled back. The most archaic racial/sexual violence reappears within new historical constellations and technological assemblages because the same problems persist. Capitalism redevelops barbaric forms; it does not do away with them. Contemporary global capitalism has demonstrated a capacity to formally subsume and unify archaic, barbaric, modern and liberal forms of exploitation and oppression (coerced imprisonment, new forms of slavery, super-exploitation, indentured labour, 'free labour', high income forms of commercial and clerical labour) and relate them all back to the unitary logic of valorisation.

BLM exploded by mounting a challenge to blatant, deadly, harrowingly arbitrary racism. Localised open revolt kicked off a movement wave. Every night, night after night, people refused to just 'Stay at Home!' Every time, reactions followed, hoping to temper its significance, to encourage ways of forgetting, through incorporation or ridicule. Liberals relate positively to protests (while condemning riots), offering solutions to fix Bad Cops: unconscious bias training, body cameras, social mobility platitudes. Conservatives saw BLM as part of a wider complex of 'identity politics', a 'liberal' diversity agenda. Some socialists barely varied this critique, except to ensure everyone knew BLM was 'liberal', not socialist.[100] Activists have tried to explain why the killings never stop, looking to longer histories.[101] People have been motivated to know more about colonialism and how it relates to the places they call home. Others stop short of systemic critiques, tending toward assimilationist and individual approaches. Many have just tried to learn why this was happening, some becoming radicalised in 'Revolutionary Time'. Imagery of celebrity 'black squares' on Instagram were used to undermine 'BLM' as a PR exercise. Parts of the mainstream and the far right converge in agreement that BLM is a top-down, command and control 'Marxist' organisation. Constant chit-chat floods the airwaves. Feedback loops create trivialisation effects, heading off attempts to preserve the historical significance of events. Some socialists reduce it all to critiques of 'commodification' or 'sell outs!' On the right, a purer conspiracism links everything together. Slogans like 'stay woke' – mainstreamed by Ferguson and Baltimore, initially faithful to how Lead Belly used it – eventually get worn out, appropriated relativistically.

Conclusion

The past is never dead. It's not even past.[1]

William Faulkner

In each chapter, we have traced how 'universals' and 'particulars' are contested. The state oversees shifts in 'identity' in order to manage the conceptual collapse it promulgates. Reifications of human experience, rights and labour, are transformed into arte-facts of 'equality', abstracted from the kinds of equality formed through 'Revolutionary Time'. The defamation of equality under capitalism is so complete it is impossible to recognise the richness of human 'inequalities' – madnesses, capacities, talents, passions, peculiar interests and needs – without them becoming re-calcified into taxonomies of abstract difference: racialised, gendered, disabled, degraded. Saidiya Hartman addresses the ambivalence of 'universals', both as correctives to violence *and* innovations of it:

> it is necessary to consider whether the effort of the dominated to 'take up' the universal does not remedy one set of injuries only to inflict injuries of another order. It is worth examining whether universalism merely dissimulates the stigmatic injuries constitutive of blackness with abstract assertions of equality, sovereignty, and individuality. Indeed, if this is the case, can the dominated be liberated by universalist assertions?[2]

Hartman's critique of 'abstract equality' was addressed in a different key by Marx in his critical exposition of the capitalist–worker relationship: 'there is here therefore an antinomy, of right against right, both equally bearing the seal of the law of exchange. Between equal rights, force decides.'[3] In the nineteenth century, universality emerged as a banner for legitimised slaughter. It contributed a transhistorical framework for theorising the 'races' and 'sexes', grounding a eugenicist political science. The most potent experiments in radical universality were expressive of fascinating, irregular temporalities, fragile and inconsistent alliances between strangers: workers, slaves, radicals.

Roediger's use of the 'Revolutionary Time' concept names this uncertain state of affairs and we have returned to it again and again to parse the strange, contradictory quality of uprisings and upheavals. The 'General Strike of the Slaves' opened a brief window, a possibility for a 'second American Revolution'. A counter-attack against the rule of private property became thinkable. Various campaigners responded to this energy by contributing their own. For a time, concrete steps towards 'equality' could be discussed as a revolutionary break with the world as it was. The uprisings of millions of enslaved people transcended the original aims of Abolitionism and makes a mockery of contemporary assertions that states like Britain and the USA played progressive roles in it. Even the most militant abolitionists could not have predicted this rupture. It was unimaginable. The unimaginable revolutionary moment is a crucial determination on historical writing, and on the revolutionary imagination. Walter Benjamin referred to revolution as the 'messianic zero-hour [*Stillstellung*] of events ... a revolutionary chance in the struggle for the suppressed past'.[4] 'Revolutionary Time' names this rupture. An exceptional temporality where a disregarded *non-conceptual* world generates a force able to overwhelm the barbarism of general law.

The risk of elevating the non-conceptual character of moments of rupture is that it can mystify or romanticise the historical content. Yet, the concept can also provide a paradox that preserves the quality of the non-conceptual rather than valorise the concept itself. 'Revolutionary Time' was a conscious framework for this book. But the histories we explore refused general frameworks and challenged our own assumptions. It is only by ending the book that we can make sense of theories of 'Revolutionary Time' as invitations to assess the historical quality of a rupture. Each chapter is an exploration of such disordered moments – upsurge, reaction, aftermath, theorisation – within a matrix of circumstances we have tried to trace. Some chapters are weighted to upsurge, some to theory, some to historical detail, some to reaction and aftermath. The project shifted from being a massive history book, packed with detail, to a bridging document. The remnants of this transition are present throughout. To the best of our abilities we have tried to create a bridge between historians and theorists who have worked with artefacts of 'Revolutionary Time' and discourses against identity politics that are fundamentally ahistorical in outlook.

The major lesson is the unpredictability of upsurges and the predictability of reaction. Solidarities can expand in defiance of pre-existing conditions and law, while claims to universality seem to break apart the moment all the pieces are legally constituted. In the midst of an upsurge, the reaction is already there but dis-oriented. The belief that there was 'already' a universal basis to human beings and class relationships, which was natural and latent, waiting to be named and profiled even more rigorously and scientifically than before, dominated the nineteenth-century ascendancy of nations, baked into its revolutionary currents. The backlash against 'Revolutionary Time' during Reconstruction reconstituted the conceptual world via legal and extralegal – that is, *normative* – violence. Constitutional Amendments universal-ised 'women', 'men' and 'whites' and 'blacks', through the discourse of rights and the formality of contract. The non-conceptual time of revolution was recast in the modular reformism of constitutional struggles. White middle-class women continued to universalise 'womanhood' as white. Workers were workers only when white and male. The 'white' universal dominated by differentiating the majority of the world it alienated. The power of a common uni-versal interest was preserved where people refused to submit to this bad version of it. Identity marks the leftover world of these struggles and those that followed, right up to our own. When these wounds are continually reopened, the reaction is palpable. Toni Morrison argued that it takes extreme collective effort to *actively forget how this world came to be*: 'certain absences are so stressed, so ornate, so planned, they call attention to themselves; arrest us with intentionality and purpose, like neighborhoods that are defined by the population held away from them'.[5] Whereas revolutionary universality is constantly recreated and struggled over, reaction-ary universalities reassert the conservative tautology: 'it is as it has always been' and clamour round this oath like a timeless article of faith. This can explain why memories of colonialism are received by so many as unwelcome guests. These spectral visitors seem to unlawfully drag themselves up from watery time, and there they sit, with a new generation of strangers, waiting for their own time to explode.

CONSPIRACIES OF 'GENDER IDEOLOGY'

If we view identity as the artefact of state identification regimes then 'reactions' to identity are not purely a matter of conservative manufacture or limited to personal displays of disgust. The hatred of identity politics can just as well be a reaction to images of capital and corporate power or mediated through displays of reason. Desire for order can come from all political traditions. Contemporary transphobia features activist philosophers, stay-at-home mums and right-wing shockjocks. These vectors of reaction are not the same. They find each other through demands on the state to regulate the threat they perceive. 'Pronouns' and anti-racist demands are treated by the media as undemocratic impositions from above.

The spectacle of the 'heretic' gender critical philosopher lining up with the state to rescue liberal democracy from corruption perhaps displays something unique to how 'identity politics' conspiracies have escalated in Britain. There's an evangelical temper to British liberalism that is especially hateful of challenges to measured debate. Struggles over concepts and historical narratives particularly agitate journalists, writers, philosophers and politicians. These circles share a belief in empirical reasoning that extends to the rule of law just as defences of the professions acts as signifiers of a free society. Anti-colonial tendencies are despised as they bring the belief in British reason into disrepute. Darcus Howe told a court in 1971, representing himself as one of the 'Mangrove Nine', that they'd captured 'a small area of a historical moment' by exposing the state prosecution case as a racist conspiracy, given legitimation through the aura of legal theatre.[6] Remembering the colonial is remembering *the violence of the reasonable*. Whenever colonial history enters public debate, received conceptions of race and sex are at risk of historicisation, as are other immediacies of class society. Leaving interpreters of the moral standard furious, and hateful. The demand for historicisation jars with the laboratories of faux empiricism, while that gentler flow and syntax of the columnist, writing the world as they see it, stutters and stumbles, as impressionistic prejudices are turned over and illuminated for what they are. No reflection on the colonial form of liberal concepts of 'sex' enters into 'gender critical' defences of it and conceptions of 'race' must be relativised to maintain this stance. Concepts are refused historicisation and this refusal is reinscribed, philosophically, as what is essential to them.

THE PAST IS NOT EVEN PAST

Writing this book, beginning around 2017, with the fundamentals of a critique of 'anti-identity politics', we have been able to map a conspiratorial turn. Robin D.G. Kelley in the 1990s noted how 'identity politics' was being blamed for division within the left. Wendell E. Pritchett in the 2000s tracked the development of the myth: ' "Identity politics", as the term is currently employed, does not provide a useful framework for understanding the recent past.' Rather, it 'is a straw man concocted by writers dissatisfied with the path of modern politics, particularly the path of the left during the second half of the twentieth century ... [and is] so vaguely defined as to be meaningless'.[7] Pritchett goes on:

> critics of what they call identity politics have had to overemphasize some aspects of the recent history of social movements while ignoring others. They have under-emphasized the complicated interaction between class and other types of identity in the years before the rise of the 1960s, overemphasized the 'break' that happened towards the end of that decade, and ignored the significant class aspects of many modern social movements.[8]

Pritchett notes how 'critics of identity attempt to create a causal connection between its "rise" and the "fall" of class politics, but this relationship is tenuous at best', underlining that we 'should not rely on simplistic understandings of a complicated past'.[9] Renato Rosaldo writes, critics maintain that identity politics is monolithic and divisive, whether it divides the working class, social movements or the nation-state. Their argument is tinged with nostalgia for the 1950s when, they think, there was a national unity that now has been balkanized by the new social movements of women, homosexuals, and people of color. I would reply that the unity of the 1950s, such as it was, was based on the exclusion of people of color, women, and homosexuals. In the latter case, it is not that there were no homosexuals at the time, but rather that homosexuality was not tolerated as a public identity. What unity are these critics talking about? Was there once upon a time unity in progressive political movements? Movements of the Left have been noted for their sectarian conflicts and are a strange case to invoke as an exemplar of unity. The critics often oppose identity politics in the name of the common good. The rhetoric of the common good, however, fails to ask who has the authority to choose and name the common good.[10]

These are some of the messy, complex pasts we have tried to interrogate. The stress of state identification regimes have the effect of abstracting class antagonisms as social antagonisms. The stories of Black and Asian reserve armies of 'free' labour integrating into the industrial centres of the USA and Britain from the late nineteenth century onwards, demonstrate how the racism of segregation and social control, popular and state violence, enforce differentiation distinctly in each case. The workers movement is shamed and weakened by a history littered with opposition to 'minorities' and 'identity groups', oppositions given the advantage of 'common sense' because their nationalised identities were made through the differentiation of others. When workers ostracised from unions – racialised, made alien, gendered as women, as domestics – challenged the basis of this universality, universality became concrete and bridgeable. British and US labour movements were, in fact, particular expressions of a more visible *minority* of workers, within a world of workers and non-workers, whose struggles have been relentlessly differentiated, if not unrecognised. Then, as now, the majority of the workers of the world are not recognised as workers.

And as Cedric Robinson argued, the defeats or capitulations of more recognised workers are costly not only to themselves:

By the beginnings of the twentieth century, the vision of the destruction of bourgeois society entertained by Western socialists had been shown to be of only partial relevance. The working classes of Europe and America had indeed mounted militant assaults on their ruling class. But in defeat they had also displayed their vulnerabilities to bourgeois nationalism and racialist sentiment.[11]

It is a powerful irony that when a subset of workers were particularised by 'race', like Britain's 'alien' Jews, they could recognise the possibility of a universal class struggle through their very *dissociation as workers*. They struggled against stereotypes that Jews were incapable of union discipline, assumed to be scabs and sneaks. It was partly through such allusions to 'cultural difference' that Jewish workers were racially differentiated. This history shows that conspiracies of 'Jewish control' were deep-rooted among British socialists and workers, not only the Churchills and Balfours with their hands at the tiller of imperial power. Conspiracies about Chinese workers in California were similar, accused of undercutting 'workingmen' but also of being used by Chinese capitalists to undermine an American sovereignty workingmen so proudly identified with. They only saw unity as possible when attempted through bonds of nation, whiteness and patriarchy. Chinese workers were, as Saxton made clear, the 'Indispensable Enemy' – indispensable as a temporary solution to the problem of composition.

The 1919 'whiteness riots' displayed the peculiar and murderous racial animus of white supremacy. In each country, a similar construction of Blackness as both ontological threat and social control conundrum preceded the violence. Each regime benefited from racialised reserve armies of labour, though how they were produced, and maintained as foreign, was over-determined by histories of white supremacy and colonial conquest particular to the evolving jurisdictions of 'Britain' and 'America'. Rigid formulations of the capital–labour relation are inadequate in accounting for this history, and for the present. Due agency must be given to the racism (and occasional anti-racism) of white workers, not only to the power of capital and state in moulding relations and terrains. State violence *and* popular racism have been the sorting techniques of history, helping to shape the representational schema of the nation: who is deserving and undeserving of its protection? Who can do which of its jobs? Who can live where? Who can marry, or touch, its daughters? These histories of violence have crystal clear resonances for us today. They show whiteness – not merely racism carried out by whites – for what it is: a culturally empty, oppositional identity that exists solely to perpetuate colonial histories of ruling class dominance. Whiteness cannot be placated, or made 'progressive'. It must be abolished through collective action. The thread of continuity through the howl of 'Britain for the British' at British Brothers League marches in 1900, the 'Back Britain, Not Black Britain' of Enoch Powell's trade unionist supporters in 1968 and the 'Take Back Control' of Brexit Britain is clear enough. As is the congruence between 'the Chinese Must Go' and calls to 'Build the Wall' to 'Make America Great Again'.

Racism continues to be indexed to national borders and racial divisions of labour. The kinds of cross-class, 'anti-establishment' alliances that first brought about immigration controls still reproduce them today. The only coherent, principled anti-racist position is the total rejection of border imperialism. This might seem impossibly unrealistic but that makes it no less true. Social movements do not all begin at the same starting blocks. There is no blank slate from which 'success' is equally easy for all, where garnering press attention or attracting numbers to demos are neutral barometers on which to compare and compete. It is far easier to build coalitions if your movement does not challenge basic categories imposed by society. It is easier to make headway if your party does not challenge the role of the police. Are the small, little-known movements, organising for decades, to decriminalise sex work or end immigration detention and deaths in custody, to be deemed failures in this zero-sum game of massification?

BLACK FEMINIST DIALOGUES

In *Undoing Border Imperialism*, Harsha Walia details how her organising network works through problems of identity:

> Instead of an anti-oppression practice that keeps us separated from each other based on our identities, we need to come together to address oppression with the purpose of working through and transcending the systemic barriers and borders that capitalism, colonialism and oppression have thrown between us to keep us from each other.[12]

Walia includes a critique of versions of intersectionality that she feels can overly essentialise or individualise, be too competitive and comparative, and lose sight of the relationality and historical contexts of oppression, rooted in questions of power and the specificities of capitalist social relations. While also rejecting 'pejorative and reactionary phrases such as identity politics or oppression olympics' as they 'ignore the materiality of oppressive hierarchies'.[13]

Members of the Combahee River Collective and the women who wrote *The Heart of the Race* have since looked back over their political lives and political work, and their roles in the development of identity politics. Barbara Smith notes:

> we came up with the term 'identity politics'. I never really saw it anywhere else and I would suggest that people if they really want to find the origin of the term, that they try to find it in any place earlier than in the Combahee River Collective statement.[14]

Smith expands on how they used it: 'What we meant by "identity politics" was a politics that grew out of our objective material experiences as Black women. This was the kind of politics that had never been ... practiced before, to our knowledge.' She reveals that their findings about Black women in US history showed them they were part of a longer tradition. 'We began to find out that there were Black feminists in the early part of this century, and also, perhaps, in the latter part of the nineteenth century.' Their updates to the work of Black feminists who came before them included 'talking about homophobia and lesbian identity',[15] allied to a more developed critique of capitalism. Smith addresses the pejorative registers later used to talk about identity politics:

> There were basically politics that worked for us. There were politics that took everything into account as opposed to saying, 'Leave your feminism, your gender, your sexual orientation – you leave that outside. You can be Black in here, but you can't be a lesbian, you can't be a feminist; or, you can be a feminist in here, but you can't be Black. That's really what we meant. We meant politics that came out of the various identities that we had that really worked for us. It gave us a way to move, a way to make change.[16]

Smith strikes an almost apologetic note, saying: 'It was not the reductive version that theorists now really criticize. It was not being simplistic in saying I am Black and you are not. That wasn't what we were doing.'[17] In Britain, Black feminism has gained more prominence in the movements and debates of students and campaigners in the last decade. The explosion of social media and BLM upsurges have brought Black feminist ideas to wider consciousness. Presumably with this in mind, a new edition of *The Heart of the Race* was published in 2018. A conversation with the authors, over 30 years on from the book's original publication, appeared as an afterword. Productive tensions emerged as Stella Dadzie, Beverly Bryan and Suzanne Scafe opened up about the movements that formed them and the basis for their book. They also spoke about identity politics, what the term meant to them and what it has come to mean since.

Stella Dadzie, early on, is critical of contemporary movements: 'nowadays it's more about identity politics, isn't it? All about "me, myself and I".'[18] Beverly Bryan, in contrast, does not 'want to be pejorative about identity politics.'[19] Dadzie laments a lack of class struggle in later anti-racist movements – always at the heart of anti-racist struggle in Britain from the 1950s–1980s. 'That "triple burden" was always at the root of our experience for me,' explains Dadzie.

But class was the bedrock of it all. These days, when people talk about identity politics and what's happened to black women in the last thirty years, the issue of class seems to have dropped down the hierarchy of oppressions.[20]

'I think identity politics is a misnomer,' Suzanne Scafe responds.

I remember when I first started teaching, the white faculty would talk a lot about identity politics and I would find myself correcting them and saying, 'what we're talking about here is actually the politics of identity'. For me, that distinction is crucial, because that is about how you are situated in terms of class, culture, gender and sexuality and so on; it's about your position in society. Whereas identity politics is a way of suggesting that your politics are based only on a very narrow definition of identity.[21]

Dadzie refers back to the text:

if you think about the areas we looked at in *The Heart of the Race*, whether it's employment, education, health, or simply the way the state deals with us in terms of housing and policing, little has changed. What *has* changed is you've got more visibility at the other end of the spectrum, more black women who are deemed to have made it. It's as if people have lost sight of the class struggle. Yet if you look at women who are at the bottom of society, they're still there, they're still predominantly black, they're still dispossessed and they're still on state benefits or struggling to hold down three jobs, coping with the same old issues.[22]

Bryan adds:

I think there *has* been change even if the mechanisms are still the same. People are still oppressed in those same ways, related to race, sex and class and it is not necessarily Caribbean women who are cleaning those offices, but the mechanisms to keep a certain set of vulnerable non-unionised workers trapped in those jobs still exist.[23]

Dadzie mentions the alliances formed during a time of 'political blackness', solidarities built between feminists of Afro-Caribbean, African, Asian and African-Asian descent and also with men of colour. 'In those days, we were looking at African-Asian unity because we saw the parallels. We also worked closely with men when the need arose.' She notes that while some contexts have changed, such coalitions are still sorely needed. 'Nowadays we might find different connectivities with different groups, but that principle of uniting with people who share a common oppression, trying to work with our commonalities rather than our differences – that remains true.'[24] Dadzie comes back to identity politics, suggesting a focus on collective issues and objective conditions is most important when addressing different approaches.

Isn't the answer that we have to ground our politics in real issues? You [Suzanne] were talking about identity politics earlier, and what you said helped me to clarify my thinking because I hadn't thought about the 'politics of identity'. I suppose what I was trying to say is that if your politics start with 'me, myself and I' and you're looking for issues because you relate to them, rather than relating to issues because they affect all of us and need addressing, then you could end up with a skewed view of politics.[25]

Bryan follows: 'you can't maintain linkages or connections just on the basis of the personal; there have to be other material ways in which you work – not just to be, but to do'.[26]

STUBBORN STRUGGLE

The CRC manifesto and *The Heart of the Race* continue to provide lessons for movements. If the working class is internally divided, so too will be its movements – movements which will include both working and middle-class strata. The basic lesson of identity politics for the CRC was: *there is no mythical unity*. Disunity must be acknowledged and understood, to be collectively addressed. This process can be accelerated through struggle and coalition, particularly during periods of 'Revolutionary Time'. The most useful way of understanding the continuing salience of raced, gendered, cis/heteronormative oppressions is not as opposable, flattened, commensurable 'identities' but as *constructed* and *constructing* relations that develop through the constantly revolutionising relations of capitalist re/production. Any study of how race and gender operate must engage with material histories of raced and gendered class composition and class struggle, through the matrix of colonialism that has formed today's world. Engaging with the variegated nature of working class composition is *never* advanced by partaking in the highly developed, politically plural whisper game that blames 'identity politics' for the difficulties posed by the composition problem.

In attempting to mount an exposition of politically diverse thinking and discourses around identity politics, and its supposed manifold plagues on democracy, nation or class struggle, we have not denied that the working class is divided. Nor do we deny that there's liberal and reactionary politics constructed around racialised, gendered or sexual identities, which sometimes cynically make use of the language of social justice. The premise we work from is that the working class – employed, unemployed, underemployed, surplus, unpaid reproductive workers – has *always been divided*. Race and gender are not 'cultural' identities separate from class but integrated, constitutive and inseparable aspects of the complex processes of class formation that are made, unmade and remade throughout the history of capitalism. Identity is expressive of past and present class antagonisms – regulated, maintained and punished by state power. This approach lets us examine the composition problem in more detail and with specificity. Reduced to 'culture', 'identity' becomes personalised rather than being an expression of class composition and the outcomes of struggle. We reject the reduction of identity to 'culture'. The culture is white supremacy. The economic coercion of subjects as bearers of capital or labour-power is impossible without the forms of identity and non-identity the colonial project produced.

No project of working-class unity, built around a particular organisational form, Leninist vanguard, nor any quests for breakthrough revolutionary subjects or single perspectives across divisions and borders, has any obvious path. Beginning with the richness of class composition, rather than the whereabouts of the working class, its division or betrayal, is a better methodology to embolden future solidarities. There is a fundamental need to recognise asymmetries – social movements must take on and ultimately dismantle whiteness, borders, patriarchy and heteronormativity, bundled relations of exploitation and oppression that harm and kill some more than others, on a planet being destroyed by capitalism. Prioritising solidarity for those most marginalised or under attack is not about guilt or charity or 'virtue-signalling'. It is part of what can get everyone free. We have seen how solidarities can form through struggle in recent years, like the committed efforts to build links between people involved in BLM and Palestinians struggling against colonialism.[27] In our chapters, we have tried to show instances of solidarity along the way, not just to give ourselves cheer, though we need it, but because solidarity is a practice, and the knowledge of history and the development of theory are part of any movement's toolkit to build on this practice. Such moments are happening all the time. The students and neighbours who rise up to resist deportations.[28] Occupations at arms manufacturers to struggle against colonialism taking place far away.[29] There is hope in the stubbornly diasporic, the everyday disobedience, the syncretism of urban culture, the mundane comfort many feel with lived multiculture, queer life and gender nonconformity. Even if this comfort has not always translated into active solidarity and political expression.

There are movements organising right now against borders and prisons, supporting each other, fighting to defend remaining welfare provision and pushing to demand more. Workplace struggles in the colonial heartlands are making inroads in hostile conditions. The measure of a new society will depend on challenging racial and gendered divisions of labour, but also a working-class 'community' model that does not depend on the family for social reproduction, and state policing to secure it. These are key sites of struggle, for communities of care and for the means of reproduction in a social context of widespread and differentiated crises of precarity and social isolation punctuated by bursts of 'Revolutionary Time'. In 2017, the movement lost one of its best, most dangerously under-read thinkers and writers in Ambalavaner Sivanandan. To honour his passing and the important legacies he left behind we can only end by quoting his blueprint for grassroots organising. As relevant today as it has ever been:

> Making an individual/local case into an issue, turning issues into causes and causes into movements and building in the process a new political culture, new communities of resistance that will take on power and Capital and class.[30]

Notes

All website and social media citations last accessed Tuesday 15 March 2022.

INTRODUCTION

1. Vron Ware, *Beyond the Pale: White Women, Racism and History* (London: Verso, 2015), 241.
2. Ber Borochov, *Class Struggle and the Jewish Nation: Selected Essays in Marxist Zionism* (New Brunswick, NJ: Transaction Books, 1984), 195.
3. BBC debating shows helped to mainstream Jordan B. Peterson in Britain, 'Jordan Peterson on the "backlash against masculinity"', *BBC News, Hardtalk* with Stephen Sackur, 7 August 2018, YouTube, https://tinyurl.com/ympcb2sr.
4. *FOX News* commentator Mark R. Levin wrote a rambling bestseller linking Marxist ideology to 'German-born Hegelian-Marxist' members of the 'Franklyn School' [sic], with Marcuse and Adorno singled out as ringleaders: Mark R. Levin, *American Marxism* (New York: Threshold Editions, 2021).
5. Glenn Greenwald, 'Contempt for it on the merits aside ...', Twitter, @ggreenwald, 20 August 2020, https://tinyurl.com/bdfhhpf4.
6. There's a long pattern of African-American vernacular and political concepts originating from Black struggle or culture – 'cancelling', 'intersectionality', 'identity politics' – being appropriated by mainstream/white 'culture', their meanings bastardised. One of the earliest written uses of 'woke' was in a 1962 *New York Times* piece by the Black novelist William Melvin Kelley. In 'If You're Woke, You Dig It', Kelley references the appropriation of Black slang by young whites and its passage into the mainstream. He notes the tendency for Black originators to stop using words as soon as whites adopt them, in an ongoing cycle of appropriation:

   > To many of these people, the words and phrases borrowed from them by beatniks or other white Americans are hopelessly out of date. By the time these terms get into the mainstream, new ones have already appeared ... A few Negroes guard the idiom so fervently they will consciously invent a new term as soon as they hear the existing one coming from a white's lips.

   William Melvin Kelley, 'If You're Woke You Dig It; No Mickey Mouse can be Expected to Follow Today's Negro Idiom Without a Hip Assist. If You're Woke You Dig It', *New York Times*, 20 May 1962, 45, https://tinyurl.com/mrvwymbr.
7. Adolph Reed, 'Antiracism: A Neoliberal Alternative to a Left', *Dialect Anthropology* 42 (2018): 105–115, https://doi.org/10.1007/s10624-017-9476-3.
8. Angela Nagle joined Tucker Carlson to discuss her article, 'The Left Case Against Open Borders', *American Affairs Journal* 2, no. 4 (2018), https://

tinyurl.com/2s38ewc6. On other shows, she has joined Carlson to mock DSA members. For a critique of Nagle's misuses of history, see Liam Hogan 'Conflation and Omission: Angela Nagle's historical negation of the racism behind the Chinese Exclusion Act', *Liam Hogan Medium*, 30 November 2018, https://tinyurl.com/35cdscmr.

9. Todd Gitlin, *The Left, Lost in the Politics of Identity*, Harper's Magazine, September 1993, https://harpers.org/archive/1993/09/the-left-lost-in-the-politics-of-identity/.

10. Robin D.G. Kelley, 'Identity Politics & Class Struggle', *New Politics* 6, no. 2 (1997), https://tinyurl.com/2p8tkzk6.

11. Nancy Fraser, 'From Redistribution to Recognition? Dilemmas of Justice in a "Post-Socialist" Age', *New Left Review* 1, no. 212 (July–August 1995), https://tinyurl.com/4frbyxh7. This argument was then revised to consider how 'questions of "identity" have fueled campaigns for ethnic cleansing', in Nancy Fraser, 'Rethinking Recognition', *New Left Review* 2, no. 3 (May–June 2000), https://tinyurl.com/yckzp6zb.

12. Eric Hobsbawm, 'Identity Politics and the Left', *New Left Review* 1, no. 217 (May–June 1996), https://tinyurl.com/553zyttm.

13. Ibid.

14. Ibid.

15. Ambalavaner Sivanandan, 'All that Melts into Air is Solid: A. Sivanandan', Part One, *Verso Books*, 13 July 2017, https://tinyurl.com/r723kpK74.

16. Ibid.

17. Sivanandan, 'All that Melts into Air is Solid: A. Sivanandan', Part Two, *Verso Books*, 13 July 2017, https://tinyurl.com/zsemtc5d.

18. Ibid.

19. This doesn't exhaust the concept of populism of relevance – it just hasn't done it any favours. For new, current and grassroots restorations of the concept in the era of climate breakdown, see, for example, Kai Bosworth, *Pipeline Populism: Grassroots Environmentalism in the Twenty-First Century* (Minneapolis, MN: University of Minnesota Press, 2022).

20. Combahee River Collective, 'The Combahee River Collective Statement', *BlackPast*, https://tinyurl.com/mpwyy95v.

21. Beverley Bryan, Stella Dadzie and Suzanne Scafe, *Heart of the Race: Black Women's Lives in Britain* (London: Verso, 2018), 25.

22. Amrit Wilson, *Dreams, Questions, Struggles: South Asian Women in Britain* (London: Pluto Press, 2006), 161.

23. Anarchists in Britain, for example, who were split by transphobic currents, leading to nostalgia for past eras of strength. During the 2017 London Anarchist Bookfair, some people distributed flyers warning about what they claimed were the dangers posed to 'women' by the proposed Gender Recognition Act. This caused heated scenes, leaving long-term comrades on different sides of the dispute. Organisers announced they would not organise the Bookfair in 2018. Sometime later, a pamphlet showed up in anarchist spaces titled 'Against Anarcho-Liberalism: and the Curse of Identity Politics', one passage read, 'rather than the destruction of that system ... the end result is Rainbow Capitalism'. Also published online, 'Against Anarcho-Liberalism

and the Curse of Identity Politics', *Void Network*, 27 April 2019, https://tinyurl.com/32dabt9x.
24. For more on this, see Jason E. Smith, ' "Striketober" and Labor's Long Downturn', *The Brooklyn Rail*, December 2021, https://tinyurl.com/3j6yz28h. In Britain, the P&O dispute showed the new spontaneity of the capitalist restructure: hundreds of workers sacked via Zoom, with many agency workers set to replace them, refusing to board. 'P&O: Agency Seafarers Quit After Hearing About Sacked Staff', *BBC News*, 18 March 2022, https://tinyurl.com/jkax463j.
25. See the film, *United Voices*, directed by Hazel Falck, about the United Voices of the World union. Lindsay Poulton and Jess Gormley, 'United Voices: An Inspiring Story of Workers' Grassroots Resistance', *The Guardian*, 12 August 2020, https://tinyurl.com/4tffmaw7.

CHAPTER 1

1. Quoted in Peter Fryer, *Staying Power: The History of Black People in Britain* (London: Pluto Press, 1984), 547.
2. Walter Benjamin, 'Theses on the Philosophy of History', in Hannah Arendt (ed.), *Illuminations* (New York: Schocken Books, 1969), 255.
3. Doug Stanglin and Melanie Eversley, 'Suspect in Charleston Church Rampage Returns to South Carolina', *USA Today*, 18 June 2015, https://tinyurl.com/f8w953c3.
4. Yamiche Alcindor and Doug Stanglin, 'Affidavits Spell Out Chilling Case Against Dylann Roof', *USA Today*, 19 June 2015, https://tinyurl.com/3d55s433.
5. See Meghan Keneally, 'Trump Says US Culture Being "Ripped Apart" by Confederate Memorial Removals', *ABC News*, 17 August 2017, https://tinyurl.com/2p83jhtd.
6. All above quotes from 'Full Text: Trump's Comments on White Supremacists, "Alt-Left" in Charlottesville', *Politico*, 15 August 2017, https://tinyurl.com/y395kyfz.
7. Larry Buchanan, Quoctrung Bui and Jugal K. Patel, 'Black Lives Matter May Be the Largest Movement in U.S. History', *New York Times*, 3 July 2020, https://tinyurl.com/ycy8r4ts.
8. Matthew Impelli, '54 Percent of Americans Think Burning Down Minneapolis Police Precinct was Justified After George Floyd's Death', *Newsweek*, 3 June 2020, https://bit.ly/3Hs6bGL.
9. 'USA: Law Enforcement Violated Black Lives Matter Protesters' Human Rights, Documents Acts of Police Violence and Excessive Force', *Amnesty International USA*, August 2020, https://bit.ly/3uoN1oO.
10. Wenei Philimon, 'Black Americans Report Hate Crimes, Violence in Wake of George Floyd Protests and Black Lives Matter Gains', *USA TODAY*, 7 July 2020, https://eu.usatoday.com/story/news/nation/2020/07/07/black-americans-report-hate-crimes-amid-black-lives-matter-gains/3259241001/.

11. 'Priti Patel: Toppling Edward Colston Statue "Utterly Disgraceful"', *Sky News*, 7 June 2020, https://tinyurl.com/2ejzdwdm.
12. 'Keir Starmer Says it was "Completely Wrong" to Topple Edward Colston Statue', *The Guardian*, 8 June 2020, https://tinyurl.com/mtabd62u.
13. For a balance sheet of the George Floyd Rebellion and the US context that argues for the historical significance of the event, see Jason E. Smith, 'The American Revolution: The George Floyd Rebellion, One Year Out', *Brooklyn Rail*, July 2021, https://tinyurl.com/ycknbdvc.
14. Vanessa Kisuule, 'Hollow', *Poetry Archives*, https://tinyurl.com/2p9yx8yk.
15. Transcripts from video interviews in Priyanka Raval, 'Reflections on the All Lives Matter Protest', *Bristol Cable*, June 2020, https://tinyurl.com/yc5v4abs.
16. Ibid.
17. Peter Oborne, a Conservative journalist, has himself been alarmed by the direction of these attacks, 'Jeremy Corbyn: British Media Waged Campaign to Destroy Me', *Middle East Eye*, 2 June 2020, https://tinyurl.com/yhvst2pz. For a comprehensive analysis of Labour antisemitism, see Michael Richmond, 'Anti-Racism as Procedure', *Protocols*, https://tinyurl.com/4bhd4bzv.
18. Kevin Rawlinson, 'Finsbury Attack Accused "Wanted to Kill Jeremy Corbyn"', *The Guardian*, 30 January 2018, https://tinyurl.com/2p9dj3f3.
19. James Tapsfield, 'Jeremy Corbyn "could do more damage to UK security in weeks than MI6 traitor Kim Philby" if he becomes caretaker PM – as ex-admiral warns he would immediately neutralise the UK's nuclear deterrent', *MailOnline*, 7 October 2019, https://tinyurl.com/bdzn9e6t.
20. See Arun Kundnani, *The Muslims Are Coming: Islamophobia, Extremism and the Domestic War on Terror* (London: Verso, 2015).
21. Cenotaph-defender at the empty Colston plinth, central Bristol, 16 June 2020.
22. A banner was unfurled, saying: 'NOT FAR RIGHT: Just ordinary people of all races from Bristol, Bath, Cardiff, Newport etc etc united to defend the cenotaph. To defend the memory of people who died so that we are able to have the freedom to protest. ALL LIVES MATTER.' See 'Scaffolder Reveals Why he Tried to Pull Colston Statue from the Water', *Bristol Live*, 15 June 2020, https://tinyurl.com/3k27v678.
23. Transcripts from Raval, 'Reflections on the All Lives Matter Protest'.
24. See Alana Lentin, *Why Race Still Matters* (Cambridge: Polity Press, 2020), 52–93.
25. Simon Clarke, 'Our History is Complex, as is Inevitably the Case for Any Nation State of at Least 1,200 Years ...' Twitter, @SimonClarkeMP, 9 June 2020, https://tinyurl.com/37fvpwvr.
26. In conversation with Nigel Farage, 'Douglas Murray ...', Twitter, @Nigel_Farage, 31 August 2020, https://tinyurl.com/6v78ur4d.
27. Sara Ahmed, 'A Phenomenology of Whiteness', *Feminist Theory* 8, no. 2 (August 2007): 154. https://doi.org/10.1177/1464700107078139.
28. Holly Brewer, 'Slavery, Sovereignty, and "Inheritable Blood": Reconsidering John Locke and the Origins of American Slavery', *The American Historical Review* 122, no. 4 (October 2017): 1038. https://doi.org/10.1093/ahr/122.4.1038.

29. Ibid., 1076.
30. Eric Williams, *Capitalism and Slavery* (London: Andre Deutsch, 1964), 181.
31. Ibid., 10.
32. Ibid.
33. Pitt's government tried to re-enslave Saint Domingue in the midst of its slave-led revolution. See C.L.R. James, *The Black Jacobins: Toussaint L'Ouverture and the San Domingo Revolution* (New York: Vintage Books, 1989), 132–152.
34. Williams, *Capitalism and Slavery*, 181.
35. Giles Fraser asked whether slaver-turned-abolitionist John Newton, writer of the hymn 'Amazing Grace', might also be targeted. He complained, 'part of the problem with the cancel culture of modern identity politics is that it makes the confession of sins so much more difficult to achieve.' Giles Fraser, 'How Cancel Culture Makes Liars of Us All', *UnHerd*, 11 June 2020, https:// tinyurl.com/yc7zjmkx.
36. James, *The Black Jacobins*, 87.
37. Robin Blackburn, *The Overthrow of Colonial Slavery: 1776–1848* (London: Verso, 1988), 323–324 and 428–433.
38. 'At least one in ten voyages experienced some form of on-board mutiny or rebellion at a rate of one or two a year.' Stella Dadzie, *A Kick in the Belly: Women, Slavery and Resistance* (New York: Verso, 2020), 41–42. See also David Richardson, 'Shipboard Revolts, African Authority, and the Atlantic Slave Trade', *The William and Mary Quarterly* 58, no. 1 (2001): 69–92, https:// doi.org/10.2307/2674419; and Adam D. Wilsey, 'A Study of West African Slave Resistance from the Seventeenth to Nineteenth Centuries', *History in the Making* 1, no. 7 (2008).
39. Cedric Robinson, *Black Marxism: The Making of the Black Radical Tradition* (Chapel Hill, NC: University of North Carolina Press, 1983), 122.
40. See Herbert Aptheker, *American Negro Slave Revolts* (New York: International Publishers, 1983).
41. Robinson, *Black Marxism*, 124.
42. As Peter Linebaugh and Marcus Rediker write:

    Sailors black, white, and brown had contact with slaves in the British, French, Spanish and Dutch port cities of the Caribbean, exchanging information with them about slave revolts, abolition, and revolution and generating rumors that became material forces in their own right.

    Peter Linebaugh and Marcus Rediker, *The Many-Headed Hydra: The Hidden History of the Revolutionary Atlantic* (New York: Verso, 2012), 241.
43. Blackburn, *The Overthrow of Colonial Slavery*, 279.
44. Fryer, *Staying Power*, 77.
45. See Olaudah Equiano, *The Interesting Narrative and Other Writings* (Harmondsworth: Penguin Classics, 2003).
46. Quobna Ottobah Cugoano, *Thoughts and Sentiments on the Evil of Slavery* (Harmondsworth: Penguin Classics, 1999), 59.
47. Ibid.
48. Ibid., 79.

49. Linebaugh and Rediker, *The Many-Headed Hydra*, 283.
50. See Eric Foner, *Politics and Ideology in the Age of the Civil War* (New York: Oxford University Press, 1980). See also Mike Davis, *Prisoners of the American Dream: Politics and Economy in the US Working Class* (New York: Verso, 2018).
51. Blackburn, *The Overthrow of Colonial Slavery*, 26.
52. See Robin Blackburn, *The American Crucible: Slavery, Emancipation and Human Rights* (New York: Verso, 2013), 977–1357.
53. W.E.B. Du Bois, *Black Reconstruction in America 1860–1880* (New York: Free Press, 1998), 57.
54. In South Carolina: 'When the planters fled, the slaves sacked the big houses and destroyed cotton gins; they then commenced planting corn and potatoes for their own subsistence.' In Eric Foner, *A Short History of Reconstruction, 1863–1877* (New York: Harper & Row, 1990), 24.
55. 'The Civil War was, among other things, a massive slave rebellion ... many at the time said so.' Stephanie McCurry, *Confederate Reckoning: Power and Politics in the Civil War South* (Cambridge, MA: Harvard University Press, 2010), 259–261.
56. See Stephanie M.H. Camp, *Closer to Freedom: Enslaved Women and Everyday Resistance in the Plantation South* (Chapel Hill, NC: University of North Carolina Press, 2004). For more, see McCurry, *Confederate Reckoning*, 241–259; and Foner, *A Short History of Reconstruction, 1863–1877*, 2–3.
57. David Roediger, *Seizing Freedom: Slave Emancipation and Liberty For All* (London: Verso, 2015), 9.
58. Ibid., 115.
59. Karl Marx, *Capital Volume I* (Harmondsworth: Penguin Classics, 1990), 414.
60. Quoted in Roediger, *Seizing Freedom*, 120.
61. Foner, *A Short History of Reconstruction, 1863–1877*, 124.
62. As stated by Saidiya Hartman,

    The emancipated also shared a different perspective on who comprised the dependent class of slavery. They argued irrefutably that they were the producing class and that the riches of their owner and the nation came from their labor. Andy McAdams said that although he was uncertain about what freedom meant, he certainly expected something different than what he experienced: 'I think they ought to have given us old slaves some mules and land too, because everything our white people had we made for them.'

    Saidiya Hartman, *Scenes of Subjection: Terror, Slavery and Self-Making in Nineteenth-Century America* (Oxford: Oxford University Press, 1997), 136.
63. Tens of thousands of Black people were murdered in riots, lynchings and massacres between 1865–1876.
64. Hartman, *Scenes of Subjection*, 6.
65. Ibid.
66. Ibid., 116–117.
67. Linebaugh and Rediker, *The Many-Headed Hydra*, 332.
68. Du Bois, *Black Reconstruction in America 1860–1880*, 357.
69. Ibid., 700.

70. Andrew Woodcock, 'Racism: Equalities Minister Says Anti-Discrimination Drives can "Create Prison for Black People"', *The Independent*, 28 October 2020, https://tinyurl.com/5b6pcvwd.
71. See Alana Lentin and Gavan Titley's *The Crises of Multiculturalism: Racism in a Neoliberal Age* (New York: Zed Books, 2011). An analysis of 'against Multiculturalism' discourses in Europe and its material effects – a big influence on our own study.
72. Quoted in John Solomos, *Race and Racism in Britain* (London: Macmillan, 1993), 228.
73. Jenny Bourne, 'Anti-Racist Witchcraft', *Institute of Race Relations*, 15 January 2015, https://tinyurl.com/3rae67pc.
74. Quoted in Solomos, *Race and Racism in Britain*, 187.
75. Eric Kaufmann, '"Racial Self-Interest" is Not Racism', *Policy Exchange*, March 2017, https://tinyurl.com/2p8bze22.

CHAPTER 2

1. Carole Boyce Davies, *Left of Karl Marx: The Political Life of Black Communist Claudia Jones* (Durham, NC: Duke University Press, 2007), 39–40.
2. Jackie Wang, 'Against Innocence', *Lies Journal*, Vol. I (2012), https://tinyurl.com/4bw93ss8.
3. Gail Mason, 'Blue Lives Matter and Hate Crime Law', *Race and Justice* 12, no. 2 (April 2022): 411–430, https://tinyurl.com/7nwnkdet.
4. Jon Skolnik, 'Nancy Pelosi Shrugs Off Criticism After Thanking George Floyd for "Sacrificing Your Life to Justice"', *Salon*, 21 April 2021, https://tinyurl.com/dxvd8bvn.
5. This has been Adolph Reed's complaint for 40 years, but universalist messaging is flexible. After the shock of the Capitol insurrection, Reed hoped 'Biden running with the Republican congresswoman Liz Cheney on a national-unity ticket' might at least 'buy time' before the working class could reorganise. See Benjamin Wallace-Wells, 'The Marxist Who Antagonises Liberals and the Left', *New Yorker*, 31 January 2022, https://tinyurl.com/yck9w5nn.
6. Paraphrasing Stuart Hall, Gilmore writes, 'action, crucially, includes the difficult work of identification – which entails production, not discovery, of a "suture or positioning"'. Ruth Wilson Gilmore, *Golden Gulag: Prisons, Surplus, Crisis, And Opposition in Globalizing California* (Los Angeles, CA: University of California Press, 2007), 236. For more on organising in a time of 'fragmentation', listen to a fantastic interview with Craig and Ruth Wilson Gilmore on *Trillbilly Worker's Party*, 'Episode 239: The Fragmented State', https://tinyurl.com/3t4w2wrr.
7. The Combahee River Collective Statement 1977, www.blackpast.org/african-american-history/combahee-river-collective-statement-1977/.
8. Kimberly Springer, *Living for the Revolution: Black Feminist Organizations, 1968–1980* (Durham, NC: Duke University Press, 2005), 2.
9. Ibid., 44 and 116.

10. Ibid., 44. See also Winifred Breines, *The Trouble Between Us: An Uneasy History of White and Black Women in the Feminist Movement* (New York: Oxford University Press, 2006), 57–58.
11. Springer, *Living for the Revolution*, 4; and Breines, *The Trouble Between Us*, 134.
12. Breines, *The Trouble Between Us*, 136.
13. Springer, *Living for the Revolution*, 29. See also Alice Echols, *Daring to be Bad: Radical Feminism in America 1967–1975*, 30th anniversary edn (Minneapolis, MN: University of Minnesota Press, 2019), xi and 106.
14. Assata Shakur, 'Women in Prison', in Joy James (ed.), *The New Abolitionists: (Neo)Slave Narratives and Contemporary Prison Writings* (Albany, NY: SUNY Press), 87.
15. Breines, *The Trouble Between Us*, 71–72.
16. Elendar Barnes, interview by Robyn C. Spencer, *The Revolution Has Come: Black Power, Gender, and the Black Panther Party in Oakland* (Durham, NC: Duke University Press, 2016), 47–48.
17. Echols, *Daring to be Bad*, 106.
18. Springer, *Living for the Revolution*, 5.
19. Breines, *The Trouble Between Us*, 122. See also Bettye Collier-Thomas and V.P. Franklin (eds), *Sisters in the Struggle: African American Women in the Civil Rights-Black Power Movement* (New York: New York University Press, 2001), 293.
20. Springer, *Living for the Revolution*, 17, 130 and 170.
21. Combahee River Collective, 'Statement', *BlackPast*.
22. Angela Y. Davis, *Women, Race and Class* (New York: Vintage Books, 1983), 53–54.
23. Gilmore, *Golden Gulag*, 188.
24. Davis, *Women, Race and Class*, 67.
25. Wendy Hamand Venet, *Neither Ballots Nor Bullets: Women's Abolitionists and the Civil War* (Charlottesville, VA: University Press of Virginia, 1991), 148.
26. Gerda Lerner, *The Grimké Sisters from South Carolina: Pioneers for Women's Rights and Abolition* (Chapel Hill, NC: University of North Carolina Press, 2004), 253.
27. McCurry, *Confederate Reckoning*, 246.
28. Beverly Guy Sheftall (ed.), *Words of Fire: An Anthology of African-American Feminist Thought* (New York: The New Press, 1995), 31.
29. Ibid.
30. Ibid.
31. Rosalyn Terborg-Penn, *African American Women in the Struggle for the Vote, 1850–1920* (Bloomington, IN: Indiana University Press, 1998), 13.
32. Sharon Harley, 'Northern Black Female Workers', in Sharon Harley and Rosalyn Terborg-Penn (eds), *The Afro-American Woman: Struggles and Imagery* (Port Washington, NY: Kennikat Press, 1978), 8–10.
33. Davies, *Left of Karl Marx*, 34 and 37.
34. Claudia Jones, 'An End to the Neglect of the Problems of the Negro Woman', 1949. https://libcom.org/article/end-neglect-problems-negro-woman.
35. Davies, *Left of Karl Marx*, 36–37 and 83–84.

36. Ibid., 31–32.
37. Ibid., 29.
38. Ibid., 42–46.
39. Ibid., 83.
40. Echols, *Daring to be Bad*, 19.
41. 'Black women in SNCC recognized the male chauvinism in the organization, but they were reluctant to confront it because of the divide erected between racial and gender struggles.' Springer, *Living for the Revolution*, 26.
42. Echols, *Daring to be Bad*, 117, 120 and 135.
43. Ibid., 28.
44. See Ibid., 53 and 83–84. Also Joy Press, 'The Life And Death of a Radical Sisterhood', *New York Magazine*, November 2017, https://tinyurl.com/a6twp4v7.
45. Echols, *Daring to be Bad*, 49.
46. Breines, *The Trouble Between Us*, 113.
47. See also, 'No More Fun and Games: A Journal of Female Liberation (v. 1, no. 1)', October 1968, Duke University Libraries, https://tinyurl.com/2sjs67fc. We commissioned Dunbar-Ortiz to write for the *Occupied Times* in 2015. https://theoccupiedtimes.org/?p=13776.
48. Echols, *Daring to be Bad*, 54.
49. Davis, *Women, Race and Class*, 142.
50. Elizabeth Cady Stanton, Susan B. Anthony, Matilda J. Gage, *History of Woman Suffrage Volume One*, Originally published 1881, 27, open source e-book access https://tinyurl.com/yckknzcp.
51. Davis, *Women, Race and Class*, 139–140.
52. Elizabeth Cady Stanton, Susan B. Anthony, Matilda J. Gage, *History of Woman Suffrage Volume Two*, 864. Originally published 1882, open source e-book access https://tinyurl.com/4263dv8u.
53. Ellen Carol Dubois, *Feminism and Suffrage* (Ithaca: Cornell University Press, 1978), 61.
54. Ellen Carol Dubois, *Woman's Suffrage and Women's Rights* (New York: New York University Press, 1998), 70.
55. Anna Julia Cooper, 'Women's Cause is One and Universal', *BlackPast*, https://tinyurl.com/3brmhshp.
56. Quoted in bell hooks, *Ain't I a Woman* (London: Pluto Press, 1982), 127.
57. Davis, *Women, Race and Class*, 82.
58. Stanton et al., *History of Woman Suffrage Volume Two*, 1241.
59. Davis, *Women, Race and Class*, 70.
60. Stanton asked how white politicians could 'make their wives and mothers the political inferiors of unlettered and unwashed ditch-diggers, boot-blacks, butchers, and barbers, fresh from the slave plantations of the South, and the effete civilizations of the Old World'. Quoted in, Nell Irvin Painter, *Sojourner Truth: A Life, A Symbol* (New York: W.W. Norton, 1997), 230–231.
61. Davis, *Women, Race and Class*, 76
62. On the Jewish immigrant women/girls who led factory strikes, rent strikes and working-class suffrage campaigns, see Annelise Orleck, *Common Sense*

and A Little Fire: Women and Working Class Politics in the US, 1900–1965 (Chapel Hill, NC: University of North Carolina Press, 1995).

63. See Allison L. Sneider, *Suffragists in an Imperial Age: U.S. Expansion and the Woman Question, 1870–1929* (Oxford: Oxford University Press, 2008).
64. See Davis, *Women, Race and Class*, 122–125.
65. Echols, *Daring to be Bad*, 65 and 153. See also Breines, *The Trouble Between Us*, 26–27, 36 and 79.
66. Breines, *The Trouble Between Us*, 4 and 116.
67. Ibid., 140.
68. Ibid., 99.
69. Echols, *Daring to be Bad*, 5.
70. See Melinda Cooper, *Family Values: Between Neoliberalism and the New Social Conservatism* (New York: Zone Books, 2017).
71. Echols, *Daring to be Bad*, xviii, 101 and 198. Radical Feminist essays and scans of original pamphlets can be freely accessed online. See 'Notes from the First Year', June 1968, Duke University Libraries, https://tinyurl.com/2rrwfnxz. See also, 'No More Fun and Games: A Journal of Female Liberation (v. 1, no. 1)', October 1968, Duke University Libraries, https://tinyurl.com/2sjs67fc. Register with Red Stockings (www.redstockings.org) to access an extensive library of radical feminist writing, https://tinyurl.com/fac6jkrk. The 'Red Stockings' stamp was designed by Shula Firestone in 1969.
72. Echols, *Daring to be Bad*, xxxi and 232–234.
73. Ibid., 204.
74. Ibid., 206–207.
75. All quotes from the appendix of Echols, *Daring to be Bad*.

CHAPTER 3

1. Hazel Carby, 'White Woman Listen! Black Feminism and the Boundaries of Sisterhood', in Heidi Safia Mirza (ed.), *British Black Feminism: A Reader* (London: Routledge, 1997), 45.
2. Ibid.
3. Ibid., 52.
4. Nim Ralph, 'Why We will Always Take a Stand Against Transphobia in the British Press', *Gal-Dem*, https://tinyurl.com/ym8nz55u.
5. Lola Olufemi, *Feminism, Interrupted: Disrupting Power* (London: Pluto Press, 2020), 58.
6. Ibid., 142.
7. Julia Serano debunks the 'bathroom predator' myth and traces its origins to Christian Right attacks on 'homosexuals', only later adapted to anti-trans moral panics. See Julia Serano, 'Transgender People, Bathrooms and Sexual predators: What the Data Say', *juliaserano.medium*, https://tinyurl.com/4y5sr643.
8. Sarah Ahmed, 'Gender Critical = Gender Conservative', *feministkilljoys*, https://tinyurl.com/2mjuwwbp.

9. Sarah Clarke and Mallory Moore, 'ALERT: Transphobic Feminism and Far Right Activism Rapidly Converging', *TransSafety.Network*, https://tinyurl.com/bdfxdftt. Moore's writing and research are crucial to understanding anti-trans ideology in Britain and its relationship to anti-trans movements elsewhere. Follow her @Chican3ry.
10. For a fine-grained survey and chronology of the development of 'Gender ideology' conspiracies, see Mallory Moore, 'Gender Ideology? Up Yours!', 23 January 2019, https://tinyurl.com/3es2bavv.
11. Terese Jonsson, *Innocent Subjects: Feminism and Whiteness* (London: Pluto Press, 2020), 36.
12. Amelia Francis, '"No Liberation Without Black Women": Gender in the Black Liberation Front', *Women's History Network*, 22 October 2018, https://tinyurl.com/3am43dy7.
13. Natalie Thomlinson, *Race, Ethnicity and the Women's Movement in England, 1968–1993* (London: Palgrave Macmillan, 2016), 65–69. See also Beverley Bryan, Stella Dadzie and Suzanne Scafe, *Heart of the Race: Black Women's Lives in Britain* (London: Verso, 2018), 148–150.
14. Bryan, Dadzie and Scafe, *Heart of the Race*, 143–144. See also Thomlinson, *Race, Ethnicity and the Women's Movement in England*, 78.
15. Gail Lewis and Pratibha Parmar reviewing books by Angela Davis and bell hooks: 'Book Reviews', *Race and Class* 25, no. 2 (October 1983), 85–91.
16. Paul Field, Robin Bunce, Leila Hassan and Margaret Peacock (eds), *Here To Stay, Here To Fight: A Race Today Anthology* (London: Pluto Press, 2019), 92.
17. Carby, 'White Woman', 47.
18. Thomlinson, *Race, Ethnicity and the Women's Movement in England*, 32.
19. Jonsson, *Innocent Subjects*, 164.
20. Thomlinson, *Race, Ethnicity and the Women's Movement in England*, 29–33; and Jonsson, *Innocent Subjects*, 15. The white feminist response has encompassed everything from erasure, the displacing of racism to outside feminism/white womanhood, the denial of history, or saying 'that's the past, things have moved on', to deep and critical engagement.
21. Quoted in Thomlinson, *Race, Ethnicity and the Women's Movement in England*, 170.
22. Thomlinson, *Race, Ethnicity and the Women's Movement in England*, 169–170.
23. Vron Ware, *Beyond the Pale: White Women, Racism and History* (London: Verso, 2015), 38.
24. Alison Phipps, *Me, Not You: The Trouble With Mainstream Feminism* (Manchester: Manchester University Press, 2020), 11.
25. Caitlin Moran, 'Women's Safety – and What Men Need to do About It', *The Times*, 16 March 2021, https://tinyurl.com/4b9kvvr5.
26. See discussion of Grunwick's place in British workers movement historiography on the brilliant *Working Class History Podcast*. 'E1: The Grunwick Strike, 1976', https://tinyurl.com/2p8fh66k. See also Evan Smith on ongoing trade union racism post-Grunwick, 'After Grunwick: Trade Unions and Anti-Racism in the 1980s', *New Historical Express*, 23 August 2016, https://tinyurl.com/yckhpdt4.

27. James Callaghan, 'Leader's Speech, Blackpool 1976', *britishpoliticalspeech*, https://tinyurl.com/2h3axwdr.
28. Jack Saunders, *Assembling Cultures: Workplace Activism, Labour Militancy and Cultural Change in Britain's Car Factories, 1945–82* (Manchester: Manchester University Press, 2019), 45. Saunders provides an extraordinary look at labour militancy in post-war Britain, tracking 1970s anti-unionism in public discourse, and the workplace cultures that emerged.
29. Simon Clarke, *Keynesianism, Monetarism and the Crisis of the State* (Aldershot: Edward Elgar), 317. Clarke provides one of the best Marxist accounts of the state.
30. For a detailed view of the changing composition of the working class in the 1970s, see Tara Martin López, *The Winter of Discontent: Myth, Memory, and History* (Liverpool: Liverpool University Press, 2014).
31. Ibid., 156.
32. Bryan, Dadzie and Scafe, *Heart of the Race*, 25.
33. Louise Raw, *Striking a Light: The Bryant and May Matchwomen and Their Place in History* (London: Continuum, 2011), 58. Raw writes:

   The overall response from the textile trades, as from the male union movement as a whole, was not to organize unskilled and female labour but to organize against incursions of women through strikes, petitions to employers, and the lobbying of parliament.

34. Sheila Rowbotham on other strikes by women workers at this time:

   Commonweal, the paper of the Socialist League, reported several other incidents of female militancy in the same year. Blanket weavers in Heckmondwike, female cigarmakers in Nottingham, girls in a tin box manufactory in London, who pelted men who continued to work after they came out with red-ochre and flour, cotton workers, and jute workers in Dundee, took action spontaneously in 1888. The reasons for striking varied, from demands for increases to resistance to cuts, or opposition to fines. Again in 1889 mill girls in Kilmarnock came out over the bad quality of yarn they were being given. At Alverthorpe, near Wakefield, woollen weavers, women and girls, rejected a reduced rate and marched in procession headed by girls with concertinas. This was broken up by the police, and the girls with concertinas – obviously regarded as 'leaders' – were fined for obstruction. Even waiters and waitresses demonstrated at Hyde Park in October 1889 though unfortunately they saw foreign workers not their employers as their foes.

   Sheila Rowbotham, *Hidden From History* (New York: Vintage Books, 1976), 77.
35. Annie Besant, 'White Slavery in London', *The Link*, no. 21, Saturday, 23 June 1888.
36. Raw, *Striking a Light*, 111–116. Fabian strategy had tended to privilege political lobbying and media campaigns for Parliamentary reform rather than industrial action.
37. Annie Besant, *An Autobiography by Annie Besant*, Project Gutenberg, 179. Open source e-book: https://tinyurl.com/2p8fj2w5/.

38. Ibid.
39. Phipps, *Me, Not You*, 155.
40. Interview by Ru Kaur with Molly Smith, 'Revolting Prostitutes: The Fight for Sex Workers' Rights', *Base Publication*, 17 November 2018, https://tinyurl.com/42hywtau.
41. Maurice Casey, 'The Suffragettes Who Became Communists', *History Today*, 4 February 2018, https://tinyurl.com/3vyxkr2t.
42. The youngest Pankhurst sister, Adela, had the most extreme trajectory of all. She emigrated to Australia where she was a founding member of the Communist Party in 1920. By 1941, she was a founding member of the fascist Australia First movement. On the Suffragettes who joined the British Union of Fascists, see Julie V. Gottlieb, *Feminine Fascism: Women in Britain's Fascist Movement 1923–1945* (London: I.B. Tauris, 2000).
43. Quoted in Barbara Winslow, *Sylvia Pankhurst: Sexual Politics and Political Activism* (New York: St. Martin's Press 1996), 16.
44. Dora Montefiore, *Justice*, 9 November 1912.
45. Amrit Wilson, *Dreams, Questions, Struggles: South Asian Women in Britain* (London: Pluto Press, 2006), 149–150.
46. Ibid.
47. Ibid.
48. For an introduction to the aims and problems of 'wages for housework', see this brilliant interview comrades Jaemie and Chloë from the erstwhile *Occupied Times* collective conducted with Selma James, 'Preoccupying: Selma James', *The Occupied Times*, 28 August 2014, https://tinyurl.com/bdhrn3dp.
49. Carby, *White Women*, 46.
50. Ibid., 47. The critique of 'white feminism' opens up a whole range of essential questions but it can risk lumping together different strands – socialist, radical, separatist – that were also engaged in fierce disagreements. Carby overlooked some of this variation in her piece but the substance of the problems identified in her early essays are shrewdly and incisively pronounced, and the call to differentiate and historicise even more so.
51. This quote is from a transcribed conference debate with Adolph Reed Jr, Ellen Meiksins Wood, Maurice Zeitlin and Steven Gregory discussing: 'How does Race Relate to Class? Not an Easy Question to Answer', https://tinyurl.com/mr42a6jk. Reed provided a better grasp of the question, with a patient enquiry wholly absent from his polemics against identity politics.
52. Jairus Banaji, *Theory as History* (Leiden: Brill, 2010), 40.
53. Carby, *White Woman*, 50.
54. On the problem with general theories of a 'slave mode of production', see Banaji, *Theory as History*, 10–11 and 352–353. See also the entirety of Chapter 2, 'Modes of Production in a Materialist Conception of History', originally written in 1977, which looks across feudal, early medieval and modern relations of production, 45–101. A truly brilliant and inspirational critique.
55. Banaji, *Theory as History*, 69.
56. Ibid., 63. For a discussion of family labour and second wave feminism's contribution to this debate, see Tani Barlow, 'From Commercial Capital to Wage

Labor Revisited: An Interview with Jairus Banaji', *episteme* 7: 'Uninvited Sexualities', https://tinyurl.com/56fr6ybe. For interesting background to Banaji's connection to Marxist and post-colonial traditions, see Sheetal Chhabria and Andrew Liu, 'Where is the Working Class? It's All Over the World Today', 18 January 2021, https://tinyurl.com/2p83d3ue.

57. Quoted in Jonsson, *Innocent Subjects*, 38–39.

58. Thomlinson, *Race, Ethnicity and the Women's Movement in England*, 73.

59. One of the best analyses of workplace militancy and the limits of union bureaucracy came from Martin Glaberman whose critique emerged from his and others' testimonies of organising conditions in the US post-war factory setting. See Martin Glaberman, 'Theory and Practice', *libcom*, 1 March 2020, https://tinyurl.com/2p8at8s8.

60. Thomlinson, *Race, Ethnicity and the Women's Movement in England*, 147.

61. Ibid., 64–65.

62. Ibid., 196.

63. Lynne Segal, 'The Hidden Powers of Injury', *New Formations* 55, no. 1 (2005): 172–187, https://eprints.bbk.ac.uk/id/eprint/188/1/Segal5.pdf.

64. Bindel's remarks from this 2016 Battle of Ideas panel 'The Personal Is Political: Is Identity Politics Eating Itself?', viewable on YouTube, https://tinyurl.com/ms92xts6.

65. Thanks to Kim Charnley for offering this neat framing.

66. Bindel, 'The Personal Is Political'.

67. 'Statement of Solidarity with the Morning Star', *Morning Star Online*, 25 May 2016, https://tinyurl.com/37va9h7z. This letter was signed by Louise Raw, whose work we refer to in this chapter. We include Raw because we think her own history of the matchwomen can be used to dismantle the conspiracist notion that trans women represent a novel 'neoliberal' rupture with 'sex-class' feminism. Other socialists and communists we once admired, like Nina Power, have travelled down an ever darker route. Sometimes these conservative turns are unsurprising, other times unexpected and sad.

68. For details on US evangelical-right pseudo-experts steering evidence in British High Court rulings, see 'Questionable expertise at Bell v Tavistock', *transsafety.network*. See also Ben Hunte, 'Britain's Equalities Watchdog Met Privately With Anti-Trans Groups', *Vice*, 2 February 2022, https://tinyurl.com/2xhu8tkj. For an analysis of legal cases concerning anti-trans challenges to trans rights, follow @truesolicitor.

69. Olufemi, *Feminism, Interrupted*, 1.

70. Jules Joanne Gleeson and Elle O'Rourke, 'Introducing Transgender Marxism', *New Socialist*, 16 October 2021, https://tinyurl.com/28m39xdc. See also Jules Joanne Gleeson and Elle O'Rourke (eds), *Transgender Marxism* (London: Pluto Press, 2021).

71. Ru Kaur interview with Molly Smith, 'Revolting Prostitutes: The Fight for Sex Workers' Rights', *Base*, 17 November 2018, https://tinyurl.com/2p-939bzd. See also Molly Smith and Juno Mac, *Revolting Prostitutes: The Fight for Sex Workers' Rights* (London: Verso, 2018).

72. Sophie Lewis, 'On Firestone', *Sophie Lewis Patreon*, 28 September 2020, https://tinyurl.com/2p8d8a37. See also, Sophie Lewis, *Full Surrogacy Now: Feminism Against Family* (New York: Verso, 2021).

CHAPTER 4

1. Cedric Robinson, *Black Marxism: The Making of the Black Radical Tradition* (Chapel Hill, NC: University of North Carolina Press, 1983), 23.
2. Bhaskar Sunkara, 'Let Them Eat Diversity: An Interview with Walter Benn Michaels', *Jacobin*, 1 January 2011, https://tinyurl.com/2p8ab4da.
3. Paul Embery, 'Labour's Conspiracy of Silence on Immigration', *UnHerd*, 4 September 2018, https://tinyurl.com/787eyrfv.
4. Ibid. Embery bemoans 'a Left that is these days far more concerned with personal autonomy, open borders and identity politics than it is community and class'.
5. Adolph Reed contributing to an immigration debate, 'A Response to "Immigration, African Americans, and Race Discourse"', *New Labor Forum* 15, no. 1 (Spring 2006), at: https://tinyurl.com/5fss7acd.
6. A. Sivanandan, *Catching History on the Wing: Race, Culture and Globalisation* (London: Pluto Press, 2008), 77.
7. Ibid., 91.
8. Ibid., 99.
9. See Luke de Noronha, 'Life After Deportation: 'No One Tells You How Lonely You're Going to Be"', *The Guardian*, 18 August 2020, https://tinyurl.com/2pmspf8w. For one of the most compelling accounts of Britain's modern border regime see the essential and harrowing, Luke de Noronha, *Deporting Black Britons: Portraits of Deportation to Jamaica* (Manchester: Manchester University Press, 2020).
10. Sivanandan, *Catching History on the Wing*, 77–78.
11. Recent attacks on the left have pushed these histories down for fear of embarrassment or manipulation. How this history is reconciled with future movements in Britain remains an open question. For more see, Michael Richmond, 'Philosemitism: An Instrumental Kind of Love', *New Socialist*, 29 January 2022, https://tinyurl.com/46zr3s3u.
12. Nadine El-Enany, *(B)ordering Britain: Law, Race and Empire* (Manchester: Manchester University Press, 2020), 45.
13. Satnam Virdee, *Racism, Class and the Racialized Outsider* (London: Palgrave Macmillan, 2014), 5.
14. TUC report, 1892, 28–29, https://tinyurl.com/munk8yxs.
15. See Giovanni Arrighi, *The Long Twentieth Century* (London: Verso, 1994), 247–335.
16. House of Commons Hansard. Parliamentary debate, 'Housing of the Working Classes', 18 February 1903, https://tinyurl.com/4ws7t74c.
17. Daniel Edmonds, 'Unpacking "Chauvinism": The Interrelationship of Race, Internationalism, and Anti-Imperialism Amongst Marxists in Britain, 1899–1933' (PhD diss., University of Manchester, 2017), 35.

18. Engels on the early SDF:

    What can you expect of a set of people who take in hand the task of instructing the world about matters of which they themselves are ignorant? There is not a single burning question which they know how to tackle; Hyndman combines internationalist phraseology with jingo aspirations.

    Yvonne Kapp explains: '[Hyndman] had read the French edition of Capital before he met Marx but "did not at the time" – nor ever after – "fully grasp all the significance of his theories".' Yvonne Kapp, *Eleanor Marx: A Biography* (New York: Verso, 2018), 162.
19. Lloyd P. Gartner, *The Jewish Immigrant in England 1870–1914* (London: Simon Publications, 1960), 127.
20. Both quoted in, Steve Cohen, 'That's Funny You Don't Look Anti-Semitic', Originally published in 1984 by the *Beyond The Pale Collective*, accessed: https://tinyurl.com/2p8273tr, 13.
21. Both quoted in Steve Cohen, *No One Is Illegal: Asylum and Immigration Control Past and Present* (Stoke-On-Trent: Trentham Books, 2003), 83.
22. Cohen, 'That's Funny You Don't Look Anti-Semitic', 23.
23. H. Snell, 'The Foreigner in England: An Examination of the Problem of Alien Immigration', Independent Labour Party, n.d., 3–5, https://tinyurl.com/uuabdasj.
24. Gartner, *The Jewish Immigrant in England 1870–1914*, 280.
25. For more on this history, see Gartner, *The Jewish Immigrant in England 1870–1914*.
26. William J. Fishman, *East End Jewish Radicals 1875–1914* (Nottingham: Five Leaves, 2004), 79.
27. Virdee, *Racism, Class and the Racialized Outsider*, 51.
28. Quoted in Cohen, 'That's Funny You Don't Look Anti-Semitic', 15.
29. Anthony Julius, *Trials of the Diaspora: A History of Anti-Semitism in England* (Oxford: Oxford University Press, 2010), 275.
30. Claire Hirshfield, 'The Anglo-Boer War and the Issue of Jewish Culpability', *Journal of Contemporary History* 15, no. 4 (October 1980): 619–631, https://doi.org/10.1177/002200948001500402.
31. Quoted in Fishman, *East End Jewish Radicals 1875–1914*, 77.
32. Quoted in Cohen, 'That's Funny You Don't Look Anti-Semitic', 21.
33. Ibid., 20.
34. Cohen, *No One is Illegal*, 82.
35. Kapp, *Eleanor Marx*, 660.
36. Quoted in Colin Holmes, *Anti-Semitism in British Society 1876–1939* (London: Routledge, 2016), 14.
37. Legal Historian Marc W. Steinberg offers a detailed investigation into 'the place of law in Marxist analysis' using concrete examples of British 'master and servant' law and how it was enforced. See Marc W. Steinberg, 'Marx, Formal Subsumption and the Law', *Theory and Society* 39, no. 2 (2010): 173–202.
38. Cohen, *No One is Illegal*, 61.
39. Fishman, *East End Jewish Radicals 1875–1914*, 247.

40. William Evans-Gordon, *The Alien Immigrant* (London: William Heinemann, 1903), 7, https://tinyurl.com/2p8wbp7b.
41. David Rosenberg, *Battle for the East End: Jewish Responses to Fascism in the 1930s* (Nottingham: Five Leaves, 2011), 23.
42. Gartner, *The Jewish Immigrant in England 1870–1914*, 62.
43. Colin Holmes, *John Bull's Island: Immigration and British Society 1871–1971* (London: Routledge, 2016), 70.
44. Cohen, *No One is Illegal*, 61.
45. David Rosenberg, 'UKIP is Nothing New: The British Brothers' League was Exploiting Immigration Fears in 1901', *The Guardian*, 4 March 2015, https://tinyurl.com/4v4rmshz.
46. By 1902, there were 32 Jewish trade unions in London, 'of which only four or five had been in existence six years earlier'. If anything, Jewish trade union organising was more successful in Leeds. See Gartner, *The Jewish Immigrant in England 1870–1914*, 119–121.
47. Quoted in Satnam Virdee, 'Socialist Antisemitism and its Discontents in England, 1884–98', *Patterns of Prejudice* 3–4, no. 51 (2017): 356–373.
48. *A Voice From The Aliens: About the Anti-Alien Resolution of the Cardiff Trade Union Congress*, originally published 1895, available on *libcom*, https://tinyurl.com/bdcv8f57.
49. Ibid.
50. Gartner, *The Jewish Immigrant in England 1870–1914*, 127–128.
51. Quoted in Virdee, *Racism, Class and the Racialized Outsider*, 49.
52. Virdee, 'Socialist Antisemitism and its Discontents in England, 1884–98'.
53. Ibid., 54.
54. David Cesarani and Irving Jacobs, *The Jewish Chronicle and Anglo-Jewry 1841–1991* (Cambridge: Cambridge University Press, 1994), 75; and Fishman, *East End Jewish Radicals 1875–1914*, 86–87.
55. Gartner, *The Jewish Immigrant in England 1870–1914*, 55.
56. Around 31,000 Jews were paid to leave Britain from 1881 to 1906. 'Community leaders' sent word to Eastern Europe that no more Jews should come to Britain. See Edmonds, *Unpacking Chauvinism*, 94. Also, Fishman, *East End Jewish Radicals 1875–1914*, 65. Finally, Gartner, *The Jewish Immigrant in England 1870–1914*, 24–25 and 49.
57. Fishman, *East End Jewish Radicals 1875–1914*, 65.
58. In the early 2000s, the Muslim Council of Britain was used by New Labour to manage the British Muslim identity. See 'Croissants and Roses: New Labour, Communalism, and the Rise of Muslim Britain', *Aufheben* no. 17 (2009), *Libcom*, https://libcom.org/library/croissant-roses-new-labour-muslim-britain.
59. Cohen, *No One is Illegal*, 110.
60. Ibid., 105.
61. Quoted in Robbie Shilliam, *Race and the Undeserving Poor* (Newcastle: Agenda Publishing, 2018), 50.
62. Ibid., 50–51.
63. Ibid., 73–79.
64. El-Enany, *(B)ordering Britain*, 69.

65. Beverley Bryan, Stella Dadzie and Suzanne Scafe, *Heart of the Race: Black Women's Lives in Britain* (London: Verso, 2018), 89.
66. Alastair Bonnett, 'How the British Working Class Became White: The Symbolic (Re)formation of Racialized Capitalism', *Journal of Historical Sociology* 11, no. 3 (September 1998): 316–340, https://doi.org/10.1111/1467-6443.00066.
67. Booth was helped in his research by his cousin Beatrice Potter (later Webb), of the Fabian Society. Charles Booth, *Life and Labour of the People in London Volume I* (London: Macmillan, 1889), 38, https://tinyurl.com/2p8zuj83.
68. William Booth, *In Darkest England and the Way Out* (New York: Funk & Wagnalls, 1890), 11–14, https://tinyurl.com/ykz8wafw.
69. Shilliam, *Race and the Undeserving Poor*, 178.
70. Ibid., 7.
71. Edmonds, *Unpacking Chauvinism*, 69.
72. Ibid., 46.
73. Ibid., 121.
74. Karl Pearson, 'National Life from the Standpoint of Science: An Address Delivered at Newcastle, November 19, 1900' (London: A&C Black, 1901), accessed at: https://tinyurl.com/2p8hnm4k.
75. Karl Pearson and Margaret Moul, 'The Problem of Alien Immigration Into Great Britain, Illustrated by an Examination of Russian and Polish Jewish Children: Part III', *Annals of Eugenics* 3, nos 1–3 (1928).
76. Cohen, *No One is Illegal*, 90–93.
77. Aamna Mohdin, 'High Fee "Removes Children's Right to UK Citizenship", Court Hears', *The Guardian*, 26 November 2019, https://tinyurl.com/48wvs2f2.
78. Cohen, *No One is Illegal*, 98.
79. Ibid., 97–98.
80. Ibid., 97.
81. Hansard, House of Commons, 25 June 1930, https://tinyurl.com/4ey3acvm.
82. Mary Davis, *Sylvia Pankhurst: A Life in Radical Politics* (London: Pluto Press, 1999), 46–47.
83. TUC report, 1900, 54–55, https://tinyurl.com/yvu9n2sp.
84. Quoted in Cohen, 'That's Funny You Don't Look Anti-Semitic', 13.
85. Edmonds, *Unpacking Chauvinism*, 81.
86. Such elements being in Labour shouldn't surprise. It has always had flirtations with the far right. As New Labour continued hollowing out industry and privatising the social state, melancholic themes were played about 'left behind' regions/people. A racially and culturally determined 'white working class' crystallised and new migrants were blamed for all and sundry. Margaret Hodge, facing competition from the BNP in her constituency, parked her tanks on fascist lawns, calling for 'policies where the legitimate sense of entitlement felt by the indigenous family overrides the legitimate need demonstrated by the new migrants'. See Deborah Summers, 'Hodge Defends Immigration Comments', *The Guardian*, 22 May 2007, https://tinyurl.com/mrxktewn. Phil Woolas, Immigration minister, said in 2008:

> We need a tougher immigration policy and we need to stop seeing it as a dilemma. It's not. It's easy. I'm going to do my best to help the British back

to work. Britain has to get working again. The easiest thing for an employer to do is to employ an immigrant. We need to help them to change that.

Alice Thomson and Rachel Sylvester, 'Phil Woolas: Lifelong Fight Against Racism Inspired Limit on Immigration', *The Times*, 18 October 2008, https://tinyurl.com/2x4rmhxy.

87. Quoted in Edmonds, *Unpacking Chauvinism*, 107–108.
88. Ibid., 108.
89. Adam Hochschild, *To End All Wars* (Boston, MA: Houghton Mifflin Harcourt, 2011), 464.
90. '[D]eeper, stronger, more primordial than ... material ties', Milner argued, 'is the bond of common blood'. David J. Wertheim, *The Jew as Legitimation: Jewish–Gentile Relations Beyond Antisemitism and Philosemitism* (Cham: Palgrave Macmillan, 2017), 138–139.
91. Roy Douglas, 'The National Democratic Party and the British Workers' League', *The Historical Journal* 8, no. 15 (1972): 535.
92. Hochschild, *To End All Wars* 179.
93. Alan Sykes, *The Radical Right in Britain* (Basingstoke: Palgrave Macmillan, 2005), 37–38.
94. Hochschild, *To End All Wars*, 462.
95. Edmonds, *Unpacking Chauvinism*, 110.
96. 'Stopping The Rot', *Peace News*, https://tinyurl.com/2p8cxvkn.
97. Virdee, *Racism, Class and the Racialized Outsider*, 30–31.
98. Hansard, Lords, 17 July 1894, https://tinyurl.com/zavtefxy.
99. Hansard, Aliens Restriction Bill, HC Deb, 15 April 1919, vol, 114 cc2745–818, https://tinyurl.com/3uybynef.
100. Ibid.
101. Cohen, *No One is Illegal*, 179.
102. 'Our leading statesmen do not care to offend the great banking houses or money kings'. Quoted in Cohen, 'That's Funny You Don't Look Anti-Semitic', 21.
103. Simon Clarke writes:

> The progressive extension of the franchise assimilated the working class to the constitution by providing a form through which workers could pursue their aspirations not as workers but as individual citizens ... It is essentially these institutions, whose developed forms were systematically rationalised in the 'welfare state', that have defined the continuing relationship between the state and the working class.

Simon Clarke, *Keynesianism, Monetarism, and the Crisis of the State* (Cheltenham: Elgar, 1988), 141.

104. Virdee, 'Socialist Antisemitism and its Discontent', 356–373.
105. Fishman, *East End Jewish Radicals 1875–1914*, 176.
106. Raw, *Striking A Light*, 165.
107. As Virdee notes:

> Not only did Eleanor Marx begin to learn Yiddish in her thirties she also started to open her speeches to the workers of the East End with the words

'I am a Jewess' … She later confided …' 'My happiest moments are when I am in the East End amidst Jewish workpeople.'
Virdee, 'Socialist Antisemitism and its Discontents', 369.

108. Virdee, *Racism, Class and the Racialized Outsider*, 50.
109. Fishman, *East End Jewish Radicals 1875–1914*, 300.
110. Joe O'Shea, 'Battle of Cable Street: When the Irish Helped Beat Back the Fascists', *Irish Times*, 24 September 2016, https://tinyurl.com/2p9f238c.
111. Fishman, *East End Jewish Radicals 1875–1914*, 104.
112. Quoted in Gartner, *The Jewish Immigrant in England 1870–1914*, 114.
113. Pankhurst would later march against Mosley in 1937. Speaking at a Jewish ex-Servicemen's League rally, she was hit by a rock thrown by a fascist. Barbara Winslow, *Sylvia Pankhurst: Sexual Politics and Political Activism* (New York: St. Martin's Press 1996), 188–189.
114. Julia Bush, *Behind The Lines* (London: Merlin Press, 1984), 178.
115. Edmonds, *Unpacking Chauvinism*, 91–92.

CHAPTER 5

1. Erika Lee, *At America's Gates: Chinese Immigration During the Exclusion Era, 1882–1943* (Chapel Hill, NC: University of North Carolina Press, 2004), 26.
2. See Phil A. Neel, *Hinterland: America's New Landscape of Class and Conflict* (London: Reaktion Books, 2018), 57.
3. Of 125 defendants after the Capitol insurrection, 60 per cent had filed for bankruptcy, unpaid tax bills or had been sued for unpaid debts, and risked foreclosure. Grace Panetta, 'The Defendants Charged in the Capitol Insurrection have Something in Common: A History of Financial Woes', *Business Insider*, no date, https://tinyurl.com/m4uk378c.
4. Editors, 'Commonsense Solidarity: How a Working-Class Coalition Can Be Built, and Maintained', *Jacobin*, 9 November 2021, https://tinyurl.com/bdf83dkx. In a YouTube breakdown, results showed 'woke progressive' messaging (emphasising racial justice) was 8 per cent less appealing than 'progressive populist' (emphasising universal messaging). It was read as a 'significant' gap for marginal states. See 'Does "Wokeness" Really Alienate Voters?', *Jacobin* YouTube, 9 November 2021, https://tinyurl.com/y5f4ba9n.
5. Barbara and John Ehrenreich, 'The Professional-Managerial Class', in Pat Walker (eds), *Between Labour and Capital: The Professional Managerial Class* (Boston, MA: South End Press, 1979), 5–45. 'If the left is to grow, it must come to an objective understanding of its own class origins and to comprehend objectively the barriers that have isolated it from the working class'; Ehrenreich and Ehrenreich, 'The Professional-Managerial Class', 6.
6. See Gabriel Winant, 'Professional-Managerial Chasm: A Sociological Designation Turned Into an Epithet and Hurled Like a Missile', *n+1*, 10 October 2019, https://tinyurl.com/2p8vw2yf.
7. Ehrenreich and Ehrenreich, 'The Professional-Managerial Class', 6. See Barbara Ehrenreich's dismay at the way this concept was being used in Alex Press, 'On the Origins of the Professional-Managerial Class: An Interview

with Barbara Ehrenreich, *Dissent Magazine*, 22 October 2019, https://tinyurl.
com/mr2hzmkp.

8. Alexander Saxton, *The Indispensable Enemy: Labor and the Anti-Chinese Movement in California* (Berkeley, CA: University of California Press, 1971), 11.

9. Quoted in Saxton, *The Indispensable Enemy*, 81.

10. Beth Lew-Williams cautions us not to accept the coolie trope:

> Though Chinese men in the United States encountered many forms of economic exploitation, they were not bound or indentured laborers. Women and girls sometimes experienced human trafficking, but Chinese men were compensated for their work, albeit scantly, and were free to leave their place of employment if they could find a better one. That said, free and unfree labor were never dichotomous categories, and at times, circumstance could push individual Chinese workers toward the unfree end of the spectrum. Some arrived in the country heavily indebted to those who had paid their passage, others were coerced into gang labor, and all encountered a dual wage system based on race. Still, Chinese workers never fully embodied the coolie trope.

Beth Lew-Williams, *The Chinese Must Go: Violence, Exclusion and the Making of the Alien in America* (Cambridge, MA: Harvard University Press, 2018), 34. On mining claims, see Saxton, *The Indispensable Enemy*, 52.

11. Quoted in Saxton, *The Indispensable Enemy*, 147–148.

12. Adam M. McKeown, *Melancholy Order: Asian Migration and the Globalization of Borders* (New York: Columbia University Press, 2011), 121.

13. Quoted in Lee, *At America's Gates*, 30.

14. Both quoted in Andrew Gyory, *Closing the Gate: Race, Politics, and the Chinese Exclusion Act* (Chapel Hill, NC: University of North Carolina Press, 2000), 18.

15. Saxton, *The Indispensable Enemy*, 73.

16. Ibid., 74.

17. Ibid., 67–91.

18. Ibid., 72.

19. Ibid., 69–70.

20. Lew-Williams, *The Chinese Must Go*, 40.

21. Judy Yung, Gordon H. Chang and Him Mark Lai, *Chinese American Voices: From the Gold Rush to the Present* (Oakland, CA: University of California Press, 2006), 17.

22. *Daily Alta*, 28, no. 9497 (6 April 1876), California Digital Newspaper Collection, Center for Bibliographic Studies and Research, University of California, Riverside, https://tinyurl.com/yckwnr2a.

23. Saxton, *The Indispensable Enemy*, 177.

24. Ibid., 176.

25. Mike Davis, *Prisoners of the American Dream: Politics and Economy in the History of the US Working Class* (New York: Verso, 2018), 87–116.

26. Saxton, *The Indispensable Enemy*, 114.

27. Davis, *Prisoners of the American Dream*, 54–55.

28. Saxton, *The Indispensable Enemy*, 118.
29. Quoted in Saxton, *The Indispensable Enemy*, 118.
30. Saxton, *The Indispensable Enemy*, 139.
31. Some of the cartoons can be viewed at 'Thomas Nast Cartoons', https://tinyurl.com/yhhsc67x. https://thomasnastcartoons.com/tag/the-wasp/
32. Lee, *At America's Gates*, 27.
33. Saxton, *The Indispensable Enemy*, 59.
34. Quoted in Saxton, *The Indispensable Enemy*, 172.
35. Most Chinese-Americans today trace their origins to this later migration. See Irene Hsu, 'The Echoes of Chinese Exclusion', *The New Republic*, 28 June 2018, https://tinyurl.com/4vdcas29.
36. For example, the El Paso Walmart shooting in 2019. The killer, an eight-chan poster, murdered 23 people, having previously expressed support for the Christchurch shooter and warned about 'hispanic invasion'. In 2021, a survivor of the massacre, Rosa, was deported by the Biden administration. See 'Hundreds Deported Under Biden, Including Witness to Massacre', *US News*, 1 February 2021, https://tinyurl.com/5n8ya7pa.
37. Chantal da Silva, 'Trump Says He Plans to Sign Executive Order to Terminate Birthright Citizenship', *Newsweek*, 30 October 2018, https://tinyurl.com/rmwdtd88.
38. Daniel Denvir, *All-American Nativism* (London: Verso, 2020), 22.
39. Silvia Foster-Frau, 'First Migrant Facility for Children Opens Under Biden', *Washington Post*, 22 February 2021, https://tinyurl.com/yckjc2n6.
40. 'Rather than a historical aberration, Briggs argues, Trump's policy built upon earlier acts of dispossession directed at black, Native, Latin American, refugee, and other historically subjugated children and families.' Paul M. Renfro, 'America's Long War on Children and Families', *Boston Review*, 23 June 2020, https://tinyurl.com/4hdpcb7s.
41. Quoted in Lew-Williams, *The Chinese Must Go*, 19.
42. Judy Yung, Gordon H. Chang and Him Mark Lai (eds), *Chinese American Voices: From the Gold Rush to the Present* (Oakland, CA: University of the California Press, 2006), 17.
43. Ibid., 4.
44. See 'Chinese Railroad Workers in North America Project', at Stanford University, 31 August 2020, https://tinyurl.com/2p8zzhc4.
45. 'Union State Convention', *Sacramento Daily Union* 33, no. 5075, 3 July 1867, https://tinyurl.com/mwyufryx.
46. Pay for at least some Chinese workers did rise shortly after the strike was defeated. It is estimated around 1,200 Chinese workers died during the construction of the Central Pacific Railroad. Eric Arnesen, *Encyclopaedia of U.S. Labor and Working-Class History, Volume 1* (Abingdon: Taylor & Francis, 2007), 242.
47. Saxton, *The Indispensable Enemy*, 10.
48. *Daily Alta* 33, no. 11349, 16 May 1881, https://tinyurl.com/ycks8k7u.
49. Chinese Exclusion inspired Hyndman and other British socialists. In 1882, he argued Chinese immigrants 'could swamp us industrially and crowd us out of almost every occupation'. Thirty years later, he complained that:

'Europeans, even in a temperate climate, cannot hold their own, in the long run, with these hard-working Asiatics; in the tropics they have no chance at all against industrious coolies from the Southern Provinces of China.' In contrast, in 1884, a year before splitting from the SDF to found the Socialist League, Eleanor Marx's column in socialist journal *Today* reported:

> there are several large strikes – that of the New York cigar makers has lasted for many weeks – but the most remarkable one, and the best deserving our careful attention, is that of the Chinamen in San Francisco. These despised Asiatics have formed a union, and following the example of their New York brethren, 3,000 Chinese cigar makers are demanding higher wages. But this is not all. The masters hope to use against these poor 'coolies', white workmen from the East!

Virdee, *Racism, Class, and the Racialized Outsider*, 49. Eleanor Marx, 'Record of the International Popular Movement', *Today*, May 1884, see www.marxists.org/archive/eleanor-marx/1884/05/record-international.htm.

50. *Daily Alta*, 36, no. 12372, 1 (3 March 1884), https://tinyurl.com/2p27xuht.
51. Ibid.
52. H.M. Lai, 'Detained on Angel Island' (Spring 1978), https://tinyurl.com/53s6mz6y.
53. See 'Angel Island Immigration Station Poetry: 1910–1940', https://tinyurl.com/mufmd3se.
54. A later exception was the IWW. See Joe Richard, 'The Legacy of the IWW: To Break Their Haughty Power', *International Socialist Review* 86 (November 2012), https://isreview.org/issue/86/legacy-iww.
55. '(1869) Frederick Douglass Describes The "Composite Nation"', *BlackPast.org*, 28 January 2007, https://tinyurl.com/y4w4yzfa.
56. Ibid.
57. Saxton, *The Indispensable Enemy*, 221.
58. Ibid., 221.
59. Ibid., 222.
60. Mae Ngai, 'Why Trump is making Muslims the new Chinese', *CNN*, 30 January 2017, https://tinyurl.com/mpd792ek.
61. Jenna Johnson, 'Trump Calls for "Total and Complete Shutdown of Muslims Entering the United States"', *Washington Post*, 7 December 2015, https://tinyurl.com/2p8rc286.
62. Chris Brooks, 'New York Taxi Workers Strike Back Against Muslim Ban', *Labor Notes*, 30 January 2017, https://tinyurl.com/2d8hamrr.
63. *Chae Chan Ping v. U.S.* (Chinese Exclusion Case), 130 U.S. 581 (1889):

> If, therefore, the government of the United States, through its legislative department, considers the presence of foreigners of a different race in this country, who will not assimilate with us, to be dangerous to its peace and security, their exclusion is not to be stayed because at the time there are no actual hostilities with the nation of which the foreigners are subjects.

See Justia, US Supreme Court, https://tinyurl.com/2p8t7vpy.
64. Sarah Wildman, 'Trump's Speech in Poland Sounded Like an Alt-Right Manifesto', *Vox*, 6 July 2017, https://tinyurl.com/4k7u3zc8.

65. Quoted in Saxton, *The Indispensable Enemy*, 180.
66. Saxton, *The Indispensable Enemy*, 202.
67. Anti-Chinese forces in Washington were led by Daniel Cronin of the Knights of Labor, among others. See Nicole Grant, 'White Supremacy and the Alien Land Laws of Washington State', *Seattle Civil Rights & Labor History Project*, 2008, https://tinyurl.com/2p9xzha3.
68. Lew-Williams, *The Chinese Must Go*, 114.
69. McKeown, *Melancholy Order*, 122–123.
70. Quoted in, Saxton, *The Indispensable Enemy*, 244.
71. Saxton, *The Indispensable Enemy*, 264.
72. Quoted in Lee, *At America's Gates*, 33.
73. Saxton, *The Indispensable Enemy*, 271.
74. In 1955, the AFL merged with the industrial CIO, both purged of radicals, prepared for an era of class compromise.

   By the late sixties, the AFL-CIO was one of the most reactionary entities in US politics, with a membership that largely supported the Vietnam War, opposed civil rights and women's liberation, and routinely tolerated corrupt sweetheart agreements with employers. The leadership had ties to the CIA and to the mafia, and the rank and file was largely dismissed by the left as having no revolutionary potential.

   Michael Staudenmaier, *Truth And Revolution: A History of the Sojourner Truth Organization* (Oakland, CA: AK Press, 2012), 16.
75. Zinn, *A People's History*, 382.
76. Quoted in Saxton, *The Indispensable Enemy*, 234.
77. Eli Watkins and Abby Phillip, 'Trump Decries Immigrants from "Shithole Countries" Coming to US', *CNN*, 11 January 2018, https://tinyurl.com/3rf2p47h.
78. Hitler praised this legislation in *Mein Kampf*: 'The American Union categorically refuses the immigration of physically unhealthy elements, and simply excludes the immigration of certain races.' See Stephen Rohde, 'The United States – A Model for the Nazis', *LA Review of Books*, September 2017, https://tinyurl.com/2nrx5b84.
79. 'Kamala Harris Tells Guatemala Migrants: "Do not Come to US"', *BBC News*, 8 June 2021, www.bbc.co.uk/news/world-us-canada-57387350.
80. Marx, *Capital Volume I* (Harmondsworth: Penguin Classics: 1990), 794.

CHAPTER 6

1. W.E.B. Du Bois, *The World and Africa: Color and Democracy* (New York: Oxford University Press, 2007), 13–14.
2. Kate Buck, 'Coventry City: "No Evidence" of Racism After Black Men Chased and Pelted with Bottles', *LBC*, 11 June 2020. https://tinyurl.com/mwzdkup6.
3. Josh Layton, 'How the Far-Right is Trying to Fan Hatred and Racism in Coventry', *CoventryLive*, 6 July 2020, https://tinyurl.com/48sbezce.
4. Known as the 'Sewell Report' or 'Commission on Race and Ethnic Disparities: The Report', March 2021, 7, https://tinyurl.com/muvhju5c.

5. Ibid., 35.
6. For this headline and other media reactions, see Mic Wright, "Cops are cool and Britain isn't racist..." The establishment marks its own work and the newspapers swallow it', *Conquest of the Useless*, 31 March 2021, https://tinyurl.com/2p9eh44s.
7. 'Sewell Report', 31.
8. Ibid., 6.
9. For a fuller survey of Britain's race reports, see Jenny Bourne, 'Sewell: A Report for Neoliberal Times', *Institute of Race Relations*, 20 April 2021, https://tinyurl.com/3kwcc4wk.
10. Liz Fekete, 'Policing in the Brexit State – Back to the 1980s', *Institute of Race Relations*, 26 March 2021, https://tinyurl.com/3bw42nz7.
11. 'Nationality and Borders Bill', 10. For quick view of Clause 9: https://tinyurl.com/2p833scd.
12. Nisha Kapoor, 'On Citizenship Deprivation: When Neo-Nationalism Meets Big Tec, *Red Pepper*, 16 December 2021, https://tinyurl.com/386455f2.
13. For more on Black resistance in Notting Hill, see 'Beating Back Mosley', *libcom*, 10 September 2006, https://tinyurl.com/2d4emkm2.
14. Peter Fryer, *Staying Power: The History of Black People in Britain* (London: Pluto Press, 1984), 383–386.
15. Evan Smith, 'Integration and Limitation: Labour and Immigration, 1962–68', *New Historical Express*, 16 March 2015, https://tinyurl.com/d9m9wkak.
16. Striking Women, 'Twice Migrants: African Asian Migration to the UK', https://tinyurl.com/3nfvxuye.
17. Alwyn W. Turner, *Crisis? What Crisis? Britain in the 1970s* (London: Aurum Press, 2013), 516.
18. Evan Smith, 'The British Left and Immigration Controls', *New Historical Express*, 27 July 2013, https://tinyurl.com/yttr8z9h.
19. Virou Srilangarajah, 'We Are Here Because You Were With Us: Remembering A. Sivanandan (1923–2018)', *Ceasefire Magazine*, 4 February 2018, https://ceasefiremagazine.co.uk/us-remembering-a-sivanandan-1923-2018/.
20. Meat Porters marched with the National Front in 1972 during the 'Ugandan Asian Crisis'. They chanted 'Britain is for the British' and 'Keep the Asians out!'; El-Enany, *(B)ordering Britain*, 122.
21. Pearman was later found to have been in 'a right-wing pressure group Moral Rearmament'. And 'Pat Duhig, another leader of the dockers' strikes turned out to be a member of the Union Movement – the successor party of the pre-war British Union of Fascists – as did Dennis Harmston who led the strikes by meatporters in both 1968 and 1972.' Harmston was Mosley's bodyguard. See Virdee, *Racism, Class and the Racialized Outsider*, 115–117.
22. Shilliam, *Race and the Undeserving*, 103. And he *was* popular. A Gallup poll days later showed 74 per cent agreed with Powell's speech. Virdee, *Racism, Class and the Racialized Outsider*, 116.
23. The 1981 Nationality Act, which removed birthright citizenship, was also an effective form of immigration control, further barring access to an increasingly cordoned off national territory for people of the colonies and

Commonwealth. See Imogen Tyler, *Revolting Subjects: Social Abjection and Resistance in Neoliberal Britain* (London: Zed Books, 2013), 48–74.

24. The 1971 Act calculated that British capital could increasingly secure returns by investing where labour-power already was, and in the EEC they had a replacement source of labour-power nearby.
25. For more, see James Trafford, *The Empire at Home: Internal Colonies and the End of Britain* (London: Pluto Press, 2020), 50–80.
26. See *Policing Against Black People* (London: Institute of Race Relations, 1987). See also Joseph A. Hunte, *Nigger Hunting in England?* (London: West Indian Standing Conference, 1966), 12, http://pg.gilroyware.com/Joseph_Hunte.pdf.
27. Field, Bunce, Hassan and Peacock, *Here To Stay, Here To Fight*, 31.
28. Part 4 of the superb *Empire's Endgame*, 'Send in the Army', explores the 'recurrent and increasingly insistent' call for domestic military intervention and how it 'reveals something important about our present crisis'. Gargi Bhattacharyya, Adam Elliott-Cooper, Sita Balani, Kerem Nişancıoğlu, Kojo Koram, Dalia Gebrial, Nadine El-Enany and Luke de Noronha, *Empire's Endgame: Racism and the British State* (London: Pluto Press, 2021), 133–170.
29. Cited in Jenny Bourne, 'The Beatification of Enoch Powell', *Institute of Race Relations*, 21 November 2007, https://tinyurl.com/2p8jfx8t.
30. *Policing the Crisis* describes how racialised framings by media, police and politicians constructed 'mugging' as a new phenomenon – 'Black crime' – an alien culture poisoning British life. Hall et al. skilfully analysed how protracted crises, and the position of unemployed Black youth as an 'ethnically distinct class fraction', were obscured by surface-level morality tales of Black degeneracy. Chapters 2 and 3 of *Empire's Endgame* delve into present discourses around 'knife crime' and 'gangs' in a way that evokes Hall's work. See Stuart Hall, Chas Critcher, Tony Jefferson, John Clarke and Brian Roberts, *Policing the Crisis: Mugging, the State and Law and Order* (London: Macmillan, 1978).
31. A. Sivanandan, *Catching History on the Wing: Race, Culture and Globalisation* (London: Pluto Press, 2008), 112.
32. CARF, 'The Summer of Rebellion: Special Report', *Institute of Race Relations*, 1 August 2001, https://tinyurl.com/4ka3zza4.
33. Ibid.
34. Arun Kundnani, 'Nine Months for White Racist Thugs who Sparked the Oldham Riots', *Institute of Race Relations*, 19 June 2003, https://tinyurl.com/2h3xr26z.
35. See Arun Kundnani, 'IRR Expresses Concern Over Excessive Sentencing of Bradford Rioters', *Institute of Race Relations*, 5 July 2002, https://tinyurl.com/3vhj6edv. See also: Arun Kundnani, 'Four Sentences Reduced, Eleven Upheld, in Appeal for Bradford Rioters', *Institute of Race Relations*, 1 February 2003, https://tinyurl.com/3d9ttb48.
36. Field, Bunce, Hassan and Peacock, *Here To Stay, Here To Fight*, 28.
37. As Natalie Thomlinson states:

> It was never true that new Commonwealth immigration was state-sponsored. Indeed, despite the individual overseas recruiting efforts by

independent bodies such as London Transport, politicians showed concerns about post-war migration from the colonies almost from its onset: George Isaacs, the Minister of Labour told the House of Commons after the Windrush docked that 'I hope no encouragement is given to others to follow their example'.

Natalie Thomlinson, *Race, Ethnicity and the Women's Movement in England, 1968–1993* (London: Palgrave Macmillan, 2016), 20.
38. David Olusoga, *Black and British: A Forgotten History* (London: Pan Books, 2017), 451.
39. Ron Ramdin, *The Making of the Black Working Class in Britain* (London: Verso, 2017), 72.
40. Jacqueline Jenkinson, 'Black Sailors on Red Clydeside: Rioting, Reactionary Trade Unionism and Conflicting Notions of "Britishness" Following the First World War', *Twentieth Century British History* 19, no. 1 (2007): 29–60, https://doi.org/10.1093/tcbh/hwm031.
41. Jenkinson, 'Black Sailors on Red Clydeside', 31.
42. Ibid., 41.
43. Hansard, House of Commons, 1 May 1919, https://tinyurl.com/y2svfb6m.
44. Jenkinson, 'Black Sailors on Red Clydeside', 55.
45. Talat Ahmed, 'The British Empire and the First World War: The Colonial Experience', *International Socialism*, https://tinyurl.com/bdfu4b8a. See also Santanu Das, 'Experiences of Colonial Troops', *British Library* website, https://tinyurl.com/4pp9thtc.
46. Robinson, *Black Marxism*, 253.
47. Jenkinson, 'Black Sailors on Red Clydeside', 56.
48. For full description of the event, see Davis, *Sylvia Pankhurst*, 102.
49. Edmonds, *Unpacking Chauvinism*, 120–121.
50. Morel Quoted in, Robert C. Reinders, 'Racialism on the Left, E.D. Morel and the "Black Horror on the Rhine"', *International Review of Social History* 13, no. 1 (1968), 7. See Judy Yung, Gordon H. Chang and Him Mark Lai, *Chinese American Voices: From the Gold Rush to the Present* (Oakland, CA: University of California Press, 2006).
51. Reinders, 'Racialism on the Left', 9.
52. Ibid., 6.
53. Likely the first Black correspondent in a British newspaper. McKay first sent his reply to *Herald* editor George Lansbury. He complained that it was too long. See Anne Donlon, '"A Black Man Replies": Claude McKay's Challenge to the British Left', *Lateral* 5, no. 1 (2016); and Reinders, 'Racialism on the Left', 16.
54. Quoted in Donlon, '"A Black Man Replies"'.
55. Claude Mckay, *The Negroes in America*, edited by Alan L. McLeod, translated from Russian by Robert J. Winter (Port Washington, NY: Kennikat Press, 1979), 77.
56. Jacqueline Jenkinson, '1919 Race Riots in Britain: Background and Consequences' (PhD thesis, University of Edinburgh, 1987), 107.
57. Ibid., 109.

58. Ibid.,113.
59. Neil Evans, 'Across the Universe: Racial Violence and the Post-War Crisis in Imperial Britain, 1919–25', *Immigrants & Minorities: Historical Studies in Ethnicity, Migration and Diaspora* (1994) 13, 2–3, 66; see also Jenkinson, '1919 Race Riots', 86–88.
60. Jenkinson, '1919 Race Riots', 88.
61. Evans, 'Across the Universe', 66.
62. Ibid., 66.
63. From a TUC report 1916, 328–329, https://tinyurl.com/ycku7sua.
64. Ibid.
65. Jenkinson, '1919 Race Riots', 233.
66. From a TUC report 1919, 373, https://tinyurl.com/5vy9me66.
67. Olusoga, *Black and British*, 457.
68. Fryer, *Staying Power*, 304.
69. Ibid., 305.
70. Variously spelled Wootten, Wooten, Wooton, Wotten in different accounts.
71. Ibid., 305.
72. Jenkinson, '1919 Race Riots', 171.
73. Near identical pogroms returned in 1948. A culmination of the National Union of Seamen's efforts to maintain its colour bar against Liverpool's Black population. Black people defended themselves with 'stones, swords, daggers, iron coshes, and axes'. See Fryer, *Staying Power*, 373–377; and Beverley Bryan, Stella Dadzie and Suzanne Scafe, *Heart of the Race: Black Women's Lives in Britain* (London: Verso, 2018), 130.
74. Ibid., 139.
75. Ibid., 211–212.
76. Fred Halliday, *Britain's First Muslims: Portrait of an Arab Community* (London: I.B. Tauris, 2010), 24.
77. Jenkinson, '1919 Race Riots', 218.
78. Ramdin, *The Making of the Black Working Class in Britain*, 73.
79. Jenkinson, '1919 Race Riots', 245.
80. Ibid., 222.
81. Evans, 'Across the Universe', 79.
82. Fryer, *Staying Power*, 318.
83. Ibid.
84. Jenkinson, *1919 Race Riots*, 200.
85. Evans, 'Across the Universe', 75.
86. Jenkinson, '1919 Race Riots', 199–200.
87. Ibid., 200.
88. Ibid., 197–199.
89. Ibid., 187.
90. Roy May and Robin Cohen, 'The Interaction Between Race and Colonialism: A Case Study of the Liverpool Race Riots of 1919', *Race and Class*, 16, no. 2 (1974).
91. Ibid., 124.
92. Olusoga, *Black and British*, 460–461.
93. Jenkinson, '1919 Race Riots', 188.

94. Ibid., 190.
95. Ibid., 95, 186 and 189.
96. Ibid., 191.
97. E.J. Hobsbawm, 'The Machine Breakers', *Past & Present*, no. 1 (1952): 57–70, https://tinyurl.com/vadeb8jb.
98. Jenkinson, '1919 Race Riots', 271.
99. Ibid., 249.
100. Neil Evans, 'Regulating the Reserve Army: Arabs, Blacks and the Local State in Cardiff, 1919–45', *Immigrants & Minorities: Historical Studies in Ethnicity, Migration and Diaspora* 4, no. 2 (1985), 108.
101. Ramdin, *The Making of the Black Working Class in Britain*, 76.
102. Karl Marx, *Capital Vol II* (Harmondsworth: Penguin Classics, 1992), 135.
103. Evans, 'Across the Universe', 81.
104. Evans, 'Regulating the Reserve Army', 80.
105. Sivanandan, *Catching History on the Wing*, 168.
106. Luke De Noronha, 'Deportation, Racism and Multi-Status Britain: Immigration Control and the Production of Race in the Present', *Ethnic and Racial Studies* (2019) 42, 14, 2413. https://doi.org/10.1080/01419870.2019.1585559.
107. Patrick Wolfe, *Traces of History* (London: Verso, 2016), 14.

CHAPTER 7

1. Claude McKay, 'If We Must Die', first published in *The Liberator* in July 1919. Can viewed online: 'If We Must Die', *BlackPast*, https://tinyurl.com/4xmm7386.
2. Lead Belly, 'Scottsboro Boys', from Lead Belly: The Smithsonian Folkways Collection (2015), find online: https://tinyurl.com/yckjzh7v.
3. Isabel Wilkerson, 'The Long-Lasting Legacy of the Great Migration', *Smithsonian Magazine*, https://tinyurl.com/25cnmewr.
4. The White House correspondence from Russel Vought can be found online through whitehouse.gov: https://tinyurl.com/2p8ryvhe.
5. See Olivia Riggio, 'The Far Right's Manufactured Meaning of Critical Race Theory', *Fair*, https://tinyurl.com/2x64822a.
6. Chibber gives his view 7 minutes in. See 'Marxism is Way Better Than Critical Race Theory – Vivek Chibber', *Jacobin*, https://tinyurl.com/4k879uzr.
7. Ibid.
8. 'Identity based critiques,' Zoé Samudzi argues, 'are simply new vocabularies employed to dismiss 'inferior' ways of knowing.' In 'Shifting Objectives: On Methodology and Identity Politics', *versobooks.com*, https://tinyurl.com/y4vc3uyf.
9. For a detailed overview of what Bills are happening and where, see Peter Greene 'Teacher Anti-CRT Bills Coast to Coast: A State by State Guide', *Forbes*, https://tinyurl.com/4dyfutvw.
10. Quoted in, Evans, 'Across the Universe', 78.
11. A research project led by historian Liam Hogan has mapped and collated 'Mob Violence, Riots and Pogroms against African American Communities' between 1824–1974. It resulted in a map littered with red dots, marking this

constant violence against Black people that scars the historic landscape. See, 'Collective Punishment', https://tinyurl.com/55ep5na8.

12. *The Clansman* by Thomas Dixon Jr.
13. D.W. Griffith, *Birth of a Nation* (1915). Film can be found online, https://tinyurl.com/4xzv8x99.
14. *The Crisis* 14, no. 5 (September 1917), https://tinyurl.com/2p8fabfm.
15. Quoted in *The Crisis* (September 1917).
16. This underlined a feature common to the whiteness riots: it 'was confined not only to men. Women were in many cases the aggressors and always ready to instigate and abet'. One woman 'wanted to "cut the heart out" of a Negro, a man already paralyzed from a bullet wound'. The *St. Louis Post-Dispatch* 'saw Negro women begging for mercy and pleading that they had harmed no one set upon by white women of the baser sort who laughed and answered the coarse sallies of men as they beat the Negresses' faces and breasts with fists, stones and sticks'. Similar was present in Britain. In Newport, a Black man, John Davies, and his white wife together owned a boarding house which was attacked by a white mob. One white woman charged with the attack, who was sentenced to three months hard labour, a Mary Sheedy, had shouted at Mrs Davies: 'You ought to be burnt, because you are a Black man's wife', *Crisis* 14, no. 5 (September 1917), 222. See also Jenkinson, '1919 Race Riots', 249.
17. *The Crisis* (September 1917).
18. Zinn, *A People's History*, 375.
19. Michael Cohen, ' "The Ku Klux Government": Vigilantism, Lynching, and the Repression of the IWW', *Journal for the Study of Radicalism* 1, no. 1 (2007): 31–56, https://tinyurl.com/ycku96j9.
20. 'Representative James F. Byrnes of South Carolina claimed the average southern Black man was "happy and contented and will remain so if the propagandist of the I.W.W., the Bolshevik of Russia, and the misguided theorist of other sections of this country will let him alone".' Becky Little, 'How Communists Became a Scapegoat for the Red Summer "Race Riots" of 1919', *history.com*, 6 August 2020, https://tinyurl.com/mt2z999b.
21. Hoover would lead a new Bureau of Investigation, monitoring the political activity of radical groups and unions. This department would become the FBI and for the next half century Hoover would run it as a fiefdom in obsessive pursuit of crushing, among other dissident strands, Black liberation movements across the country.
22. 'Reds Try to Stir Negroes to Revolt', *New York Times*, 28 July 1919, https://tinyurl.com/yckzk98p.
23. Little, 'How Communists Became a Scapegoat for the Red Summer "Race Riots" of 1919'.
24. Rollin Kirby, '*New York World*', Cartoon, 30 September 1919, https://tinyurl.com/4rm37e2p.
25. Peter Perl, 'Race Riot of 1919 Gave Glimpse of Future Struggles', *Washington Post*, 1 March 1999, https://tinyurl.com/2wckez5v.
26. Congressional Record: Proceedings and Debates of the First Session of the 66th Congress of the United States, Volume LVIII – Part 6, 13 September–4 October 1919, 6082.

27. There were at least four mass mob attacks in Philadelphia alone between 1834–1849, targeting Black and white abolitionists, Black homes, churches, orphanages. Between 1877–1950, 4,084 Black people were lynched in the South. Lynchings – ritualistic, organised affairs, not 'crimes of passion' – were advertised in newspapers, attended by eager out-of-towners arriving via expanding railroad networks. For more, see Lynching in America: Confronting the Legacy of Racial Terror by the Equal Justice Initiative: https://lynchinginamerica.eji.org/.
28. Perl, 'Race Riot of 1919'.
29. Ibid.
30. Ibid.
31. Ibid.
32. The Crisis 19, no. 2 (December 1919), 62, https://tinyurl.com/2m22avxy.
33. Omaha Daily Bee, 26 September 1919, https://tinyurl.com/5f4zdh9f.
34. Ibid., 1.
35. Ibid., 1.
36. Ibid., 5.
37. 'Criticize Chief of Police', Omaha Daily Bee, 1 October 1919.
38. Omaha Daily Bee, 26 September 1919, 6.
39. Nicolas Swiercek, 'Stoking a White Backlash: Race, Violence, and Yellow Journalism in Omaha, 1919', James A. Rawley Graduate Conference in the Humanities. 31. University of Nebraska, 12 April 2008, https://core.ac.uk/download/pdf/188059225.pdf.
40. Quote sourced from Swiercek, 'Stoking a White Backlash', 12.
41. See James Baldwin, 'A Report from Occupied Territory', The Nation, 11 July 1966, https://tinyurl.com/yx587c6z.
42. Daniele Selby, 'From Emmett Till to Pervis Payne – Black Men in America Are Still Killed for Crimes They Didn't Commit', Innocence Project, 25 July 2020, https://tinyurl.com/2p89macz.
43. The Messenger 2, no. 9 (September 1919), 13.
44. Dominic J. Capeci, 'Race Riot Redux: William M. Tuttle, Jr. and the Study of Racial Violence', Reviews in American History 29, 1 (2001), 165–118, https://tinyurl.com/5n7ejphy.
45. For more, read Maya Gonzalez, 'Notes on the New Housing Question', End Notes 2, 55–60, https://tinyurl.com/acxnuw8m.
46. Similar policies operated in Britain in the 1960s and 1970s. Black and Asian kids were bussed to far away schools as many local authorities decided no school should have more than 30 per cent immigrant students. White kids were not bussed. See 'The Child Immigrants "Bussed" Out to School to Aid Integration', BBC News, 30 January 2017, https://tinyurl.com/yazuh73s.
47. Jonathan Kozol, 'When Joe Biden Collaborated With Segregationists', The Nation, 6 June 2019, https://tinyurl.com/2e9fvwek.
48. Saidiya Hartman on the lasting trauma for Black kids:

> it brought to mind all the young people who were a part of the school desegregation movement in the American South. Elizabeth Eckford was never the same after being assaulted by a mob of white adults when she

tried to enter Little Rock Central High School. Other children burnt their schoolbooks and experienced severe depression and had breakdowns after the intensity of navigating such hate and hostility. Those narratives trouble the one-dimensional portrait of these young people as solely heroic or triumphant. They paid a great psychic cost for trying to desegregate their schools.

See 'Errant Daughters: A Conversation between Saidiya Hartman and Hazel Carby', *The Paris Review*, 21 January 2020, https://tinyurl.com/5dzapw6y.

49. Bruce Gellerman, '"It was Like a War Zone": Busing in Boston', *WBUR*, 5 September 2014, https://tinyurl.com/2p9w97tr.

50. Jonathan Kozol writes, 'The proportion of black students in majority-white schools stands at "a level lower than in any year since 1968"', see 'Jonathan Kozol on Apartheid Education', *Practical Theory*, 4 December 2005, https://tinyurl.com/5e3r9dhv; and Jonathan Kozol, 'Overcoming Apartheid', *The Nation*, 1 December 2005, https://tinyurl.com/2p933t8k.

51. Dianne Harris, 'Race, Space, and Trayvon Martin', *Society of Architectural Historians*, 25 July 2013, https://tinyurl.com/3585yh7p.

52. Jelani Cobb, 'The Killing of Renisha McBride', *The New Yorker*, 16 November 2013, https://tinyurl.com/2b256p5h.

53. Maanvi Singh, 'Georgia Overhauls "Citizen's Arrest" Law After Ahmaud Arbery Killing', *The Guardian*, 1 April 2021, https://tinyurl.com/2p8ncf2p.

54. Charles E. Cobb Jr, *This Nonviolent Stuff'll Get You Killed* (Durham, NC: Duke University Press, 2016), 72–73.

55. *The Messenger*, September 1919, 3.

56. Ibid., 20.

57. *The Crisis* 18, no. 5 (September 1919), 231, https://tinyurl.com/9y6vnnuh.

58. *The Crisis* 2, no. 6 (October 1919), 297, https://tinyurl.com/2p8ceyd5.

59. *The Messenger* 2, no. 2 (December 1919), 4, https://tinyurl.com/2vcbtft7.

60. *The Messenger*, September 1919, 4.

61. Ibid., 4–5 and 20–21.

62. Ibid., 29.

63. Perl, 'Race Riot of 1919'.

64. Ibid.

65. *The Messenger*, September 1919, 11.

66. Ibid., 11–13.

67. Harry Haywood, *Black Bolshevik: Autobiography of an Afro-American Communist* (Liberator Press, 1978), 82.

68. Ibid., 1.

69. See Adolph Reed: 'Fetishizing Agency is at Bottom a Thatcherite Project', *Jacobin*, 6 October 2015, https://tinyurl.com/2rtj9wjc. Working-class history is partly about recognising people's agency in their historical circumstances – with the potential to fight for, or unravel, working-class solidarity. The heavy focus put on opportunism in socialist historiography can mean sidestepping this issue. It has the effect of reducing working-class subjectivity to a repository of revolutionary 'energy' subject to manipulation by reactionary strategists (therefore requiring socialist counter-strategists). If people

really were so pliant and easily manipulated there would have been no need for complex forms of social control through identities of oppression and exploitation. We require 'agency', therefore, as a methodological starting point to assess *both* moments of resistance and a fuller picture of acquiescence and conformity.

70. *The Crisis*, December 1919, 56.
71. Francine Uenuma, 'The Massacre of Black Sharecroppers That Led the Supreme Court to Curb the Racial Disparities of the Justice System', *Smithsonian Magazine*, https://tinyurl.com/235n4r4w.
72. *The Crisis*, December 1919, 60.
73. *The Brinkley Argus*, 2 October 1919. *Chronicling America: Historic American Newspapers*, Library of Congress, https://tinyurl.com/3m2n8twx.
74. Ida B. Wells-Barnett, 'The Arkansas Race Riot', 1920, 13, https://tinyurl.com/28sxkckn.
75. Ibid., 15.
76. Robin D.G. Kelley, *Hammer and Hoe: Alabama Communists During The Great Depression* (Chapel Hill, NC: University of North Carolina Press, 1990), 30.
77. Ibid., 29.
78. Du Bois, *Black Reconstruction*, 680.
79. Ibid., 674.
80. Uenuma, 'The Massacre of Black Sharecroppers'.
81. Grif Stockley, *Blood in Their Eyes: The Elaine Race Massacres of 1919* (Fayetteville, AR: University of Arkansas Press, 2001), 81.
82. Philip S. Foner, *History of the Labor Movement in the US*, Vol. 8 (New York: International Publishers, 1988), 1.
83. Ibid., 22–23.
84. *The Messenger*, often full of praise for the IWW, dedicated a cover story in 1919 to solidarity shown by white workers to Black workers in Louisiana: 'All hail to the white workers of Bogalusa! You are learning! You are on the road. Your enemy is the Southern white employing class, not the Negroes. Your only weapon is the solidarity of the working class, Black and white.' Foner, *History of the Labor Movement in the US*, 196.
85. A government committee in 1919 praised AFL leaders for being 'free from the revolutionary radicalism'. They were congratulated for not following the British example of founding a labour party. Foner, *History of the Labor Movement in the US*, 33.
86. *The Crisis*, September 1917, 216.
87. Quoted in *The Crisis*, September 1917, 221.
88. Foner, *History of the Labor Movement in the US*, 137.
89. Ibid.
90. Ibid.
91. Ibid.
92. Ibid.
93. Martin Glaberman, 'The Dodge Revolutionary Union Movement', *Marxists. org*, https://tinyurl.com/386vjx33. There is a whole archive of materials on

the League of Revolutionary Black Workers at *libcom*, 14 October 2006, https://tinyurl.com/mr3hkppn.

94. Adam Cohen and Elizabeth Taylor write:

    Daley's role ... is likely lost to history, in part because the police and prose-cutors never pursued the white gang members who instigated the violence. At the least ... Daley was an integral member of a youth gang that played an active role in one of the bloodiest antiblack riots in the nation's history – and that within a few years' time, this same gang would think enough of Daley to select him as its leader.

    Excerpt from Adam Cohen and Elizabeth Taylor, 'American Pharaoh: Mayor Richard J. Daley – His Battle for Chicago and the Nation', https://tinyurl.com/4pf5vy5j.

95. 'Nation: Should Looters Be Shot?', *Time*, 26 April 1968, https://tinyurl.com/mr3afh9r.

96. Bobby Vanecko, 'A Letter to My Cousins: Coming to Terms with Family History When Your Family Name is "Daley"', *Southside Weekly*, 11 November 2020, https://tinyurl.com/2ewhtvp4.

97. 'Folk politics' was an expression popularised by Nick Srnicek and Alex Williams, *Inventing The Future: Postcapitalism and a World Without Work* (London: Verso, 2015).

98. What got the goods? Nous: 'What I'll do is study a group of friends and go to the leader of the pack. Whatever the leader says, the rest of the group is going to do.' Working through the divisions that exist: 'Cassio [Mendoza] talks to all the Latino workers in the building.' Empathy: 'I knew that we would win because of Maddie [Wesley ... She's so empathetic, so she can connect with a lot of people in the building. She was one of the key leaders.' Luis Feliz Leon, 'Amazon Workers in Staten Island Clinch Historic Victory', *Labor Notes*, 1 April 2022, https://tinyurl.com/yckpxz5h.

99. Theodor W. Adorno, *Metaphysics: Concept and Problems* (Cambridge: Polity, 2015), 65.

100. See, for example, Cedric Johnson, 'The Triumph of Black Lives Matter and Neoliberal Redemption', *nonsite*, 9 June 2020, https://tinyurl.com/465enyph.

101. See Derecka Purnell's excellent *Becoming Abolitionists: Police, Protests, and the Pursuit of Freedom* (London: Verso, 2021), where the author combines autobiography, organising accounts and long-view histories to take the reader on her journey to finding an abolitionist politics.

CONCLUSION

1. William Faulkner, *Requiem for a Nun* (New York: Random House, 1951), 85.

2. Saidiya Hartman, *Scenes of Subjection: Terror, Slavery and Self-Making in Nineteenth-Century America* (Oxford: Oxford University Press, 1997), 123.

3. Marx, *Capital Volume I* (Harmondsworth: Penguin Classics, 1990), 344. Marx remains a lucid guide to the 'rule of abstraction' that characterises capitalist society, but the solutions required to overcome its laws are ours to solve. As Robinson wrote in his introduction to *Black Marxism*: 'The European

proletariat and its social allies did not constitute the revolutionary subject
of history, nor was working-class consciousness necessarily the negation
of bourgeois culture.' See Cedric Robinson, *Black Marxism: The Making of
the Black Radical Tradition* (Chapel Hill, NC: University of North Carolina
Press, 1983).

4. Walter Benjamin, 'On the Concept of History', *Marxists.org*, https://tinyurl.
com/35urp8rr.

5. Morrison, in a lecture titled, 'Unspeakable Things Unspoken: The Afro-
American Presence in American Literature', puts it this way:

> We can agree, I think, that invisible things are not necessarily 'not-there';
> that a void may be empty but not be a vacuum. In addition, certain
> absences are so stressed, so ornate, so planned, they call attention to them-
> selves; arrest us with intentionality and purpose, like neighborhoods that
> are defined by the population held away from them. Looking at the scope
> of American literature, I can't help thinking that the question should never
> have been 'Why am I, an Afro-American, absent from it?' It is not a par-
> ticularly interesting query anyway. The spectacularly interesting question
> is 'What intellectual feats had to be performed by the author or his critic
> to erase me from a society seething with my presence, and what effect has
> that performance had on the work?'

Toni Morrison, 'Unspeakable Things Unspoken: The Afro-American
Presence in American Literature', *The Tanner Lectures on Human Values*,
University of Michigan, 7 October 1988, 136, https://tinyurl.com/3ftpaj3h.

6. Darcus Howe quoted in this extract from an article titled 'Why I'll Fight the
Heavy Mob', *Post Mercury*, 17 December 1971, https://tinyurl.com/3v6sn4vk.

7. Wendell Pritchett, 'Identity Politics, Past and Present', *International Labor
and Working-Class History*, no. 67 (2005), 33–34, https://doi.org/10.1017/
S0147547905000049.

8. Ibid.

9. Ibid., 37 and 40.

10. Renato Rosaldo, 'Identity Politics: An Ethnography by a Participant', in
Linda Martín Alcoff, Michael Hames-García, Satya P. Mohanty and Paula
M.L. Moya (eds), *Identity Politics Reconsidered: An Introduction* (New York:
Palgrave Macmillan, 2006), 119.

11. Robinson, *Black Marxism*, 239.

12. Harsha Walia, *Undoing Border Imperialism* (Oakland, CA: AK Press, 2013),
193–194.

13. Ibid., 193.

14. Barbara Smith, interview with Susan Levine Goodwillie, 1994, quoted in
Duchess Harris, 'Conclusion: Defining the Politics of Identity', in Bettye Col-
lier-Thomas and V.P. Franklin (eds), *Sisters in the Struggle: African American
Women in the Civil Rights-Black Power Movement* (New York: New York
University Press, 2001), 300.

15. Ibid.

16. Barbara Smith, quoted in Duchess Harris, 'Black Feminist Politics – Kennedy
to Clinton', in Bettye Collier-Thomas and V.P. Franklin (eds), *Sisters in the*

Struggle: African American Women in the Civil Rights-Black Power Movement (New York: New York University Press, 2001), 28.

17. Ibid.
18. Beverley Bryan, Stella Dadzie and Suzanne Scafe, *Heart of the Race: Black Women's Lives in Britain* (London: Verso, 2018), 242.
19. Ibid., 245.
20. Ibid., 246.
21. Ibid.
22. Ibid., 248.
23. Ibid., 249
24. Ibid., 250.
25. Ibid., 255–256.
26. Ibid., 256–257.
27. For a detailed discussion of this connection, see Kristian Davis Bailey, 'Black-Palestinian Solidarity in the Ferguson-Gaza Era', *American Quarterly* 67, no. 4 (2015): 1017–1026, https://doi.org/10.1353/aq.2015.0060.
28. 'Thousands of French Students Protest Against Deportation of Roma High School Student', *Hurriyet Daily News*, 17 October 2013, https://tinyurl.com/yxp3t35y. See also Chris H., 'Glasgow's Tradition of Resisting the Home Office', *New Socialist*, 19 May 2021, https://tinyurl.com/4yk66xyr.
29. Nadine Talaat, '"Can You Stop Us or Will We Stop You?": Inside Palestine Action, the Group Shutting Down Israel's Largest Weapons Company', *The New Arab*, 11 February 2022, https://tinyurl.com/2p89ymp4.
30. Ambalavaner Sivanandan, *Catching History on the Wing: Race, Culture and Globalisation* (London: Pluto Press, 2008), 54.

Index

origins 46,
statement 11–12, 52, 215
see also Black feminism
Commonweal 108
Communist Party 54–5, 193, 196,
198–200
Conservative Party 8, 18, 22, 36, 38, 84,
99, 101, 103, 105, 153–5, 157, 159
Cooper, Anna Julia 62
Corbyn, Jeremy 10, 20, 99
Coventry 150–1
Covid-19 pandemic 124, 136
Crisis, The (journal of the NAACP)180,
188, 191, 195, 198
Cugoano, Ottobah 28–9
'culture war' 1, 12, 15, 39, 216
critical race theory (CRT) 36, 178–9

Dadzie, Stella 12, 213–15
Daily Alta, The 131, 139
Daily Herald, The 163–4
Daily Mail, The 151
Daley, Richard J. 200–1
Danielewicz, Sigismund 141–2
Davis, Angela 46, 48, 59, 62
Davis, Mike 130–1, 133
deaths in custody 9–10, 169, 211
Democratic Party 4, 10, 44, 61, 126–7,
188, 200
De Noronha, Luke 176
Denvir, Daniel 138
Depo Provera 90
Dodge Revolutionary Union Movement
(DRUM) 199
Douglass, Frederick 30, 50, 63, 140–1
Dunbar-Ortiz, Roxanne 58
Du Bois, W. E. B. 31, 33, 36, 55, 150, 188,
191–2, 196
see also Black agency
Dubois, Ellen Carol 61

East St. Louis 181, 198–9
Echols, Alice 57–8, 66–67
Edmonds, Daniel 113, 116
Ehrenreich, Barbara and John 124–5
Eight hour day movement 32, 131–2, 134
Elaine, Arkansas 179, 194–7
El-Enany, Nadine 99, 110
Embery, Paul 96–7, 148
Equiano, Olaudah 28–9

eugenics 71, 110–13, 147–8, 204
Evans, Neil 175
Everard, Sarah 78

Fabian Society 81–2, 102–3, 117
fascism 2, 9, 14, 125, 136–7, 144, 163, 211
backlash against BLM 20–1, 150–1
Charleston Massacre 16, 28
Charlottesville 'Unite the Right' rally
17
'gender critical' crossover 73, 93–4
mainstreaming 152–3, 203
overlap with liberalism 20–1, 42, 158,
203
relationship to racism 152–4
wartime patriotic labour 116–18, 120
see also Ku Klux Klan
Fawcett, Millicent 83
Fekete, Liz 152
feminism 11–13, 42–69, 70–95, 212–18
see also Black feminism; carceral
feminism; radical feminism; socialist
feminism; 'white feminism'
Ferguson, Missouri 4, 202–3
Fineberg, Joe 106
Finn, Joseph 107
Firestone, Shulamith 58–9, 61, 66, 94
First World War 116–18, 159–63, 177,
182–3, 190, 193
Fisher, Victor 117–18
Fishman, William 103
Floyd, George 18, 21, 26, 44
Fraser, Nancy 7, 9
Fryer, Peter 24, 153, 167

Gal-Dem 71
Garrison, William Lloyd 53
Garvey, Marcus 171, 182, 192
'gender critical' feminism 72–4, 91, 93,
207–8
'gender ideology' 1, 49, 73–4, 93, 207–8
Gilmore, Ruth Wilson 44–5
Glasgow 160–2, 165
Goldman, Emma 119, 182
Gompers, Samuel 147–8, 198
Gordon, Major William Evans 105
Great Migration 47, 177, 180, 188, 198–9
Greenwald, Glenn 3
Griffith, D. W. 181
Grimké, Angelina 51

Haitian Revolution 28, 52
Hall, Stuart 8
Hardie, Keir 102
Harlem Six 187
Harley, Sharon 53–4
Harper, Frances W. 62, 64
Harris, Kamala 148
Hartman, Saidiya 34, 204
Haskell, Burnette 136
hate crime 37–8, 43, 73
'hate strike' 18, 32, 81, 167
Haywood, Harry 193, 199–200
Heart of the Race, the 12, 80, 111, 212–15
see also Black feminism
Hercules, F. E. M. 171–2
Hobsbawm, Eric 7, 173–5
Holmes, Colin 105
Hoover, J. Edgar 183
'Hostile Environment' 114
see also bordering
Howe, Darcus 158, 207
Hyndman, H. M. 101, 108, 112–13, 116, 122

identity politics
Black feminist origins 10–13, 45–6, 49, 52, 54, 56, 62, 70–1, 91, 212–15
prehistories 13–14, 41, 52, 56, 206, 216
see also anti-identity politics
immigration controls 109–10, 113–15, 145, 152, 172, 198–9
against Jews in Britain 96–110
against radicals 118–19, 182
Aliens Act (1905) 99, 105,
Anglo-Jewish elites, supporting 109
as basis for future legislation 114, 149, 156, 175
Aliens Order (1920) 175
Commonwealth Immigrants Act (1962) 98, 153
Commonwealth Immigrants Act (1968) 153
crime and disease control 105, 118, 145
divide and rule 101, 107, 115
following urban uprisings 153, 175
Hart-Celler Act (USA, 1965) 137
leading to further bordering 114, 145–9, 156, 175–6, 182
Nationality and Borders Bill (2021) 152

public messaging 101, 104, 107, 115, 119
racist street movements 105
racist street violence 154, 157–8, 174
Special Restriction (Coloured Alien Seamen) Order (1925) 175
see also borders and bordering
Independent Labour Party (ILP) 101–3, 164
Industrial Workers of the World (IWW) 182, 198–9
intersectionality 12, 91, 212
Irish immigrant workers 80, 82–4, 100–1, 111, 118, 121, 126–8, 133, 138, 141–2, 188
Islamophobia 20–1, 37, 118, 158

Jacksonian Democracy 126–7
Jacobin Magazine 4, *96*, *124–5*
Jamaica 25, 52, 78, 80, 164, 170–1, 179
James, C. L. R. 16, 25
Japanese immigrants 140–1, 145–8
Jenkinson, Jacqueline 160, 173
Jewish Chronicle, The 109, 114, 119
Jewish immigration to Britain 13, 99, 102–4, 109–10
Jewish self-activity 103, 105–7, 109, 120–1
Jewish workers 13, 84, 99, 102–10, 120–1
John Bull (magazine) 161–2
Johnson, Andrew 33
Jones, Claudia 42, 54–6
Jonsson, Terese 60, 74, 77
'July Days', The 132–3
Justice (SDF journal) 101, 119, 163

Kahan, Zelda 106
Kalloch, Isaac S. 135
Kapoor, Nisha 152
Kearney, Denis 133–4, 146, 148
Kelley, Robin D. G. 6, 196, 208
Kin, Huie 138
King Jr., Martin Luther 37, 154, 200
Kisuule, Vanessa 19
Ku Klux Klan (KKK) 33, 151, 181–2
see also fascism
Knights of Labor 130, 144
Kropotkin, Peter 106
Kundnani, Arun 21

Labor Enquirer, The 146

labour
British colonial differentiation of 159,
174–6
'coolie' 128, 135
craft unionism 100, 104, 123, 128, 130,
133, 146, 147
deskilling 7
racism, one form of 98, 200
differentiation, by race and gender
53–6, 64, 68, 71, 72, 75, 79, 112, 149,
159, 165, 173, 179, 209–10, 213–17
see also bordering
domestic 50, 54
forms of exploitation, theories of 71,
74, 86–90
see also slavery and slave trade
housework 80, 86, 90, 94
indentured 23–4, 27, 89, 203
sex workers and rights 28, 76, 82–3, 94,
105, 135, 148–9, 211
see also trade unions
Labour Leader (ILP Journal) 102, 116
Labour Party 8–9, 18, 20, 92, 99
1970s crisis management 78–80
immigration control 1950–70s 153,
157
see also bordering and immigration
controls
New Labour 8, 21, 37–8, 157–8
origins, early figures 101–3, 115, 161,
163–4, 176
support for First World War 116–17
Lansbury, George 163
Lead Belly 177, 187, 203
League of Revolutionary Black Workers
199
Lee, Erika 123, 135
Leeds 102, 107, 157
Lentin, Alana 22
Lew-Williams, Beth 131
Lewis, Gail 75
Lewis, Sophie 94
Lieberman, Aaron 1, 121
Linebaugh, Peter 35
Liverpool 167–71, 188
Lloyd George, David 117–18, 159
London 8, 25–6, 54, 167
dockers and union 26, 83, 100, 103,
121 154–6, 161, 164–5

far right/racism 20, 28, 103–5, 114,
164–5, 170, 171–2
radical East End 81–3, 102–6, 111, 119,
121, 148
solidarity 121, 165, 180
López, Tara Martin 80
Los Angeles Times, The 147
lynching 180
in USA
anti-Black 78, 183–4, 186, 191–2
anti-Chinese 134, 138
in Britain
anti-Black 153, 168

Macdonald, Ramsey 102
Manchester 26, 77, 102, 119, 121, 159,
168
Mangrove Nine 207
Mann, Tom 83, 103
marronage 27, 52
Martin, Trayvon 190
Marx, Eleanor 106–8, 115, 119, 121
Marx, Karl 94–5, 101, 119
against borders 148
anti-slavery 32
on the capitalist-worker relationship
204
on transportation 175
Marxism 1, 2, 8, 9, 39, 94, 101, 107, 173,
203
Black feminist engagement 48–9, 54–5,
74, 86–7, 91, 120
universalising 5, 7, 14, 86–9, 179
mass incarceration 43–4, 66, 74, 78, 96,
123–4, 137, 149, 158, 180, 187, 201,
203
'Matchgirls' Strike (1888) 81–3, 85–6, 100
McBride, Renisha 190
McCurry, Stephanie 52
McKay, Claude 164, 177, 179, 192
McKeown, Adam M. 129, 145
Meiksins Wood, Ellen 87
Messenger, The 180, 188, 190–2, 198
Michaels, Walter Benn 96
Milner, Viscount Lord Alfred 117–18,
171
misogyny,
as *the worst* oppression 59, 63, 85,
in Black movements 48, 57, 75
misogynoir 42, 55–6, 64, 68, 73–5,

INDEX

Vanecko, Bobby 200–1
Vesey, Denmark 16, 28
Virdee, Satnam 99, 108
'Virginity Testing' at Heathrow Airport 89

Walia, Harsha 212
Wang, Jackie 42, 44
Ware, Vron 1
Washington D.C. 57, 136, 181, 184–5, 192
Wasp, The 135
Webb, Beatrice 103
Welfare State 13, 46, 66, 79, 96–8, 105, 109–114, 174, 217
Wells, H. G. 117
Wells-Barnett, Ida B. 194–5
'white feminism'
  in Britain
    as colonial-imperial 71–2, 74, 78, 84–5, 87–8, 93
    exclusionary by practice 71–4, 76–8, 84
    exclusionary by theory 71–4, 76–8, 80, 84, 86–8, 90, 92–3, 206
    as racist-nationalist 72–3, 78, 84–5, 87–8, 92–3
    as transphobia 71–4
    innocence 43, 77–8, 82–3
  in USA
    erasure, appropriation 58–62, 64
    exclusionary by practice 48, 50, 59–62, 65, 67
    exclusionary by theory 47, 49, 52–3, 59–65, 67–8, 206
    racist discourses 51–3, 60, 63–4, 68–9
    tokenisation 65
white gangs 150–1, 167, 183, 188, 199–200
white phosphorus poisoning ('Phossy Jaw') 85–6
'white slavery' 81–2
White, Walter 188, 191
whiteness
  becoming white 36, 81, 111–12, 120, 127, 132, 135, 154, 173–5, 183–4, 188–9, 210
  eternalisation 22, 206
  innocence 43, 60

mutability 81, 111–12, 120, 127, 147, 149, 153, 188–9, 211, 217
state anti-racism in Britain 36–40, 151–3
white historiographies of abolition 22–30
class 124–5
feminist 'waves' 92–3
hereditary-thinking 20–3
marxist 'stages' 86–9
universality 6–8
welfare state 96–7
whiteness riots 14, 153–4, 158–60, 163–75, 177–86, 188–97, 199–200, 210–1
  see also anti-Blackness
Wilberforce, William 23, 25, 29, 39
Williams, Eric 23–5
Williams, Eugene 188
Wilson, Amrit 12, 85–6
Wilson, Harold 153
Wilson, Joseph Havelock 118, 161, 166–7
Wilson, Woodrow 181
Winant, Gabriel 125
'Windrush Generation' 98
'woke'
  appropriation of 4, 177–8, 187, 203
  original meaning 177–8, 187
Wolfe, Patrick 176
Worker's Dreadnought, The 84, 164–5, 180
Women's Liberation Movement (WLM) 13, 46–7, 55–6, 64–9, 70–4, 76–7, 79, 92–3
Women's Loyal League 51
Women's Social and Political Union (WSPU) 84
women's suffragism 49–51, 54–5, 57, 59–61, 64–5, 68, 71, 73, 83–5, 93, 115, 164
Wootton, Charles 168, 171, 188
Workingmen's Party 132–6

Yemen/Yemenis 142, 166, 169, 179
'Yorkshire Ripper' murders 77–8

Zinn, Howard 50
Zionism 99, 121–2

‖‖‖‖‖‖‖‖‖‖‖‖‖‖‖‖‖

9780745346564